Killing
Detente

Anne Hessing Cahn

Killing Detente

The Right Attacks the CIA

The Pennsylvania State University Press
University Park, Pennsylvania

Anne Hessing Cahn is Scholar in Residence at The American University in Washington, D.C. She has served on the staff of the Arms Control and Disarmament Agency and the Department of Defense and, from 1982 to 1988, was President and Executive Director of the Committee for National Security. Her articles have appeared in leading newspapers, including the *New York Times* and *Los Angeles Times,* and in a wide variety of professional journals. She has also testified before Congress on numerous occasions on security issues.

Library of Congress Cataloging-in-Publication Data

Cahn, Anne H.
    Killing detente : the right attacks the CIA / by Anne Hessing
Cahn.

        p.   cm.
    Includes bibliographical references and index.
    ISBN 0-271-01790-2 (acid-free paper)
    ISBN 0-271-01791-0 (pbk. : acid-free paper)
    1. Intelligence service—United States.   2. United States.
Central Intelligence Agency.   3. Strategic forces—Soviet Union.
4. United States—Foreign relations—1969–1974.   5. United States
—Foreign relations—1974–1977.   6. Detente.   7. Cold
War.   I. Title.
JK468.I6C33   1998
327.1273—dc21   97-49346
                                                        CIP

Copyright © 1998 The Pennsylvania State University
All rights reserved
Printed in the United States of America
Published by The Pennsylvania State University Press,
University Park, PA 16802–1003

It is the policy of The Pennsylvania State University Press to use acid-free paper for the first printing of all clothbound books. Publications on uncoated stock satisfy the minimum requirements of American National Standard for Information Sciences—Permanence of Paper for Printed Library Materials, ANSI Z39.48–1992.

Contents

Acknowledgments   vii

Introduction   1

1   Setting the Stage   6

2   The Demise of Detente: Domestic Considerations   17

3   The Demise of Detente: International Causes   50

4   The CIA as a Vulnerable Institution   70

5   National Intelligence Estimates   86

6   PFIAB into the Fray   100

7   Team B Is Born (or How Did We Get Here from There?)   122

8   The Teams at Work   141

9   Team B Panel Report on Soviet Strategic Objectives   163

Epilogue   185

Appendix   197

Glossary   199

Bibliography   203

Index   218

Acknowledgments

This book could not have been written without the benefit of the Freedom of Information Act. I wrote to the Central Intelligence Agency in February 1989, seeking material on the threat-assessment process. That request was stonewalled for more than two years. Then former assistant secretary of defense David McGiffert offered to obtain a lawyer to file a suit on my behalf, seeking disclosure of the records I had requested. It was my great good fortune that attorney Mark Lynch of McGiffert's law firm, Covington and Burling, provided his wise counsel pro bono; due to his diligence and expertise the requested documents began to arrive within two months of filing the suit. I owe a profound debt of gratitude to David McGiffert, Mark Lynch, and Covington and Burling.

The research for the book was made possible by a generous Grant for Research and Writing from the John D. and Catherine T. MacArthur Foundation. My sincere appreciation for their generosity and their patience. Both the Center for International and Security Studies at the University of Maryland and the School for International Service at American University provided hospitable intellectual environments during the long gestation of this book and are gratefully acknowledged.

Without the cooperation of the eighty people who permitted me to interview and pester them, repeatedly in some cases, this book would certainly have been the poorer. Their names and the dates of their interviews appear at the end of the bibliography.

Many other people were most helpful. A special thanks is due Barbara Green, who provided much encouragement and support and made helpful comments on the entire manuscript. Joan Dash, Thomas Hirschfeld, Spurgeon Keeny, Lisa Lerman, Sharon McGrayne, Martha Mautner, Oliver Penrose, Philip Schrag, Mari Slack, Nancy Slack, Howard Stoertz, Gail Ullman, Paul Warnke, and the late William Colby all read partial drafts of the manuscript and offered insightful suggestions.

Others who helped in one way or another are Scott Armstrong, Charles Babcock, Kai Bird, Betty Bumpers, David Callahan, Robert Crowley, Robert Ducas, Robert English, Saul Friedman, Raymond Garthoff, Harry Gelman,

Sanford Gottlieb, Roy Jonkers, James Klurfeld, Peter Kornbluh, Donald Lenker, Kirsten Lundberg, Michael Nacht, Stanley Morris, Lt. Col. Rick Oborn, Mark Pekula, John Prados, Jeffrey Richelson, Quinn Shea, David Skidmore, Leon Sloss, Thomas Street, and Robert Toth.

My daughter, Lorie Cahn, my son, Andrew Cahn, and my daughter-in-law, June Blender Cahn, provided useful comments on early drafts. Finally, my most profound thanks to my best friend and husband of forty-seven years, John, who extended encouragement at all times and without whose support and prodding this book would never have been completed.

Of course, I alone bear the responsibility for any shortcomings that may be within.

Introduction

In the 1970s, a profound change occurred in American public opinion. Starting with President Richard Nixon's historic first trip to Moscow in 1972, the American public began to turn dramatically away from favoring confrontation with the Soviet Union and toward approving cooperation with them. By the time of General Secretary Leonid Brezhnev's return visit to the United States in 1973, a large majority of Americans believed the United States should go further in negotiating with the Soviet Union to reduce armaments on both sides. By 1974, the general mood in the United States concerning the Soviets was positive and upbeat. By and large, public opinion approved of the Nixon administration's policy of improving relations with the Soviet Union. This policy came to be known as detente.

This book is about attempts to destroy these improved relations between the United States and the Soviet Union in the 1970s. Those opposed to the easing of tensions between the two countries used every means available, including accusing the Central Intelligence Agency (CIA) of understating the threat posed by the Soviets. The very idea of thus charging the CIA seems preposterous now, given what we recently learned about the confessed CIA spy Aldridge Ames, who for nine years gave Moscow the names of a number of Soviets recruited by the CIA. Some of these men came to be controlled by the Soviet intelligence agency, the KGB, and fed the CIA systematic overassessments of Soviet economic, technological, and military might. These threat assessments, transmitted to U.S. policymakers with no indication of their questionability, may have resulted in the Defense Department's spending billions of dollars to defend the country against false threats.

For the opponents of detente in the 1970s, the CIA was never a target per se, but threat assessments that didn't paint a bleak enough picture of the impending danger posed by the Soviets were. In the highly politicized and ideologically charged atmosphere of the Cold War, overstated threat assessments were not uncommon.

Why worry now about past threat inflations? We won the Cold War, didn't we? In the words of former secretary of defense Casper Weinberger, "Yes, we used worst-case analysis. You should always use a worst-case analysis in this business. You can't afford to be wrong. In the end, we won the cold war, and if we won by too much, if it was overkill, so be it."[1] But in our zeal to meet the oversold threat, in the 1980s we undertook a military buildup on a scale unprecedented in peacetime, which left present and future generations with the most crippling debt in our nation's history. As a result of the buildup, we neglected our schools and cities, our health-care system, our roads and bridges and parks. Once the world's greatest creditor nation, we became the greatest debtor—all to defend against a nation that was even then collapsing. As we now struggle with the results, we are a country politically and economically depleted, less able to cope with internal and external problems than we might have been had we spent less on unnecessary armaments during the Cold War.

If we want to avoid returning to the chilly atmosphere of a Cold War mentality, we need to learn about the demise of detente and the role played by many actors—organized labor, neoconservatives, conservatives, lifelong liberals—who, some wittingly and some unwittingly, coalesced into a movement strong enough to derail detente. Along the way, they decided that the CIA was a vulnerable institution that could be used to drive the nail in the coffin of improved relations with the Soviet Union. In order to understand the threat assessment phenomena, we need to place them in their specific context. Inflated assessments resulted from the Cold War and contributed to the demise of detente.

Detente in the 1970s came about because the United States and the Soviet Union needed each other. The Vietnam War occurred during a period when American power was weakening and that of the Soviet Union was growing. President Nixon and National Security Adviser Henry Kissinger hoped that the Soviets would help extricate the United States from Vietnam. By the time of Nixon's election in 1968, even the *Wall Street Journal* had begun to question the wisdom of the war in Indochina. Congress rescinded the bipartisan blank check it had given the White House in the Gulf of Tonkin Resolution, suspended appropriations for the expanded war in Cambodia in 1970, instructed the president to cease all Indochinese military operations in mid-1973, and passed the War Powers Act later that year, placing restraints on the president's ability to wage undeclared wars like those in Korea and Vietnam. Given these events, Nixon and Kissinger concluded that cooperation with the Soviets was necessary. To obtain this they were

---

1. Quoted in Tim Weiner, "Military Accused of Lies over Arms," *New York Times*, June 28, 1993, 10.

ready explicitly to acknowledge the Soviet Union's status as one of the world's two superpowers.

The Soviet Union needed detente for a variety of reasons as well. As the *New York Times* in July 1971 began to print the "Pentagon Papers," the classified history of the Vietnam War, Nixon and Kissinger surprised the world with a stunning announcement. Kissinger had just met with the leaders of the People's Republic of China in Beijing and arranged for Nixon to visit China early the following year. The principal reason, although unstated, for Nixon's opening to China was to facilitate U.S. withdrawal from Vietnam without precipitating the collapse of the South Vietnamese government.

Rapprochement with China became possible when a major conflict between the Soviet Union and the People's Republic broke out in the Ussuri River border region in March 1969. There were battles between their armed forces and casualties on both sides. This created an opportunity to exploit the split, and Nixon and Kissinger proceeded to practice triangular diplomacy.

The opening to China made possible rapprochement with the Soviet Union as well. The rift between the People's Republic and the USSR was keeping large amounts of Russian conventional and nuclear forces tied up in northern Asia, thus significantly reducing Russia's capability to wage war in Europe. With detente, the Soviets could concentrate their resources on the Chinese challenge without jeopardizing their security in Europe. The U.S. diplomatic efforts in China made the Soviet Union more interested in improving relations with the United States as the Soviets strove to prevent a full-fledged Sino-American alliance.

Before detente overstated threat assessments occurred repeatedly. Early in 1950, in the wake of the first Soviet nuclear test, "NSC 68," a comprehensive U.S. national security review, stated that "the integrity and vitality of our system is in greater jeopardy than ever before in our history." The Kremlin was portrayed as "inescapably militant" and requiring "the ultimate elimination of any effective opposition. . . . [The United States] is the principal enemy whose integrity and vitality must be subverted or destroyed . . . if the Kremlin is to achieve its fundamental design."[2]

In 1957 the Gaither Committee, originally established by President Dwight Eisenhower to study the requirements for civil defense, broadened

2. "United States Objectives and Programs for National Security" (April 14, 1950), in *Foreign Relations of the United States, 1950*, 1:262–63.

its own mandate and concluded that American deterrence and survival were both in jeopardy. The report, titled "Deterrence and Survival in the Nuclear Age," warned of a "missile gap" and stated that if the United States failed "to act at once, the risk . . . [would] be unacceptable."[3] This document reached President Eisenhower a few weeks after the launching of Sputnik in 1957, and its dire and ultimately unfounded warnings about the Soviet strategic threat were leaked to the press, to Eisenhower's consternation. The report remained classified until 1973.

Both of these reports were threat assessments; that is, they assessed for U.S. policymakers the threats posed by the Soviet Union. Whereas NSC 68 had designated 1954 "the year of maximum danger," the Gaither Report pointed to 1959 as the new "year of maximum danger." The similarity in language is not coincidental, since Paul Nitze, a man for all Cold War seasons, was a principal author of both documents.

Both NSC 68 and the Gaither Report appeared during the height of the Cold War. In the early 1970s detente between the Soviet Union and the United States gathered momentum. This caused critics of detente, who were numerous, to revive the specter of Soviet superiority and raise it to new prominence, because this time the goal was to discredit the threat assessments of the entire intelligence community.

Every year the intelligence community produced many assessments of possible threats to U.S. national security. The most important of these dealt with Soviet strategic forces, and it was this assessment that came under attack. In 1976 an alternative to that assessment was prepared by a group of very influential outsiders, who came to be known as Team B to differentiate them from the regular intelligence analysts who were preparing yearly assessments of Soviet capabilities. Team B asserted that the Soviet Union surpassed the United States in overall military strength and was bent on a first-strike policy. The indefatigable Paul Nitze was again a participant, but this time not the principal author. That honor went to Harvard professor Richard Pipes.

This book addresses how the intelligence community and outsiders assessed the threat from the Soviet Union during the rise and fall of detente in the 1970s and how those assessments affected its demise. Chapter 1 sets the stage by examining the heyday of detente in the mid-1970s. This was a

3. "Deterrence and Survival in the Nuclear Age: Report to the President of the Security Resources Panel of the Science Advisory Committee," November 7, 1957 (printed for the use of the Joint Committee on Defense Production, 94th Cong., 2d sess.), 25.

time of great hope for the majority of Americans and of great fear for cold warriors. The next two chapters try to determine what caused the demise of detente. I first look at domestic factors contributing to detente's end. Paramount among these were the Jackson-Vanik amendment to the trade bill, the arrival of Aleksandr Solzhenitsyn in the United States, and, most important, the presidential campaign of 1976, when Ronald Reagan mounted a serious challenge to the renomination of incumbent president Gerald Ford. Chapter 3 examines the international stage, where actions by the Soviet Union in the Third World were significant factors in changing the U.S. public's perceptions about detente.

The fourth chapter focuses on the CIA. It is not immediately obvious why, if one wants to attack detente, one would pick on the Central Intelligence Agency. In Chapter 5, I look at National Intelligence Estimates and what they are. How are they prepared and disseminated, and why are they important? Chapter 6 examines the President's Foreign Intelligence Advisory Board, the official watchdog over the intelligence community and the primary impetus behind alternative threat assessments. The seventh chapter follows the tangled course of bureaucratic decision making in the intelligence community regarding alternative threat assessments. In Chapter 8 I look at three alternative threat assessments, the Team B panel reports, their members and how they were chosen, and how their reports were presented to the intelligence community. The ninth chapter looks at what the Team B panel on Soviet strategic objectives said, how this differed from the National Intelligence Estimate of that year, whether that estimate was toughened up in response to Team B's criticisms, and who leaked the Team B report. What was the aftermath of this experiment in competitive threat assessments? The last chapter deals with the short- and long-term consequences of these inflated threat assessments.

For more than a third of a century, perceptions about U.S. national security were colored by the view that the Soviet Union was on the road to military superiority over the United States. For more than a third of a century, that view prompted calls for the United States to "rearm." Now that such calls are heard again, we need to understand how those perceptions are formed and manipulated.

1

Setting the Stage

In the United States 1974 was a memorable year. The Watergate cover-up unraveled, President Richard Nixon resigned, and later President Gerald Ford pardoned him. Gasoline lines and shortages were prevalent. Ella Grasso of Connecticut became the nation's first woman governor. Kidnapped Patricia Hearst joined the Symbionese Liberation Army. Streaking became a U.S. fad. Unleaded gasoline was introduced. Television hits were *All in the Family*, *The Waltons*, *MASH*, and *Maude*. The most popular movies included *Blazing Saddles*, *Chinatown*, *Lenny*, and *The Parallax View*. On Broadway the hottest tickets were for *Equus*, *A Moon for the Misbegotten*, and *The River Niger*. Best sellers were *Jaws*, *All the President's Men*, and *The Diary of Anaïs Nin*. Oakland won the World Series in five games over Los Angeles.

And what about the international scene? Moscow expelled the noted author Aleksandr Solzhenitsyn. The United States established diplomatic relations with East Germany. Eight-dollar American blue jeans cost $80 on the Soviet black market. Mikhail Baryshnikov defected to the United States, and Eisaku Sato and Seán MacBride shared the Nobel Peace Prize.

Insofar as Americans thought about foreign relations and the relationship between the two superpowers—the United States and the Soviet Union—a profound change had occurred. After President Nixon's trip to Moscow and the signing of the Strategic Arms Limitation Talks (SALT) and Anti-Ballistic Missile Treaties, American public opinion toward the Soviet Union changed. The number of Americans who took a favorable view of the Soviet Union rose from 5 percent in 1954 to 34 percent in April 1973.[1] Nixon changed the course of U.S. foreign policy radically, and Americans, by and large, approved.

On the eve of Leonid Brezhnev's return visit to the United States in 1973, 78 percent of Americans responding to a Gallup poll believed the United States should go further in negotiating with the Soviet Union to reduce armaments on both sides. Nearly half the respondents, 48 percent, thought the United States and the Soviet Union were about equal in military strength, and nearly the same number, 44 percent, believed that the two countries would be equally strong in five years. The danger of nuclear war within five years was deemed "not very much" by four out of ten, while 37 percent thought there was no such danger at all.[2] Thus, Brezhnev's visit took place at a time when American attitudes toward the Soviet Union were more favorable than at any time since World War II.

By the fall of 1974 inflation was the dominant concern of Americans, and nearly half believed the United States was spending too much for defense and military purposes. About one person in eight said the amount being spent was too little, while 32 percent believed the amount was "about right."[3] Although the two countries were actively involved in negotiating a second SALT Treaty, nearly half of the respondents said they paid no attention to the talks, and 37 percent followed them "casually."[4] By the end of 1974, a strong majority, 68 percent, favored expanding Soviet-American trade, while only 21 percent opposed.[5]

Thus, in 1974, the general mood in the United States was positive and upbeat concerning our relations with the Soviet Union. We didn't worry too much about nuclear war and thought the two countries were about equally strong and would still be so in five years. We believed that arms control negotiations were beneficial, and favored broadening trade and cultural rela-

1. Poll conducted by the Gallup Organization, May 1973. Unless otherwise noted, all polling data was provided by the Roper Center for Public Opinion Research, University of Connecticut.
2. Poll conducted by the Gallup Organization, April 1974.
3. Poll conducted by the Gallup Organization and Louis Harris and Associates, December 1974.
4. Poll conducted by the Roper Organization, July 1974.
5. Poll conducted by Louis Harris and Associates, December 1974.

tions between the two countries. By and large, public opinion approved of the Nixon administration's policy of detente.

But in the 1970s a rift grew between policymakers within the Nixon administration and influential conservatives outside. To Nixon and Kissinger, detente "was a political, military and economic strategy to stabilize relations. It was to be embedded in a new and more stable international structure."[6] This strategy included an end to the war in Vietnam, accommodation of the new West German policy of accepting the division of Germany and the legitimacy of a Communist government in East Germany, and increased commercial, scientific, and cultural relations between the two superpowers. In the early and mid-1970s, four summit meetings were held, eleven bilateral commissions were created, and over 150 agreements on subjects ranging from health improvement to strategic arms limitation were reached.[7]

For the policymakers, these many interchanges soon led to an easy camaraderie, as illustrated by the following exchanges between Brezhnev and Secretary of State Kissinger at a meeting in Brezhnev's office, in the Council of Ministers Building, at the Kremlin on March 26, 1974.

According to the official memorandum of conversation, Brezhnev began by teasing, "I just got a code message from President Nixon. He is very displeased with you." Kissinger replied, "It happens every Tuesday afternoon." Following a discussion about ending underground nuclear tests, peaceful nuclear explosions, and banning the use of chemical weapons, Brezhnev concluded that "Foreign Ministers speak in such an interesting way but resolve nothing." Kissinger noted, "That gives them job security." The banter continued until Brezhnev noticed National Security Council staffer Peter W. Rodman taking notes, at which time Kissinger observed that the notes were "for our diplomatic language training . . . our Foreign Service charm course."[8]

After a brief break, Jan Lodal, of the National Security Council, came in. "Brezhnev roughed up Lodal's hair and commented that he needed a haircut; Kissinger agreed. Dobrynin [Anatoly F. Dobrynin, Soviet ambassador to the United States] pointed out that Lodal's hair was not long by American standards. On his way back to his seat, Brezhnev picked up Mr. Rodman's case

---

6. William G. Hyland, *Mortal Rivals: Superpower Relations from Nixon to Reagan* (New York: Random House, 1987), 8.

7. Raymond Garthoff, *Detente and Confrontation: American-Soviet Relations from Nixon to Reagan* (Washington, D.C.: Brookings Institution, 1985), 21.

8. The White House, memorandum of conversation, March 26, 1974, obtained through the Freedom of Information Act (FOIA) and provided by the National Security Archive.

containing Dr. Kissinger's briefing books and walked off into the next room. Mr. Rodman followed him. Brezhnev turned around and came back. Mr. Rodman retrieved the case. Mr. Gromyko [Andrei A. Gromyko, foreign minister of the USSR] affirmed that it was a joke. The meeting then resumed."[9]

The following day, even the extremely serious subject of how many warheads were on each side's missiles became a subject for humor. Again, from the official memorandum of conversation: "Tea is brought in. Brezhnev counts the slices of lemon. 'How many warheads here? One-two-three . . . six! You tested one like this."

KISSINGER	No, it was five yesterday.
BREZHNEV	You have one with twelve.
KISSINGER	No, ten.
BREZHNEV	Twelve.
KISSINGER	Ten. When you come to the U.S. in 1975 we will show you.
BREZHNEV	We will show you ours too. The maximum we have is three.
KISSINGER	That is on a good day.
GROMYKO	Two and a half.
KISSINGER	That is why I say, on a good day it is three.

Brezhnev ends the repartee by declaring, "But truly this question is a very serious one and it warrants very serious discussion."[10]

In contrast to this palpable sense of goodwill, by 1974 many conservatives were becoming increasingly critical of the general policy of detente with the Soviet Union. A group of them who called themselves "strategic thinkers and worriers" met for dinner at the Santa Monica, California, home of James and Mary Jane Digby on Tuesday evening, June 4, 1974. Albert and Roberta Wohlstetter were the co-hosts. The guests—Paul Nitze, Johan Holst, Joseph Kraft, Joseph Fromm, Robert Bartley, and Jason and Deborah McManus—dined on spinakopites, tyropites, poached salmon with dill sauce, poulet au riz basquaise, dilled tomatoes, Italian green beans, and frozen zabaglione while sipping a 1971 Steinberger Spatlese and a 1964 Clos de Vougeot.[11]

The host, James Digby, was a senior research engineer at the RAND Cor-

9. Ibid.
10. The White House, memorandum of conversation, March 27, 1974, obtained through FOIA and made available by the National Security Archive.
11. Menu kindly supplied by James Digby, October 2, 1990.

poration (a think tank formed by the Air Force after the end of the Second World War), and co-host Albert Wohlstetter was a well-known and influential strategic thinker and professor at the University of Chicago. Paul Nitze had been director of the Policy Planning Staff at the State Department during the Eisenhower administration, where he was the chief architect of National Security Council 68 (NSC 68), the influential policy paper that recommended a major U.S. military buildup to forestall the danger of Soviet superiority within four to five years and that called for the United States to bring about an internal change in the Soviet system and to liberate those under Kremlin domination. Later Nitze was secretary of the navy and deputy secretary of defense and, until the week before the dinner, a member of the SALT Treaty negotiating team. Nitze had just tendered his resignation to President Nixon, but it had not yet been accepted. Johan Holst, a tall Norwegian (who later became his country's defense and foreign minister and hosted the secret Israeli-Palestinian talks in 1993 shortly before his death), was already a familiar figure in arms control and national security intellectual circles.

Another guest, short, wiry Joseph Fromm, a senior journalist with *U.S. News and World Report,* had just returned from several years in Europe to resume writing about arms control matters. In my conversations with him, Fromm remembered that at the dinner he "realized with a jolt that in the United States, the debate about detente, arms control, and strategic matters had become vicious. There was now an ideological doctrinaire struggle going on."[12]

The three other journalists at the dinner table covered the political spectrum from Left to Right. Joseph Kraft, by then a syndicated columnist, had been a strong advocate of detente. However, during the 1973 Middle East war, Kraft felt that Secretary of State Kissinger had "been taken in by the Soviets."[13] Within a year of this dinner, Kraft was to conclude that "the detente strategy may have run its course. So this country needs to be looking about for an alternative to detente."[14] Tall, lanky Jason McManus, age forty, was a senior editor at *Time.* A colleague recalled, "As a writer he could whip out a cover story overnight."[15] Iowa-born Robert Bartley had become editorial-page editor of the *Wall Street Journal* two years earlier, after being

12. Telephone interviews with Joseph Fromm, September 27, 1990, and October 17, 1993.
13. Henry Kissinger, *Years of Upheaval* (Boston: Little, Brown, 1982), 531.
14. Joseph Kraft, "The Limits of Detente," *Washington Post,* August 7, 1975, 15, quoted in Hyland, *Mortal Rivals,* 126.
15. Edwin Diamond, "Time Warner Marches On," *New York,* May 21, 1990, 23–24.

on the editorial-page staff since 1964. He was a self-described conservative who was to win a Pulitzer Prize for editorial writing in 1980. Bartley later acknowledged the importance of attending such meetings: "On certain issues, the editorial writers have better news sources than our reporters who've been covering that topic simply because there are some issues our editorial writers have been at longer. As an editorial writer, you can pick something, some topic, and get to know two or three people in the forefront of the field and they'll call you."[16]

The morning after the dinner, the guests, plus about forty other strategic thinkers and worriers, attended a conference on "Arms Competition and Strategic Doctrine" sponsored by the California Arms Control Seminar. The two-day conference was held at the Beverly Hills Hotel and was convened by the Seminar's Working Group on National Aims, International Agreements, and Strategic Forces. The conference chairman, Albert Wohlstetter, had a surprise planned for the participants. The opening session was chaired by William Bader, an urbane project officer at the Ford Foundation. Bader introduced the opening speaker, Albert Wohlstetter, whom he knew well. Bader spent much of his time at the Ford Foundation's Paris office. Wohlstetter's brother was part-owner of the Sloan Wohlstetter winery in Bordeaux, and Wohlstetter often invited Bader there. Bader assumed his task that morning would be easy—to introduce a friend and to chair the session.[17]

Wohlstetter, in addition to holding a position at the University of Chicago, was also a sometime fellow of All Souls College, Oxford University, a member of the RAND Research Council, and a former professor at the University of California at Los Angeles and at Berkeley. The author and coauthor of numerous articles and book-length studies about military and strategic matters, Wohlstetter was highly regarded in many influential circles. Tall, energetic, and self-assured, Wohlstetter strode to the podium.

He began by declaring that much of the public debate over the arms race had been fueled by myths, particularly the myth of overestimation. Wohlstetter challenged the conventional wisdom that nations in an arms race invariably exaggerate the strength of their opponents. Over the next forty-five minutes, Wohlstetter drilled his point home. He accused the Department of Defense of systematically underestimating Soviet deployments of strategic missiles, strategic warheads, and bombers. He declared that "in spite of the

16. Interview by Peter Benjaminson, October 31, 1979, in *Contemporary Author*, ed. Frances C. Locher (Detroit: Gale Research Company, 1981), 97:33.
17. Telephone interview with William Bader, October 23, 1990.

myth of invariable U.S. overestimation, we systematically underestimated the number of vehicles the Russians would deploy for a period that dwarfs the three years or so when we expected a 'missile gap.' "[18] Using information from the secretary of defense's annual posture statements from 1962 to 1972, information that was specially declassified at his request, Wohlstetter presented charts and figures comparing forecasts to actual deployments. Worse still, according to Wohlstetter, the size of the miscalculations increased throughout the decade, even as the quality of U.S. intelligence-collection programs improved. A few years earlier, however, Wohlstetter had admitted that "predicting exact calendar dates at which technologies will be available to adversaries and what their strategic significance will be is very hard, and we are not very good at it."[19]

At the Los Angeles meeting, Wohlstetter was stating in an open forum what some inside the administration had been saying for some time. A classified Defense Posture Panel of the Defense Science Board, in their 1970 summer study, asked, among other questions, "What is the predictive accuracy of intelligence forecasts of defense posture and how can this accuracy be improved?" According to the chairman of that panel, Albert Wheelon, "What we did was very simple. We took the [CIA] estimates for the prior years and measured them against the reality year by year and what we discovered was something that Wohlstetter wrote up in a paper . . . in a disguised way." Wheelon believed that Wohlstetter saw this report and claims Wohlstetter "has many times said he publicized what 'you guys [the Defense Posture Panel] did.' "[20]

Wohlstetter claimed that, far from engaging in an arms race, U.S. strategic budgets and the destructiveness of U.S. strategic forces had been going down, not up. According to Wohlstetter, "[T]he net thrust of major qualitative change in the strategic field has been to redeploy and cut rather than to increase resources devoted to the strategic force; to increase political control of the force; to reduce its vulnerability; and therefore also to reduce the instabilities that could lead to a nuclear holocaust. Almost the exact reverse of the stereotype."[21]

18. Albert Wohlstetter, "Is There a Strategic Arms Race?" *Foreign Policy* 15 (summer 1974): 5.

19. Albert Wohlstetter, testimony before the Senate Armed Services Committee on ABM, 91st Cong., 1st sess., April 23, 1969, *Congressional Record*, 115, pt. 8:10956.

20. Quoted in Kevin Roy Cunningham, "Scientific Advisers and American Defense Policy: The Case of the Defense Science Board" (Ph.D. diss., University of Michigan, 1991), 286.

21. Albert Wohlstetter, "Legends of the Strategic Arms Race, Part I: The Driving Engine," *Strategic Review* 2 (fall 1974): 67–92.

The usually unflappable Bill Bader remembers the morning session well because of his demonstrable inability to get Wohlstetter to yield the floor to the next speaker. According to Bader, "Albert waxed and never waned. He was an uncontrollable missile. He wouldn't accept notes, he wouldn't take glances, he wouldn't take nudges."[22] Another attendee at the meeting, Lynn Davis, later undersecretary of state, also remembered Wohlstetter "going on and on and Bader not being able to stop him." She thinks Wohlstetter spoke all morning and into the afternoon.[23]

At the conference, other participants from universities such as Stanford, the University of California, and Harvard, and from think tanks like the Hudson Institute and RAND, presented papers on "Alternatives to MAD-ness" (a pun on the acronym for the official targeting policy of the United States, Mutual Assured Destruction); "The U.S. Strategic Defense Posture in an Arms Limitation Environment"; and "SALT [Strategic Arms Limitation Talks]: Technological Impact on Progress and Prospects." Nathan Leites of RAND issued a warning in his title "Once More About What We Should Not Do Even in the Worst Case: The Assured Destruction Attack." But the only paper still remembered by national security and arms control aficiona-dos twenty years later is Albert Wohlstetter's accusation of systematic under-estimation of Soviet strategic deployments.

Not all of the participants at the meeting were impressed by Wohlstetter's presentation, nor should they have been. Sidney Drell's reaction was "that his conclusions were the result of his choosing the right year for starting his comparisons."[24] Wohlstetter's curve depicting U.S. warhead deployments stopped with 1972, but a substantial number of warheads were coming into the American force in 1974, and Wohlstetter and many in the audience had known that for several years. The Soviet inventory of intercontinental ballis-tic missiles reached its peak of 1,600 in 1975 and dipped to 1,400 by 1979. Their submarine fleet declined from 370 to 257 during the decade, as they retired many of their diesel subs. The numerical balance of conventional forces between the Soviets and their Warsaw Pact allies and the United States and its NATO allies changed little during the 1970s.[25]

Alton Frye, a thoughtful and carefully spoken participant in many such conferences, believed "Albert was showboating for a political purpose."[26] But

22. Telephone interview with William Bader, October 23, 1990.
23. Telephone interview with Lynn Davis, October 9, 1989.
24. Sidney D. Drell, letter to the author, October 5, 1990.
25. Richard A. Stubbing, *The Defense Game* (New York: Harper & Row, 1986), 15–16.
26. Interview with Alton Frye, November 1, 1990.

many who attended thought it was an important meeting. James Digby believes that "the presence of some quite serious reporters added to the drama."[27] And Wohlstetter and other "hard-liners" promptly publicized his conclusions.

The week after the Los Angeles meeting, the first of two articles by Wohlstetter detailing the arguments he made at the Los Angeles meeting appeared in the widely read and highly regarded journal *Foreign Policy*. In 1993 the editor of that journal could still recall those articles clearly. "It was the most difficult single editing job of my entire life, and I have edited everyone from Kennan to Nitze," Richard Holbrooke, later an assistant secretary of state and ambassador to Germany, reminisced. According to Holbrooke, "They were hell to edit, because Albert is a very precise man and they were very long. I kept trying to make them more accessible to the general reader, and he kept arguing the precision of language and so on."[28]

Wohlstetter's charges of perennial underestimation of Soviet deployments immediately became widely discussed. Robert Bowie, then a senior professor at Harvard, recalled, "At Harvard, we talked about the validity of his arguments. They seemed to establish a pattern of underestimation that was troubling."[29] Paul Nitze, in his first public testimony after resigning from SALT, cited the work of his friend Wohlstetter in support of his warning that "the U.S. has for many years underestimated future Soviet offensive deployments."[30] In the fall of 1974, an expanded version of Wohlstetter's argument appeared in two installments in *Strategic Review*,[31] and he authored an op-ed piece on the same subject in the *Wall Street Journal*.[32]

Wohlstetter's articles in *Foreign Policy*[33] elicited a lengthy debate in subsequent issues of the journal, which ended with a final article by Wohlstetter, "Optimal Ways to Confuse Ourselves."[34] Perhaps most important, Wohlstet-

27. James Digby, letter to the author, September 20, 1990.
28. Telephone interview with Richard Holbrooke, July 9, 1993.
29. Interview with Robert Bowie, December 15, 1989.
30. Strobe Talbott, *The Master of the Game: Paul Nitze and the Nuclear Peace* (New York: Knopf, 1988), 140.
31. Wohlstetter, "Legends of the Arms Race, Part I," 67–92, and idem, (part II) "The Uncontrolled Upward Spiral," *Strategic Review* 3 (winter 1975): 71–86.
32. Albert Wohlstetter, "Clocking the Strategic Arms Race," *Wall Street Journal*, September 24, 1974, 24.
33. Wohlstetter, "Is There a Strategic Arms Race?" 3–20; "Rivals but No 'Race,' " *Foreign Policy* 16 (fall 1974): 48–81.
34. Comments by Paul H. Nitze, Joseph Alsop, Morton H. Halperin, and Jeremy Stone, *Foreign Policy* 16 (fall 1974): 82–92; Johan Jorgen Holst, "What Is Really Going On?" *Foreign Policy* 19 (summer 1975): 155–63; Michael L. Nacht, "The Delicate Balance of Error," *Foreign*

ter's critique led William Colby, the ramrod director of the CIA, to send the first Wohlstetter article to his staff for comments. In interview, Colby, dapper in his white-collared blue shirt with a power red tie, said that he had found the article "pretty compelling" and had not been happy with the "defensive stuff" he got back.[35]

However, in a letter to the chairman of the Chicago Council on Foreign Relations, Colby wrote: "Professor Wohlstetter himself somewhat oversimplified the historical record of intelligence projections in the last decade. The broader context includes projections of weapons technology, i.e., qualitative factors as well as numbers of launchers deployed, and defensive systems, such as ABMs, as well as offensive weapons. Viewed in this broader context, the record of intelligence projections is considerably more mixed than Professor Wohlstetter's article suggests. There are about as many examples of overestimation as there are of underestimation."[36]

Although Wohlstetter never mentioned the CIA in his talk or articles, all the strategic thinkers and worriers knew that the data Wohlstetter used came from National Intelligence Estimates. These yearly estimates, described in detail in Chapter 4, are prepared by the entire intelligence community, but are signed by the director of the CIA in his capacity as the director of Central Intelligence (DCI), which includes all the intelligence agencies.[37] Contrary to a widespread impression, the CIA and the intelligence community are not the same thing. The "Community," as it is called, consists of all the various intelligence services in the U.S. government, including Army, Navy, Air Force Intelligence, the Defense Intelligence Agency, and the National Security Agency, as well as the Bureau of Intelligence and Research in the State Department and the counterintelligence unit of the FBI.

Wohlstetter's charges were the opening salvo of a movement determined to destroy detente and to steer U.S. foreign policy back to a more militant stance vis-à-vis the Soviet Union. The critics of detente were certain that the Cold War was far from over and were determined that American hegemony should not disappear. They believed the world still required a paramount policeman and that he should wear an American uniform. To these conservatives, economic and social problems, due to their complexity, often could not be addressed effectively until military solutions first imposed political

Policy 19 (summer 1975): 163–88; Albert Wohlstetter, "Optimal Ways to Confuse Ourselves," Foreign Policy 20 (fall 1975): 170–98.

35. Interview with William Colby, August 18, 1989.

36. William Colby, letter to John E. Rielly, July 25, 1974, obtained through FOIA.

37. The terms CIA director and DCI are used interchangeably throughout this book.

stability. "They believed that America still had the power and the responsibility to play that role and needed only to regain the will to wield that power. As a consequence, they committed themselves to the remilitarization of American foreign policy. The American military shield, refurbished and rebuilt, would contain the expansion of Russia's 'evil empire,' which they viewed as the fountainhead of revolution, terrorism, and all things unseemly in the world."[38] Through articles, op-ed pieces, speeches, letters to the editor, and lobbying, these hard-liners, who viewed themselves as modern Paul Reveres attempting to awaken a sleeping nation, kept up a steady onslaught on the policy of detente.

Along the way they were aided by a loose coalition of labor, neoconservatives, Eastern European refugees and their elected representatives, liberals disillusioned by "realpolitik," human rights activists, and champions of Jewish emigration from the Soviet Union. Many people and organizations strove to overturn detente. Eventually one vehicle emerged that delivered the final coup d'état. Wohlstetter's charges of chronic underestimation led to the creation of a group of "outsiders" whose specific charge from the Ford administration was to look at the same data and information used by the CIA and the rest of the intelligence community to assess Soviet strategic forces, and to see if they could come up with different, that is, more frightening, conclusions. The men eventually selected by the administration to perform this competitive analysis came to be known as Team B.

38. Thomas J. McCormick, *America's Half-Century: United States Foreign Policy in the Cold War* (Baltimore: Johns Hopkins University Press, 1989), 196.

2

The Demise of Detente: Domestic Considerations

Background

During the heyday of detente, American power weakened while that of the Soviet Union grew. President Nixon and National Security Adviser Kissinger hoped that the Soviets would help extricate the United States from Vietnam. To do so, Nixon and Kissinger concluded that cooperation with the Soviets was necessary. The Soviets, for their own reasons, were ready to improve relations with the United States and to be acknowledged as one of the world's two superpowers.[1]

Nixon and Kissinger also sought to create rules of conduct, rules and procedures to define the limits of acceptable behavior in the important fields of arms control and crisis management. Walter LaFeber states, "[T]hey believed that a new means for controlling the Communists had to be found. In their hands, detente was to be the containment of Soviet power by different—and cheaper—means."[2]

1. John Lewis Gaddis, *The United States and the End of the Cold War* (New York: Oxford University Press, 1992), 38.
2. Walter LaFeber, *The American Age: United States Foreign Policy at Home and Abroad Since 1750* (New York: W. W. Norton, 1989), 616.

By 1971, the Soviets were admitting that their badly run economy had slowed to a crawl. It needed a jump start, and the United States could best provide it. Nixon and Kissinger intended to use "linkage" to provide the Soviet Union with the necessary economic boost. In return for abiding by new rules of conduct, the Russians would be given access to the trade, technology, and investment capital needed to modernize their economy. Soviet leader Leonid Brezhnev also required arms control so that more money could go into the basic economy.

Early Opposition

Domestic opposition to detente was muted at first. Senator Henry Jackson (D-Wash.), who later became an implacable foe of the policy, called National Security Adviser Kissinger after the 1972 Moscow summit and offered to cooperate in securing passage of the SALT and ABM arms control treaties signed at the summit.[3] However, on the day the agreements were signed in Moscow, Jackson charged, "The present agreements are likely to lead to an accelerated technological arms race with great uncertainties, profound instabilities and considerable costs."[4] Right from the start Jackson actively sought to amend the treaty limiting strategic weapons. On August 3, 1972, he introduced an amendment requiring that future agreements be based on numerical equality, a direct repudiation of the just-negotiated treaty in which Soviet quantitative advantages were offset by the U.S. qualitative edge.

The Interim Agreement (SALT I) limiting offensive arms seemed to give the Soviet Union a decided advantage: 1,618 ICBMs, 62 ballistic missile submarines, and 950 sea-launched ballistic missiles; the comparable U.S. figures were 1,054, 44, and 710. To reach these ceilings, however, the Soviets would have to deactivate 210 older, pre-1964 ballistic missiles, and the United States 54. In addition, the United States had three times as many long-range bombers as the Soviet Union and seven thousand nuclear weapons in Europe. Moreover the United States had a two-to-one advantage in nuclear warheads, which was expected to grow to four to one by the time

3. William G. Hyland, *Mortal Rivals: Superpower Relations from Nixon to Reagan* (New York: Random House, 1987), 53.
4. Quoted in Peter J. Ognibene, *Scoop: The Life and Politics of Henry M. Jackson* (New York: Stein & Day, 1975), 202.

the Interim Agreement expired in 1977. What the SALT I Treaty in effect did was to give the Soviets a numerical advantage in missiles, which was offset by the American technological and numerical lead in warheads.

Nevertheless, the White House began negotiating with Jackson immediately. Kissinger reportedly spoke with Jackson three and four times daily.[5] Jackson knew that Kissinger and others opposed his amendment, fearing it would reduce future U.S. negotiating flexibility. Jackson girded for battle. But the White House surrendered without a fight. Nineteen seventy-two was an election year, and Jackson was well known for his animosity to George McGovern, the likely Democratic nominee. Nixon also was indebted to Jackson for his steadfast support of the war in Vietnam and Defense Department programs. The Jackson codicil therefore passed with the administration's blessing, and the treaties eventually cleared the Senate by a vote of eighty-eight to two.[6]

Other concessions were extracted by Jackson and his conservative allies as well. One was congressional approval of Secretary of Defense Melvin Laird's request for an accelerated offensive program, namely the B-1 bomber and the Trident submarine. The home base for the Trident, originally planned for the East Coast, was relocated to the state of Washington, Senator Jackson's state. Laird also won a presidential commitment to increase spending on strategic weapons by more than 16 percent—some $1.2 billion—in the 1973 Defense Department budget, the largest such increase since the Vietnam War.[7]

A third quid pro quo was a purge of the SALT negotiating team at the State Department, the Arms Control and Disarmament Agency (ACDA), and even at the Pentagon. Senator Jackson had never looked kindly upon ACDA and in 1961 had joined forces with Senate conservatives in an unsuccessful attempt to prevent its formation.[8] Gerard Smith was forced out as the director of ACDA, and fourteen senior ACDA officials who had worked on the treaty were fired as well. In addition, ACDA lost one-third of its budget, 50 of its 230 employees, and much of its influence. Fred Ikle, a hard-line strategic analyst who was chairman of the Social Science Department at the RAND Corporation, was persuaded to become the new director after the

5. Ibid., 41.

6. Stanley Karnow, "Jackson's Bid: Walking the Long Road to the White House," *New Republic*, May 25, 1974, 17–21.

7. Seymour M. Hersh, *The Price of Power: Kissinger in the Nixon White House* (New York: Summit Books, 1983), 537.

8. Ognibene, *Scoop*, 200.

office had been vacant for three months. The appointment of Swiss-born Ikle, a former professor at MIT, reportedly had Jackson's blessing.[9] When confirmed, Ikle brought in several like-minded critics of detente.

Ray Garthoff, the SALT delegation's executive secretary, was fluent in Russian and highly regarded. He, too, was purged, despite the fact he was supposed to return to SALT II as the State Department's representative, which would have been a promotion. Garthoff, however, was informed that he would be reassigned to duties not involving SALT. Again Jackson was fingered as responsible.[10]

Gen. Royal B. Allison, the principal military delegate on the SALT team, not only was removed from the SALT delegation, but was offered an assignment considerably below what an officer of his rank and experience would normally get. When he learned that Senator Jackson had demanded his removal, he made an appointment to see the senator, not to plead for reinstatement, but to ask for a few months' grace so that he could obtain a suitable assignment. When it became clear to Allison that Jackson wanted him not only off the SALT delegation but also out of the air force, Allison resigned.[11]

These concessions were opening salvos in the concerted attack on detente. Many factors conspired to ensure that the policy of detente would be strongly challenged and eventually abandoned. According to Henry Kissinger, "conservatives who hated Communists and liberals who hated Nixon came together in a rare convergence, like an eclipse of the sun."[12] One of the important elements not mentioned by Kissinger was a general disdain for Kissinger himself. The debate over detente, writes Harvard professor Stanley Hoffman, "served as a peg on which the most diverse opposition to or hatreds of Kissinger's person and policy could hang."[13]

Administration Foes of Detente

Within one week of the signing of the SALT and ABM treaties, the Watergate burglary occurred, and President Nixon soon became embroiled in try-

9. Ibid., 213.
10. Ibid., 214.
11. Ibid.
12. Henry Kissinger, *Years of Upheaval* (Boston: Little, Brown, 1982), 983; Walter Isaacson, *Kissinger: A Biography* (New York: Simon & Schuster, 1992), 608.
13. Isaacson, *Kissinger,* 610.

ing to save his presidency. Therefore, most of the job of selling detente to the American people fell on the shoulders of Kissinger. Kissinger's haughty and imperial manner soon became a lightning rod for anyone in the administration less than enthusiastic about the new policy of cooperation with the Soviet Union. Kissinger's deputy at the National Security Council (NSC), William Hyland, relates, "Much of the time it was a war of all against all: the NSC against the State and Defense departments and a struggle for power within the NSC staff for Kissinger's favor."[14]

Even before President-elect Nixon offered Kissinger the job of national security adviser, they discussed running foreign policy from the White House and shunting aside the State Department.[15] Fifty-year-old William P. Rogers, a distinguished lawyer and a long-time friend of Nixon's, told the president-elect when the job of secretary of state was first mentioned that he knew little about foreign affairs. "It was that ignorance," Nixon replied, "that made the job his."[16] Kissinger, in his memoirs, remarks, "Few Secretaries of State can have been selected because of their President's confidence in their ignorance of foreign policy."[17] Rogers states that he "was prepared to play a subordinate role" and thus could be counted on to be loyal and to keep the State Department preoccupied with minor matters while Nixon and Kissinger conducted policy.[18]

Anatoly Dobrynin, Moscow's ambassador to six U.S. presidents, in his memoirs remarked, "Keeping the secretary of state in the dark about such important matters [Nixon's impending trip to Moscow] was unprecedented, and it certainly sounded very strange to Moscow." According to Dobrynin, "even Brezhnev's personal messages to Nixon were edited before they were shown to Rogers, and any references to the confidential channel [between Kissinger and Dobrynin] were cut out. Some messages were not shown to him at all."[19]

The interactions between Kissinger and Rogers concerning the SALT negotiations were marked by animosity and distrust. Kissinger's unflattering estimate of the secretary was gleefully echoed by NSC staffers. "The only time Rogers opens his mouth is to change feet" was a typical comment at

14. Hyland, *Mortal Rivals*, 7–8.
15. Isaacson, *Kissinger*, 136.
16. Hersh, *Price of Power*, 32.
17. Henry Kissinger, *The White House Years* (Boston: Little, Brown, 1979), 26.
18. LaFeber, *American Age*, 601; Hersh, *Price of Power*, 32.
19. Anatoly Dobrynin, *In Confidence: Moscow's Ambassador to America's Six Cold War Presidents (1962–1986)* (New York: Times Books, 1995), 232 and 240.

the NSC. Several of Rogers's aides retaliated by caricaturing Kissinger as a power-mad Dr. Strangelove. "What country is Herr Doktor nuking today?" they would ask.[20]

Instead of seeking to make the secretary of state his ally in selling detente to the American public, Kissinger delighted in besting Rogers in petty bureaucratic games. For two months during the summer of 1973, Kissinger withheld intelligence reports concerning possible Soviet violations of the SALT accords from the secretary of state by removing Rogers's and others' names from the CIA circulation list. Edward Proctor, deputy director for intelligence at the CIA, became so concerned that he wrote to acting CIA director Vernon Walters, "At a minimum, I think you should seek Dr. Kissinger's assurance that he has informed or will inform the President of this situation and the concern it generates."[21] Proctor's predecessor, Ray Cline, told a congressional committee that systematic suppression of intelligence had become routine under Kissinger.[22]

Another official who deeply resented being kept "out of the loop" was Adm. George Anderson, chairman of the President's Foreign Intelligence Advisory Board, the official "watchdog" of the intelligence community. Anderson, a former chief of naval operations, complained, "We found that access to certain facets of the total foreign intelligence problem was being circumscribed. Then on further examination we found that access to what was important intelligence information was sometimes denied to people who were responsible for producing intelligence. Let me be specific. Discussions taking place with the Assistant to the President for National Security were not being made available to the intelligence community."[23] Kissinger's highhanded treatment of intelligence reports helped convince Anderson and others that alternative access to intelligence reports about the Soviets was needed.

An early, highly placed foe of detente was James Schlesinger, who became secretary of defense in July 1973 with the strong backing of Senator Jackson.[24] The forty-one-year-old, nearly white-haired Schlesinger was known

20. Marvin Kalb and Bernard Kalb, *Kissinger* (Boston: Little, Brown, 1974), 112.

21. Nicholas Horrock, "1973 Arms Cover-up Is Laid to Kissinger," *New York Times*, December 18, 1975, 1.

22. Rhodri Jeffreys-Jones, *The CIA and American Democracy* (New Haven, Conn.: Yale University Press, 1989), 189.

23. Adm. George W. Anderson, discussion in *Intelligence Requirements for the 1980s: Analysis and Estimates*, ed. Roy Godson (New Brunswick, N.J.: Transaction Books, 1980), 75.

24. Arthur Macy Cox, *Russian Roulette: The Superpower Game* (New York: Times Books, 1982), 68.

for wearing rumpled suits, scrawny ties, and sagging socks. Essentially a pessimist concerning the West's willingness to stand up to the Soviets, Schlesinger once remarked, "Spengler [the philosopher who wrote *The Decline of the West*] was an optimist." As soon as he became secretary of defense, Schlesinger began to push for huge, unprecedented peacetime increases in the military budget. A month after his confirmation as secretary of defense, Schlesinger told a group of newsmen, "The Soviets . . . have a mailed fist. It is now encased in a velvet glove. . . . I have the responsibility to figure out what that mailed fist means inside the velvet glove. The detente is the velvet glove."[25] According to one of his critics, Schlesinger "always saw the Russians or their missiles coming over the horizon in such hordes that the underground circle of cynics in the Pentagon named him 'Dr. Doom.' "[26] He also came to be known as "the thinking man's cold warrior."[27]

As the Soviets began to test the limits of detente, taking advantage of vague language in the SALT Treaty steadily to augment their strategic offensive nuclear forces, Schlesinger became one of the first in the executive branch to voice alarm about the Soviet buildup. As secretary of defense, Schlesinger strongly emphasized a growing Soviet military threat and advocated a much harder line in the SALT negotiations.[28]

When Gerald Ford became president in August 1974, Schlesinger's anti-detente voice within the administration was a lonely one. The new president had misgivings about the secretary of defense right from the beginning. At his first cabinet meeting, on Saturday, August 10, the day after being sworn in, Ford looked around at his cabinet and later wrote in his memoirs: "As for Secretary of Defense James Schlesinger, I respected his intellect, but I wasn't sure how effective he would be in dealing with the Congress. People on Capitol Hill often found him patronizing or arrogant."[29] Ford continued:

> In the wake of Nixon's resignation, the newspapers were full of bizarre stories about his conduct in the final days. Some of them indicated that Schlesinger was so concerned about Nixon's mental stability that he had taken steps to make sure the President couldn't

25. Tad Szulc, "Pentagon Cool," *Washingtonian Magazine* 10, no. 1 (1974): 115, 116.

26. A. Ernest Fitzgerald, *The Pentagonists: An Insider's View of Waste, Mismanagement, and Fraud in Defense Spending* (Boston: Houghton Mifflin, 1989), 75.

27. "Arming to Disarm in the Age of Detente," *Time*, February 11, 1974, 15–24.

28. Raymond Garthoff, *Detente and Confrontation: American-Soviet Relations from Nixon to Reagan* (Washington, D.C.: Brookings Institution, 1985), 440.

29. Gerald Ford, *A Time to Heal: The Autobiography of Gerald R. Ford* (New York: Harper & Row, 1979), 132.

give orders to the Armed Services unilaterally. The story made me
furious because I was assured no such measures had been taken. I
talked to [Alexander] Haig [White House chief of staff] about it,
and we concluded that it had been leaked deliberately from the
highest level of the Pentagon. That made me madder still. Haig was
present when Schlesinger walked into the Oval Office. "Jim," I said,
"I'm damn disturbed by these rumors about what was done in the
Pentagon during the last days of the Nixon Administration. Obviously, they come from the top and I want the situation straightened
out right away." Schlesinger didn't admit that he had been the
source of the leak, but the significant thing was that the leaks did
stop, at least for a while. As President, that was the first run-in I
had with Schlesinger. I hoped it would be the last, but I suspected
otherwise.[30]

Schlesinger and Kissinger, Harvard classmates, both with strong egos and
disdainful airs, soon became intellectual rivals. In his memoirs, Kissinger
wrote: "And if he was at least my equal in intelligence, I conceded him pride
of place in arrogance."[31] As the U.S. government began discussions on a
follow-up SALT treaty (SALT II), Kissinger exacerbated the rivalry by excluding Defense Department and uniformed military representatives from
participating, just as he had earlier shut out the State Department.

Schlesinger had a deliberate, thoughtful manner of speech, often fumbling
with his pipe, which conveyed an impression of profundity. He began em-
phasizing "throw weight," the lift capacity of a missile, which determines
what weight and number of warheads it can carry. Since the Soviets lacked
the United States' technological skills at miniaturization and advanced elec-
tronics, they emphasized heavy missiles and thus had a big throw-weight
advantage. Schlesinger used to come to meetings with impressive scale models illustrating the disparity. "The throw-weight issue began to drive Henry
wild," Schlesinger recalled with a faint smile, "and so did I."[32] After he was
fired by President Ford in November 1975, Schlesinger, in a parting shot,
publicly endorsed a "detente without illusions" that was coupled with a
strong defense. It was a scarcely veiled criticism of what he regarded as the
Kissinger-Ford pursuit of a detente with illusions and insufficient attention
to military programs. Schlesinger claimed that "Kissinger is always tough

30. Ibid., 136. See also Szulc, "Pentagon Cool."
31. Kissinger, Years of Upheaval, 1155.
32. Quoted in Isaacson, Kissinger, 623.

with everybody but the Russians."[33] Ronald Reagan, soon to challenge Ford for the Republican nomination, charged that Ford fired Schlesinger because he was "afraid to tell the American people the truth about our military status."[34]

Other Influential Foes of Detente

Kissinger's penchant for conducting foreign policy through "back channels," outside the normal diplomatic corridors, was, quite naturally, bitterly resented by the negotiators. Paul Nitze, for many years a member of the SALT negotiating team, expressed his disgust at Kissinger's antics by composing a draft memorandum titled "The Last Twenty Minutes of a Negotiation Are the Most Important," which satirized Kissinger's closely held negotiating techniques, phrased here, by way of example, as instructions: "[A]rrange to have top negotiations in your capital. . . . Have no typewriters nor Xerox machines available when needed. Give other side as minimum secure communications facilities as possible."[35]

The "depressing reality" of Watergate was the reason given by Nitze for his resignation from the SALT negotiations on June 14, 1974. In his statement to the press, Nitze declared that after nearly three decades of working on national defense issues and nearly five years of working on SALT, he now saw "little prospect of negotiating measures" that would enhance U.S. general security.[36] His resignation meant that Nitze was now free to criticize the Soviet Union and detente, and he lost no time in doing so. In testimony before the House Armed Services Subcommittee on Arms Control on July 2, 1974, Nitze reproached Kissinger and cited the work of his friend Albert Wohlstetter. He repeated Wohlstetter's charges of habitual underestimation of future Soviet offensive deployments and warned that the Soviet Union was well on its way to achieving usable strategic superiority over the United States.[37]

33. Quoted in Richard J. Whalen, "The Ford Shakeup: Politics vs. Policy," *Washington Post*, November 9, 1975, D1.

34. Ford, *Time to Heal*, 346.

35. Hersh, *Price of Power*, 546n.

36. "U.S. Negotiator on Arms Quits, Citing the Effects of Watergate," *New York Times*, June 15, 1974, 4; Strobe Talbott, *The Master of the Game: Paul Nitze and the Nuclear Peace* (New York: Knopf, 1988), 139.

37. Talbott, *Master of the Game*, 140.

Nitze's personal animosity toward Kissinger ran deep. At a wedding reception in New York a few months later, he was innocently asked by another guest whether he knew Henry Kissinger. "That man is a traitor to his country," Nitze sputtered as he turned and walked away.[38]

Although Kissinger assiduously wooed the press, not all journalists were convinced about the merits of detente. Richard J. Whalen of the *Washington Post* wrote, "This consistent private appeasement and public falsification of the Soviets enabled Kissinger to be full of optimism concerning detente and its prospects, while Schlesinger, the unsparing realist, played the unpopular role of Cassandra."[39]

Conservatives

Conservatives, of course, feared that detente would sap the will of the American people to stand up to the "godless" Communists. As Kissinger wrote, "They foresaw an erosion of all distinctions, a decay of convictions, when American and Soviet (or for that matter Chinese Communist) leaders were displayed in easy camaraderie on American television screens. They wondered how we would maintain our vigilance—whatever the saving clauses in Presidential statements—when we proclaimed a new era. They doubted whether America could sustain both the willingness to confront and the readiness to cooperate at the same time."[40]

One of the earliest and most prominent conservative critics was Eugene Rostow, a former undersecretary of state in the Kennedy-Johnson administrations and a professor at Yale Law School. In 1972 Rostow had helped form the Coalition for a Democratic Majority to back the presidential quest of Senator Henry Jackson. Many of the people associated with Rostow in that endeavor—Max Kampelman, Lane Kirkland, Norman Podhoretz, and Midge Decter—joined with him a few years later in his attack on detente. By 1974 Rostow was warning: "We confront two implacable facts: the Soviet military buildup is continuing at an ominous rate and Soviet political policy is more and more obviously fixed in a mood of muscular imperialism."[41]

38. Quoted in ibid., 141.
39. Whalen, "Ford Shakeup."
40. Kissinger, *White House Years*, 1256.
41. Eugene V. Rostow, "Defining Detente in Terms of the United Nations Charter," *New York Times*, April 27, 1974, 31.

In 1974 a Foreign Policy Task Force of the Coalition for a Democratic Majority, chaired by Rostow, accused the Nixon administration of creating "a myth of detente" instead of adequately warning Americans about the threats posed by the Soviet Union. The report was a broadside attack on Kissinger's negotiations and maintained that the Russians couldn't be trusted. Foreshadowing language that would be much used in the 1976 presidential campaign, the report asserted, "The goal of detente has not been achieved in any sense of the term Americans can accept. There is no evidence that Soviet objectives have changed."[42] "The myth of detente" soon became the mantra of conservatives.

On Thanksgiving Day, 1975, inspired, in his words, "by a couple of bloody Marys,"[43] Rostow wrote a letter to Paul Nitze and others, proposing that like-minded private citizens should band together to alert the nation to the growing Soviet threat.[44] "By God, why don't we just do it?" the letter asked.[45]

The group held an organizing lunch at the Washington, D.C., Metropolitan Club on March 12, 1976. Chaired by Rostow, the meeting was attended by Richard Allen, who had been passed over as Nixon's national security adviser and was to attain that post under President Reagan; former treasury secretary Henry Fowler; Professor Edmund Gullion of the Fletcher School of Law and Diplomacy; Max Kampelman, a prominent lawyer and close aide to Senator Hubert Humphrey (D-Minn.); labor leader Lane Kirkland; Charles Burton Marshall, a former member of the Policy Planning Staff at the State Department; Paul Nitze; former deputy secretary of defense David Packard, who became a major contributor to the group; former secretary of defense James Schlesinger; Charles Tyroler, the former director of the Citizens Committee for Peace and Freedom in Vietnam; former undersecretary and deputy secretary of the treasury Charls Walker, who once prompted Lyndon Johnson to refer to him admiringly as an "S.O.B. with elbows";[46] and former chief of naval operations Adm. Elmo Zumwalt, who, while running for the Senate earlier, had lashed out at the SALT II negotiations and Soviet compliance with SALT. Not at the meeting but committed to formation of the committee were Sol Chaiken of the AFL-CIO, Ronald Reagan, George Shultz, for-

42. Bernard Gwertzman, "Democrats Score Nixon on Detente," *New York Times*, August 1, 1974, 7.

43. Quoted in William Delaney, "Trying to Awaken Us to Russia's 'Present Danger,'" *Washington Star*, April 4, 1977, 1.

44. Talbott, *Master of the Game*, 147.

45. Quoted in Jerry W. Sanders, *Peddlers of Crises* (Boston: South End Press, 1983), 152.

46. Quoted in Kay Bartlett, "Letting Light into the Lobby Club," *Milwaukee Journal*, July 7, 1974, pt. 5, p. 3.

mer secretary of state Dean Rusk, Harvard professor Richard Pipes, and Herbert Stein.[47] They were all white middle-aged males, and most were relatively wealthy. All were well-known hawks with long histories of anti-Communist activism. They agreed to reestablish the Committee on the Present Danger (CPD) to alert the public to the "growing Soviet threat."

The original Committee on the Present Danger was formed in 1950 at the time of the Korean War to urge the country to build up its conventional forces through universal military training.[48] The charge given by one of the founders, James Conant, was, "Get a group of distinguished citizens together, put it before the public, get people to write Congress and, in general, respond to the gravity of the situation."[49] The same mission would be followed now, twenty-four years later, as the dormant committee was revitalized.

The resuscitated committee struck a familiar tone of grim alarmism. Where the original committee warned that "the naked aggression by powerful Communist forces" constituted a "grave threat to the survival of the United Nations and a peril to the very security of these United States,"[50] the new committee thundered about "the ominous Soviet military buildup" and "the unfavorable trends in the U.S.-Soviet military balance."[51]

Right from that first luncheon "there was a great sense of urgency" to get the Soviet threat campaign rolling.[52] The first draft of the committee's initial statement was circulated to its members within a month. According to Charles Tyroler, who became the group's director, the driving force behind the formation of the committee was Rostow. He chaired the meeting at the Metropolitan Club, as well as all subsequent committee meetings for the next five years. By the time of that March lunch, Rostow had already circulated thirteen drafts of the committee's policy statement.[53] The committee was formally launched on November 11, 1976, three days after Jimmy Carter won the presidency.

The founder of the earlier CPD, James Conant, once wrote, "There is no

47. Max M. Kampelman, *Entering New Worlds: The Memoirs of a Private Man in Public Life* (New York: Harper Collins, 1991), 233.

48. S. S. Schweber, "The Hawk from Harvard," *Washington Post Book World*, February 6, 1994, 10.

49. James Conant, letter to Tracy Voorhees, August 1950, quoted in James Hershberg, *James B. Conant: Harvard to Hiroshima and the Making of the Nuclear Age* (New York: Knopf, 1993), 491.

50. Ibid., 506.

51. Charles Tyroler, ed., *Alerting America: The Papers of the Committee on the Present Danger* (Washington, D.C.: Pergamon-Brassey's, 1984), xv.

52. Sanders, *Peddlers of Crises*, 153.

53. Tyroler, *Alerting America*, xv.

such thing as plagiarism in the propaganda field."[54] The later CPD took this to heart, endlessly repeating the same charges of "the myth of detente," Soviet superiority in weaponry, Soviet cheating on the SALT Treaty, and Soviet military intervention in the Third World. The new committee's first pamphlet, "What Is the Soviet Union Up To?" was drafted by Richard Pipes, the chairman of one Team B panel, about which much more will be said later in this book. The CPD report ominously warned, "The ultimate Soviet objective—a Communist world order—requires the reduction of the power, influence, and prestige of the United States," and "Soviet nuclear offensive and defensive forces are designed to enable the U.S.S.R. to fight, survive and win an all-out nuclear war should it occur."[55]

The committee was not alone. Frank Barnett, a longtime hard-line anti-Communist and crusader for a strong defense, formed the National Security Information Center. Inviting Eugene Rostow to join, Barnett wrote, "You are fully aware, of course, that in terms of the shifting military balance, the U.S. today is about where Britain was in 1938, with the shadow of Hitler's Germany darkening all of Europe." In accepting the invitation Rostow replied, "We are living in a prewar and not a postwar world."[56] Barnett's Center sponsored briefing sessions for the press, featuring speakers such as Leon Goure of the University of Miami and Gen. Lyman Lemnitzer, both members of the CPD.

During this time, the American Security Council's film *The Price of Peace and Freedom,* supplied free as a "public service," was aired 180 times on television stations around the country. The film shows "young strong-jawed Soviet officers pushing buttons that send missiles soaring in an arc of destruction and displays the efficiency of Soviet tanks, bombers, radar and other military hardware. It is laced with somber warnings by high-ranking U.S. officers and extensive use of a pessimistic speech by Alexander Solzhenitsyn."[57]

Through newspaper advertisements, news briefings, radio and television programs, mailings, and speeches, conservative foes of detente gathered momentum during the mid-1970s. The indefatigable Eugene Rostow pointed to one indicator of their success. When the reconstituted committee was formed, it was identified as "hawkish," and its members as "cold warriors"

---

54. Quoted in Hershberg, *James B. Conant,* 522.

55. Quoted in Tyroler, *Alerting America,* 10–15.

56. Quoted in Linda Charlton, "Drive for Stronger U.S. Defense," *International Herald Tribune,* April 5, 1977, 3.

57. Ibid.

or "representatives of the military-industrial (or intellectual) complex." Six months later, the committee was described as "nonpartisan," as "a public interest group," "a study group," and "a group of nationally prominent individuals, including Democrats, Republicans, labor leaders, liberals, conservatives."[58] When Ronald Reagan became president thirty-two administration officials were members of the CPD, including Reagan himself, CIA director William Casey, National Security Adviser Richard Allen, U.N. ambassador Jeane Kirkpatrick, navy secretary John Lehman, and Assistant Secretary of Defense Richard Perle.[59] Reflecting back on the CPD, Max Kampelman wrote, "I know of no private public affairs organization that has had a greater influence in such a short period of time on U.S. foreign and defense policy issues."[60]

Neocons

Active opposition to detente also came from former liberals, some of whom had been part of the antiwar and pro–civil rights movements. Spearheaded by Jewish intellectuals and other strong supporters of Israel, they came to be known as neoconservatives, or "neocons." Their main concern was that America's post-Vietnam anti-interventionist mood combined with an eagerness to curry favor with Moscow would make the United States a less staunch defender of Israel. According to Richard Perle, one of the group's mandarins, "The Jewish–neo-conservative connection sprang from that period of worries about detente and Israel."[61]

The Yom Kippur, or October, War of 1973 in the Middle East seemed to confirm the worst fears of these strong supporters of Israel. Many Americans thought that the Soviet Union should have warned Washington of the impending Egyptian attack across the Suez Canal. After the attack, just before Israel could complete its encirclement of the Egyptian army, the Soviet Union wanted the United States to join it in enforcing a cease-fire. When the Soviets threatened to intervene unilaterally, the United States accused

58. Eugene V. Rostow, Memorandum to Members of the Board of Directors, Committee on the Present Danger, June 2, 1977, Papers of Clare Boothe Luce, Manuscript Division, Library of Congress.

59. Martin Walker, The Cold War: A History (New York: Henry Holt, 1993), 248.

60. Kampelman, Entering New Worlds, 234.

61. Quoted in Isaacson, Kissinger, 609.

the Soviets of violating the recently negotiated Agreement on the Prevention of War and called a worldwide alert of American military forces. Nevertheless, from the Israeli perspective, there were two disturbing developments: First, the United States joined the USSR in cosponsoring the U.N. resolution that demanded a cease-fire before Israeli objectives were reached. Second, the United States sternly threatened to end its resupply operation if Israel did not stop violating the cease-fire and agree to a truce.

Thomas J. McCormick writes,

> The lesson drawn by Israel's supporters . . . [was that] despite the Soviet-American tension during the American military alert, detente by and large worked. It worked, however, in ways contrary to Israel's long-term desire to maximize its freedom to pursue its own security. Detente in operation had demonstrated that the two superpowers might collude in ways inimical to chosen Israeli policy. . . . The political effect of the October War was to intensify and enlarge the coalition of anticommunist ideologues, military-industrial politicos, and American supporters of Israel.[62]

Neocons raised the human rights banner in their attack on the mistreatment of dissidents and minorities within the Soviet Union and criticized the "amorality" of the Nixon-Kissinger policies of detente.[63] Most members were Jewish, often former liberals mutating into conservatives (neoconservatives), and many were prominent in opinion-influencing fields. They included Irving Kristol, editor of *Policy Review*, Martin Peretz, editor of the *New Republic*, Norman Podhoretz, editor of *Commentary*, and Ben Wattenberg of the American Enterprise Institute. Podhoretz, for example, wrote that Secretary of State Kissinger "often sounds like Churchill and just as often acts like Chamberlain." Podhoretz accused Kissinger of promoting a new and insidious form of isolation. To these neocons, the future looked bleak: "If it should turn out that the new isolationism has indeed triumphed among the people as completely as it has among the elites, then the United States will celebrate its two-hundredth birthday by betraying the heritage of liberty which has earned it the wonder and envy of the world from the moment of its founding to this, and by helping to make that world safe for the most deter-

---

62. Thomas J. McCormick, *America's Half-Century: United States Foreign Policy in the Cold War* (Baltimore: Johns Hopkins University Press, 1989), 180.

63. E. J. Dionne Jr., *Why Americans Hate Politics* (New York: Simon & Schuster, 1991), 72.

mined and ferocious and barbarous enemies of liberty ever to have appeared on the earth."[64]

Aleksandr Solzhenitsyn

In February 1974, fifty-six-year-old Soviet novelist and Nobel laureate Aleksandr Solzhenitsyn was expelled from the Soviet Union and went into exile in Switzerland. There he became a powerful opponent of detente. In 1975 Solzhenitsyn traveled in the United States for two months. Based on Kissinger's advice that meeting with the famous Russian author and dissident might jeopardize progress at the forthcoming meeting with Brezhnev, President Ford declined to meet Solzhenitsyn. In a shabby moment, anonymous Ford aides raised the question of Solzhenitsyn's "mental stability." The liberal *New Republic* editorialized, "[A] meeting between Gerald Ford and Aleksandr Isayevitch Solzhenitsyn would have been the most convincing of semaphores signaling to the Russians that we have not forgotten all that has happened to this man (and to millions of others)—his years in Soviet slave labor camps, his defiance of Soviet authorities after his release from those camps and his determination to inform the world of what he has witnessed and endured."[65] According to former president Ford, "As soon as I saw the damage that my 'snub' was causing me among conservatives, I told [Jack] Marsh to tell [Senator Jesse] Helms that I'd be glad to see Solzhenitsyn when I returned from Helsinki. The Soviet author had an 'open' invitation. And this was the curious aspect of the whole affair. As soon as I issued the invitation, everyone seemed to lose interest in arranging the meeting. Helms never pushed it again, and Solzhenitsyn himself was reported to be too busy to come to Washington."[66]

On June 30, Solzhenitsyn was invited as guest of honor and dinner speaker at an AFL-CIO dinner in Washington, D.C. At the dinner, in a ninety-minute talk, Solzhenitsyn warned, "I have come to tell you the situation in the world is not just dangerous, not just threatening; it is catastrophic." He

64. Norman Podhoretz, "Making the World Safe for Communism," *Commentary*, April 1976, 31–41, quoted in H. W. Brands, *The Devil We Knew: Americans and the Cold War* (New York: Oxford University Press, 1993), 154.
65. "No Time to Say Hello, Goodby," *New Republic*, July 26, 1975, 5–6.
66. Ford, *Time to Heal*, 298.

also exclaimed, "It is not a detente while, over there, people are groaning and dying, and in psychiatric hospitals are being injected three times a day with drugs which destroy their brain cells."[67] Solzhenitsyn never mentioned the rearming of Germany, NATO, SEATO, CENTO, the missile race, or the anti-Communist rhetoric endemic to American politics for a generation. To an uneasy audience he implored, "Interfere more and more. Interfere as much as you can. We beg you to come and interfere."[68] While President Ford did not attend the dinner, Secretary of Defense Schlesinger, however, was there, and his prominent presence was thought by some to be one of the reasons for his dismissal a few months later.[69]

President Ford also turned down a public offer by conservative senators to bring Solzhenitsyn to the White House on July 4. Ford's decision was based on personality as well as policy: He considered the Russian to be "a god-damned horse's ass."[70] Kissinger, in his memoirs, claims that when Solzhenitsyn had expressed fears for his life, he (Kissinger) had repeatedly raised the matter with Soviet ambassador Dobrynin and had promised that if Solzhenitsyn were permitted to leave the Soviet Union, the administration "would not exploit his presence in the West for political purposes."[71]

For Senator Jackson and other detente critics, Solzhenitsyn was a godsend. Jackson saw to it that the invitation to a reception in Solzhenitsyn's honor at the Capitol in July was extended by a bipartisan group of twenty-four senators, including Senators Biden, Bumpers, Church, Glenn, Inouye, Magnuson, Stevenson, Javits, Packwood, Case, and Taft Jr.[72] In a press release, Jackson stated, "If Kissinger and Ford had met with Solzhenitsyn rather than cowering in fear of the Soviet reaction to such a meeting, they would have learned that all Solzhenitsyn is asking for is a detente without illusions, for an American-Soviet relationship that promotes the cause of human rights and a genuine peace."[73]

67. Aleksandr Solzhenitsyn, "No More Concessions!" *Reader's Digest* 107, no. 642 (1975): 73–78.

68. Quoted in Roger Morris, "Solzhenitsyn with a Grain of SALT," *New Republic*, August 16 and 23, 1975, 10–12.

69. Clarence A. Robinson, "Cabinet Shifts May Speed SALT," *Aviation Week and Space Technology*, November 10, 1975, 12.

70. Isaacson, *Kissinger*, 658.

71. Kissinger, *Years of Upheaval*, 986.

72. Press release, July 9, 1974, Box 11, no. 106, Henry M. Jackson Papers, University of Washington Libraries.

73. Press release, July 16–17, 1974, Box 11, no. 112, Henry M. Jackson Papers, University of Washington Libraries.

Liberals

Almost all liberals applauded detente and, although they hated to admit it, recognized Kissinger as its architect. For example, an editorial in the *New Republic*, early in 1974, asked whether "detente isn't preferable to the days of Berlin blockades, missile crises and bomb shelters."[74] Writing in the *New Republic*, John Osborne expressed his "gratitude to President Ford for keeping Kissinger in the dual role that Richard Nixon created for him. Henry Kissinger continues to be both assistant to the President for national security affairs and Secretary of State and all of us are lucky that he does."[75]

But Kissinger's belief in power politics and the necessity for trade-offs in foreign affairs became distasteful to some liberals. They preferred to stick to certain principles, and to pursue them consistently. For example, while generally applauding Nixon's openings to China and the Soviet Union, many were dismayed with the U.S. tilt toward Pakistan in the Indian-Pakistan War of 1971, which killed as many as one million persons. Although many Americans could understand that humoring Pakistan made sense while its president, Agha Yahya Khan, was acting as a go-between for the United States and China, once "the door to China ha[d] been opened, it [was] impossible to excuse or explain Washington's continuing supply of arms to Islamabad and its persisting ambiguity in the face of a deepening tragedy."[76] Likewise, once the secret bombing raids in Cambodia became known, liberals were outraged.

Liberal organizations that had excoriated successive administrations for the Vietnam War, the Cold War mentality shaping U.S. foreign policies, the failure to pursue a comprehensive test ban, and the arms buildup, now faced cross pressures. As relations between the superpowers improved, they felt freer to turn their attention to internal developments in the Soviet Union. They abhorred much of what they saw there but remained committed to the policy of detente between the United States and the Soviet Union.

Liberals and conservatives found common ground in their support for Soviet and Eastern European human rights and national self-expression, neither of which mattered much to Kissinger. As repression in the Soviet Union continued unabated at the onset of detente, some pundits worried whether

74. "Kissinger on Balance," *New Republic*, March 30, 1974, 5–7.

75. John Osborne, "Arming Up," *New Republic*, December 14, 1974, 9–10.

76. "Himalayan Confrontation?" editorial, *New York Times*, August 1, 1971, Week in Review, 10.

detente itself might be a cause of recurrent harassment of Soviet dissidents. "The recent campaign against the dissident intelligentsia has the purpose of depriving Soviet society of any free-thinking individuals who could interpret the new state of affairs and the arrival of thousands of American specialists in any way differing from the official line," wrote Richard Lourie. He continued, "It is probably too much to expect that they [Soviet dissidents] be remembered by the men in power now making deals and rearranging maps. But surely it is a moral obligation for the kinds of people likely to read this note that they remember not only Sakharov and Solzhenitsyn but also the other Russian dissidents, less well-known, but not less significant, who speak for freedom."[77]

Philip Handler, president of the National Academy of Sciences, had worked hard to develop scientific contacts and exchanges between American and Soviet scientists. When word came that Andrei Sakharov was being harassed and threatened by Soviet authorities, Handler cabled the protest of the National Academy to its Soviet counterpart: "Were Sakharov to be deprived of his opportunity to serve the Soviet people and humanity, it would be extremely difficult to imagine successful fulfillment of American pledges of binational scientific cooperation, the implementation of which is entirely dependent upon the voluntary effort and good will of our individual scientists and scientific institutions."[78]

The Federation of American Scientists issued a similar warning. The new president of the American Psychiatric Association began protesting directly to Moscow against the continued use of psychiatric torture on dissidents.[79] The liberal organization SANE also opposed nuclear weapons testing, the arms race, and the Cold War. Yet in September 1973, board members hand-delivered to Soviet ambassador Anatoly Dobrynin a letter stating: "We are disturbed by the Soviet government's chilling persecution of such dissidents as Andrei Sakharov, Aleksandr Solzhenitsyn, and many other individuals we have considered our counterparts in the Soviet Union. . . . When Soviet scientists and intellectuals are threatened, jailed or exiled, we see the spokesmen for detente with humanist values under attack. When your dissidents are attacked by your government, we are concerned about the kind of peaceful coexistence your government has in mind."[80]

77. Richard Lourie, "Soviet Dissidents and Balance of Power," Dissent 21 (winter 1974): 15–17.
78. Quoted in Joseph Clark, "Notes on Detente," Dissent 21 (summer 1974): 443–46.
79. I. F. Stone, "The Sakharov Campaign," New York Review of Books, October 18, 1973, 3–6.
80. Quoted in Fitzgerald, The Pentagonists, 134.

Theodore Draper, who had been a consistent critic of Lyndon Johnson's Vietnam policy, denounced detente as "an unmitigated snare and delusion" and described the Nixon-Kissinger policy as appeasement. Detente, according to Draper, was American give and Soviet take. Draper concluded that "detente with the East has beguiled us while deterioration in the West has beset us."[81]

Liberals certainly were never in favor of resuming the Cold War, but as the historian H. W. Brands writes, "The alienation of the liberals would matter later in the decade . . . the evident cynicism of detente's implementation at the hands of Nixon and Kissinger—combined with the liberals' thorough distaste for Nixon as an individual—left them less than enthusiastic about the President's policies. When the conservatives struck back against detente, the liberals would scatter quickly."[82]

Labor

Organized labor had long opposed improving relations with the Soviets. In 1959 the AFL-CIO opposed President Eisenhower's invitation to General Secretary Khrushchev to visit the United States.[83] The longtime outspoken anti-Communist octogenarian president of the AFL-CIO, George Meany, thought detente was "an absolute fraud." "Detente," he said, "is appeasement. Nothing else pure and simple, but appeasement. It's a giveaway in search of profits for our corporations through a combination of American capital and Soviet slave labor."[84] According to Meany, "The detente delirium which has seized so many American opinion-molders never stopped the Russians from rushing arms to the Arabs during the Yom Kippur War, or from urging other Arab nations to enter the fray or from encouraging the Arab oil boycott."[85]

From the beginning, labor worked closely with Senator Jackson in his

81. Theodore Draper, "Detente," *Commentary*, June 1974, 25–47, quoted in Brands, *The Devil We Knew*, 152.

82. Brands, *The Devil We Knew*, 133.

83. Fred Halliday, *The Making of the Second Cold War* (London: Verso, 1983), 117.

84. Quoted in Paula Stern, *Water's Edge: Domestic Politics and the Making of American Foreign Policy* (Westport, Conn.: Greenwood Press, 1979), 132.

85. George Meany, "How Much Is Enough?" June 8, 1974, Legislation Department, Records, 1906–78, Box 0034, Folder 024, The George Meany Memorial Archives.

antidetente activities. Jackson acknowledged this in a letter to Andrew Bie-miller, AFL-CIO director of the Legislative Office: "Dear Andy: I want you to know how grateful I am for your support and backing in the effort to get a favorable Senate vote on our amendment to the SALT Interim Agreement resolution. Only the future will reveal the importance of the action we took. You were there when needed and I deeply appreciate your help."[86] One of labor's biggest battles against detente revolved around trade issues.

Meany opposed trade with Communist Russia for ideological reasons. Meany had a powerful ally in the maritime unions, particularly the International Longshoremen's Association, headed by AFL-CIO vice-president Thomas W. Gleason. When Gleason and his fellow unionists in the maritime trades announced their intention to refuse to load American wheat bound for the Soviet Union, Meany declared, "Foreign policy is too damn important to be left to the Secretary of State." But he went on to link this statement with concern for trade union and consumer interests. He said, "Very simply, we are not going to load any grain to the Soviet Union unless and until a policy is set forth and agreed to that will protect the American consumer and also the American shipping interests."[87] The longshoremen's union balked at loading grain destined for the Soviet Union, because only 11 percent of American wheat going to the USSR went over in American boats, in violation of the 1972 wheat agreement, under which American ships were supposed to carry one-third of this wheat.[88]

U.S.-Soviet trade tripled between 1971 and 1973 to about $650 million (with American exports accounting for $546 million of the total). But according to Walter LaFeber, in half the trade of 1972–73 the Soviets had "cleverly and secretly entered the American grain market to buy up at low prices wheat and corn that U.S. taxpayers had paid farmers high subsidies to produce. As U.S. grain dealers made a fortune and Brezhnev obtained shiploads of cheap farm products, Nixon did nothing."[89] In 1972 late monsoons caused severe crop failures in South Asia and China and drought in parts of Africa. As a result, the price of wheat doubled between 1972 and 1974. As American bread prices increased dramatically, U.S. politicians grew furious

---

86. Henry M. Jackson, letter to Andrew J. Biemiller, September 15, 1972, Legislation Department, Records, 1906–78, Box 079, Folder 67, The George Meany Memorial Archives.

87. Quoted in John Herling, "George Meany and the AFL-CIO," *New Republic*, October 4, 1975, 15–19.

88. Ibid.

89. LaFeber, *American Age*, 618.

at the way Americans had been taken by Communist buyers. In his memoirs, Kissinger admitted that the Soviets had outwitted the United States and that the wheat deal was a mistake for the Americans.[90]

In 1975, when oil prices were rising steeply, Meany suggested swapping American grain for Russian oil instead of selling it at the market's low tide: "Should we not say, 'as you do with the oil which we need, so shall we do with our grain, which you need?' " One editorial opined that Meany's "judgment on bargaining with the Soviets, or with anybody else, has a good deal more experience and common sense to commend it than Gerald Ford's."[91]

Meany's unions also opposed extending government credits for Soviet-American transactions, believing that this encouraged the transfer of U.S. plants and technology to the Soviet Union, thus spurring Soviet competition against products made by American workers.[92] Meany objected to liberalizing trade if it failed to stop job losses for American workers. In a telegram sent to all members of the House Ways and Means Committee in the summer of 1973, Meany stated:

> The AFL-CIO strongly opposes the granting of most-favored-nation status to Communist countries. Such a move would be contrary to the best interests of the people of the United States and would be an abandonment of this nation's principles to support free nations, free economies and free peoples. MFN (most-favored nation) will insure massive increases in imports from countries which repress their populations and thwart formation of free trade unions and stifle legitimate dissent. . . . MFN will be used to expand and modernize Soviet industry to further the U.S.S.R.'s ambitions and power in the world. . . . Urge you vote against including MFN benefits for Communist countries in trade bill and we also urge that you vote to prohibit any credit or loans to Communist countries.[93]

90. Kissinger, *White House Years*, 1269–70, quoted in Dan Caldwell, *American-Soviet Relations from 1947 to the Nixon-Kissinger Grand Design* (Westport, Conn.: Greenwood Press, 1981), 118.

91. "On the Money," *Pine Bluff Commercial*, September 15, 1975, 4, Legislation Department, Records, 1906–78, Box 0034, Folder 022, The George Meany Memorial Archives.

92. Stern, *Water's Edge*, 210.

93. George Meany, telegram to members of House Ways and Means Committee, summer 1973, Legislation Department, Records, 1906–78, Box 0034, Folder 022, The George Meany Memorial Archives.

(MFN is a misnomer, since it provides for nondiscriminatory, rather than favored, treatment. Nations not granted MFN are subject to tariffs designed to inhibit trade.)

Enter Senator Jackson

The skillful politician who was able to meld together these disparate elements of the antidetente coalition—conservatives, neocons, Vietnam War liberals, organized labor, and human rights activists—was Senator Henry ("Scoop") Jackson, Democrat of Washington. A longtime anti-Communist, supporter of Israel, and defender of the defense industry ("the senator from Boeing," some said derisively), Jackson, whom John F. Kennedy passed over as his choice for vice-president in 1960, still harbored serious presidential ambitions. By identifying himself with the attack on detente, Jackson hoped to broaden his political base and to tap into the wide ideological diversity present in the strange bedfellows' coalition.

The Soviet Union did not generally permit its citizens to emigrate, but made exceptions for Jews who wanted to go to Israel. After the 1967 Arab-Israeli war, the number of Soviet Jews arriving in Israel jumped from 379 in 1968 to 13,000 in 1971 and 33,000 in 1973.[94] In August 1972 the Kremlin inadvertently handed Jackson the vehicle with which to unite the multifaceted opposition to detente. That month, at the height of Soviet-American goodwill about improved relations between the two superpowers, the Soviet government levied a new, prohibitively high "education tax" on all Soviet citizens who emigrated. The tax, to be paid before emigration, was ostensibly reimbursement for state-funded schooling.

The idea of linking freedom of emigration from the Soviet Union to trade concessions did not originate with Jackson. Paula Stern, the authoritative chronicler of the history of the Jackson amendment to the trade bill, writes that Louis Rosenblum, chairman of the Union of Councils for Soviet Jewry, came up with the idea in 1969. In 1971 the National Center for Jewish Policy Studies assigned a student to assess the Soviet need for trade from the West.[95] Senator Jackson then grabbed the idea as his own and ran with it for the next two and one-half years.

94. Stern, *Water's Edge*, 217.
95. Ibid., 11.

According to his aide Richard Perle, Jackson thought, "The whole MFN (most-favored nation) and trade agreement was bullshit. You can't have a truly reciprocal trade agreement with a nonmarket economy."[96] Jackson was profoundly skeptical about detente and not at all reluctant to see it held "hostage" to the issue of human rights inside the Soviet Union, particularly if this might advance his own 1976 presidential ambitions.[97] At a Gridiron Dinner in 1974, Jackson, who was not Jewish, half jokingly, half seriously intoned, "Actually, I'd be elected in a walk, if Brezhnev would let my people go."[98] President Ford wrote that he thought Jackson "was playing politics to the hilt."[99]

Stern reports that the question of Soviet Jews was not discussed at the 1972 Moscow summit. She quotes Kissinger counseling speechwriter William Safire and presidential aide Robert Haldeman to "say nothing while we're here. How would it be if Brezhnev comes to the United States with a petition about the Negroes in Mississippi?"[100]

Jackson's plan to link Jewish emigration from the Soviet Union with MFN status for that nation upset Kissinger's game plan. Kissinger's intentions with regard to "linkage" were modest. If the Soviets played by the American rules of the international game and cooperated in limiting arms, resolving the war in Vietnam (that is, helped the United States to reach, in Kissinger's words, "an elegant bug-out"),[101] and managing other crises, they would be rewarded with most-favored-nation trade status, technology transfers, and generous access to credits from the Export-Import Bank. Such was the intent of the comprehensive trade agreement reached between the United States and the Soviet Union in October 1972. In the agreement the United States consented to seek congressional approval to extend MFN status to the Soviet Union, and the Soviets promised to repay $722 million of its World War II lend-lease debt.[102] To the Nixon administration the trade agreement was an integral part of detente. But Kissinger doubted whether the Russian need for economic concessions was sufficient to get them to relax internal controls. At Vladivostok in 1974, Brezhnev proved Kissinger

96. Quoted in Isaacson, *Kissinger*, 613.

97. Gaddis, *The United States and the End of the Cold War*, 42; Garthoff, *Detente and Confrontation*, 412, 456.

98. Jackson speech, Box 10/120, Acc. 3560–6, University of Washington Libraries.

99. Ford, *Time to Heal*, 180.

100. Stern, *Water's Edge*, 15.

101. James Chace, "The Kissinger Years: A Gravely Flawed Foreign Policy," *New Republic*, November 9, 1974, 30–33.

102. Stern, *Water's Edge*, 44.

prescient: "No one should try to dictate to other people, on the basis of foreign policy considerations of one kind or another, the manner in which they ought to manage their internal affairs."[103]

To Senator Jackson, linkage was an instrument with which to secure greater respect for human rights inside the Soviet state and to make it easier for Soviet Jews and dissidents to leave the Soviet Union. On October 4, 1972, just as Congress was recessing for the presidential election, Senator Jackson introduced an amendment to the trade bill that would extend MFN status to the Soviets. Shortly thereafter, the bill was cosponsored in the House of Representatives by Ohio Democrat Charles Vanik, who had many Eastern European constituents. Vanik, a third-generation Czech, represented a Cleveland district that was 11 percent Jewish. Over the years, Vanik had intervened on behalf of hundreds of his Slavic constituents who were trying to arrange reunification of families with members trapped behind Communist borders.[104] Jackson's amendment, to block all trade advantages for the Soviet Union until emigration from that country was liberalized, soon had 72 cosponsors in the Senate, and Vanik garnered 238 cosponsors in the House. Although annual Jewish emigration from the Soviet Union had recently increased to about thirty-five thousand, it fell significantly short of the sixty thousand that Jackson publicly demanded.

To Kissinger's surprise, the Soviets quickly abandoned the education tax. But when Jackson and other senators were invited to the White House and shown the Soviet note agreeing to eliminate the education tax, Jackson said, "Mr. President, if you believe that, you're being hoodwinked." George Meany issued a statement that "the Soviet Union has an unbroken record of breaking its word."[105] Not only would the Soviets have to revoke the education tax, but to satisfy Jackson and Meany, they would also have to guarantee a sizable increase in the number of exit visas granted each year.[106]

In an unusual move, the renowned Soviet physicist Andrei Sakharov endorsed the Jackson amendment in an open letter to the U.S. Congress dated September 14, 1973. He characterized the amendment as "an attempt to protect the right of emigration of citizens in countries that are entering into new and friendlier relations with the United States."[107]

---

103. Quoted in S. R. Ashton, *In Search of Detente: The Politics of East-West Relations Since 1945* (New York: St. Martin's Press, 1989), 130.

104. Stern, *Water's Edge*, 54.

105. Both quoted in ibid., 70.

106. Ibid., 70; Isaacson, *Kissinger,* 613.

107. "An Open Letter to the Congress of the United States from Andrei Sakharov," Sep-

Sakharov's action opened the floodgates of opposition to expanding East-West trade. The historian and former Kennedy administration official Arthur M. Schlesinger up to then had been a staunch supporter of such trade. Now he wrote in the *Wall Street Journal*, "Always trust the man on the firing line."[108] I. F. Stone, the iconoclastic and fiercely independent journalist opined, "[W]hen a man as humane as Sakharov, who knows what is going on in the Soviet Union far better than we do, calls on us to back the Jackson amendment as the last hope for some liberalization in the U.S.S.R., I think we have no choice but to support him."[109] Sixty-five intellectuals sent joint telegrams to Sakharov and Aleksandr Solzhenitsyn praising their "courageous efforts on behalf of peace and freedom" and in a cable to Brezhnev denounced the Soviet Union's violation of human rights.[110]

In an October 1973 address at a Pacem in Terris Conference at the Sheraton Park Hotel in Washington, D.C., Jackson said:

> On Monday night the Secretary of State and the Chairman of the Senate Foreign Relations Committee—who agree on little else— came before you to share their belief that it is wrong for the U.S. to condition trade concessions to the Soviet Union on adherence to the free emigration provision of the Universal Declaration of Human Rights. Senator Fulbright, who is beguiled by the Soviets and Dr. Kissinger, who believes he is beguiling them, manage to find common ground in rejecting Dr. Andrei Sakharov's wise counsel against promoting a "detente" unaccompanied by increased openness and trust.[111]

The issue of Jewish emigration from the Soviet Union elicited enormous interest, sympathy, and newsprint for several years. Between 1973 and 1975, the *New York Times* index listed more than five hundred articles dealing with emigration. The pages of the *Bulletin of Atomic Scientists* were filled with stories of Soviet scientists refused permission to travel abroad to attend scientific meetings and of resolutions passed at those meetings decrying such ac-

---

tember 14, 1973, reprinted in Senate Committee on Finance, *The Trade Reform Act of 1973, Hearings*, 93d Cong., 2d sess., 1974, 2254–55.

108. Arthur M. Schlesinger, "The Price of Detente," *Wall Street Journal*, September 27, 1973, 18, quoted in Kissinger, *Years of Upheaval*, 988.

109. Stone, "The Sakharov Campaign," 4.

110. Stern, *Water's Edge*, 86.

111. Jackson speech, Pacem in Terris Conference, October 11, 1973, Box 10, Folder 80, Acc. 3560-30, University of Washington Libraries.

tions.[112] Scientists from many disparate fields signed appeals on behalf of Soviet scientists and often sent them to Soviet ambassador Anatoly Dobrynin.[113]

Throughout 1973 labor unions worked closely with Jackson to defeat the administration's trade bill. In a letter sent to all congressmen, Andrew Biemiller of the AFL-CIO wrote, "The AFL-CIO considers the Administration's trade bill one of the most damaging pieces of legislation to come before the House in recent years."[114] A few months later, Meany urged all members to vote for the Vanik amendment and then *"vote to defeat the entire bill"* (emphasis in original).[115]

By 1974 Kissinger was conducting shuttle diplomacy between Senator Jackson and the Soviets about the Jackson-Vanik amendment, and Jackson was able to boast, "Kissinger is afraid of me."[116] Kissinger hoped to extract enough concessions on Jewish emigration to satisfy Jackson and then to persuade the senator to support a provision to waive the effect of his amendment for a year or so.[117] But Jackson wanted assurances that a specific number of Jews would be allowed to leave each year, and the Soviets were insulted at the very notion of guaranteeing that a large number of its citizens would emigrate. "It was the beginning of a dialogue that made me long for the relative tranquillity of the Middle East," Kissinger recalled.[118]

When Gerald Ford became president in August 1974, he met with Soviet ambassador Dobrynin and said that the trade bill would contain some form of the Jackson-Vanik amendment. Dobrynin said that the Soviets could give an implied oral assurance that fifty-five thousand Jews or so could emigrate each year but that they "wouldn't put that guarantee on paper and let Jackson use it for his own political purposes."[119] Ford thought that number was suitable. And so a complicated deal was worked out. Kissinger would write to Jackson that he had assurances that Moscow would permit freer emigra-

112. See, for example, Sally Jacobsen, "On the Freedom of Emigration," *Bulletin of Atomic Scientists* 30, no. 2 (1974): 36; Earl Callen and Edward A. Stern, "Abuses of Scientific Exchanges," *Bulletin of Atomic Scientists* 31, no. 2 (1975): 32–35.

113. See, for example, "Evgeny Levich—An Appeal," *Bulletin of Atomic Scientists* 29, no. 10 (1973): 2.

114. Andrew J. Biemiller, letter, October 19, 1973, Legislation Department, Records, 1906–78, Box 020, Folder 36, The George Meany Memorial Archives.

115. George Meany, letter, December 5, 1973, Legislation Department, Records, 1906–78, Box 020, Folder 36, The George Meany Memorial Archives.

116. Quoted in Karnow, "Jackson's Bid," 17–21.

117. Isaacson, *Kissinger*, 615.

118. Ibid.

119. Ford, *Time to Heal*, 139.

tion; then Jackson would reply that this meant at least sixty thousand Jews would be permitted to exit each year; and then Kissinger would write back that he did not disagree with Jackson's interpretation.[120] The Soviets and the administration wanted the texts to remain confidential; Jackson wanted them all to be made public.[121]

On October 18, 1974, Senator Jackson, Senator Jacob Javits of New York, and Congressman Vanik met with President Ford and Kissinger in the White House to sign with fanfare the two letters that would resolve the trade-emigration issue. Jackson implied that the Soviets had capitulated to his campaign. He even drew special attention to the shaky sixty-thousand figure as a "benchmark" for Soviet behavior and predicted that it would be only a baseline.[122] Far from behaving in a low-key fashion as the Soviets and Kissinger had hoped, Morris Amitay of Senator Abraham Ribicoff's staff and Richard Perle of Senator Jackson's staff distributed copies of the letters at a press conference, precisely the type of "official release" the Soviets had rejected.[123]

When Kissinger arrived in Moscow the following week, Brezhnev was "livid" and "raged" at Jackson's crowing over the Soviet capitulation and stretching the general "assurances" reported by Kissinger into a "guarantee" of sixty thousand or more Jewish emigrants annually.[124] Within a week, a commentary from *Tass*, the official Soviet news agency, stated that the Soviet Union would "flatly reject as unacceptable any attempts . . . to interfere in internal affairs that are entirely the concern of the Soviet state and no one else."[125] Shortly after the trade bill, with the Jackson-Vanik amendment, passed in the Congress, the Soviet Union officially informed the United States that it would not seek most-favored-nation status or comply with the provisions of the bill, thus pounding another nail into the coffin of detente. The Jackson-Vanik amendment remained in effect for twenty years, until President Bill Clinton, in September 1994, signed a declaration freeing the former Soviet state from the law tying trade conditions to emigration.[126]

Also in 1974 the Senate passed an amendment by Senator Adlai Stevenson III (D-Ill.) to limit Export-Import Bank credits for the USSR to a total

120. Isaacson, *Kissinger*, 617.
121. Garthoff, *Detente and Confrontation*, 455.
122. Ibid., 455.
123. Isaacson, *Kissinger*, 618.
124. Garthoff, *Detente and Confrontation*, 457.
125. Ibid., 459.
126. Douglas Jehl, "Clinton Frees Russia from Curbs on Trade," *New York Times*, September 21, 1994, 3.

of $300 million over a four-year span, a sum far less than Russia already enjoyed without the trade-reform legislation. A major impetus for passage of the Stevenson amendment was the announcement by the Export-Import Bank in May that it had approved a $180-million loan to the USSR at the bargain interest rate of 6 percent to help finance a $400-million natural gas and fertilizer plant. The loan was one of the largest in the agency's forty-year history and, at the time, was issued at barely more than half the prevailing prime bank rate for big business.[127]

Ironically, the chairman and president of the Export-Import Bank who approved this generous loan to the USSR without congressional approval was William J. Casey, later to become the vehemently anti-Soviet director of the CIA in the Reagan administration. Together, the Jackson-Vanik and Stevenson amendments killed MFN status and export-import credits for Russia and gutted the economic component of detente. They also altered the meaning of linkage. Henceforth, detente would depend on proper Soviet behavior not only in its foreign policy but also in its internal policies toward Jews and dissidents in general.

Perhaps most important, the Jackson-Vanik-amendment battle succeeded in uniting American Jews, other ethnic and religious groups with cohorts under Soviet rule, some liberal organizations (such as the Americans for Democratic Action), as well as artistic, professional, intellectual, and scientific groups with hard-liners like George Meany and traditionally conservative anti-Soviet groups in opposing increased trade between the two countries.

Domestic Politics

When Gerald Ford became our nation's thirty-eighth president on August 9, 1974, he was firmly committed to the policy of detente. At a cabinet meeting on August 6, three days before Nixon's resignation, Vice-President Ford said to the president: "You have given us the finest foreign policy this country has ever had. A super job, and the people appreciate it. Let me assure you that I

---

127. "Ex-Im Bank Lets Soviets Borrow $180 Million at 6%," *Wall Street Journal*, May 22, 1974, 5, quoted in Harry Gelman, *The Brezhnev Politburo and the Decline of Detente* (Ithaca, N.Y.: Cornell University Press, 1984), 251.

expect to continue to support the Administration's foreign policy and the fight against inflation."[128]

The day before he was sworn in, Ford met with Henry Kissinger. Later, Ford recalled, "The one bright spot I remember in our session that day was the possible chance to reach agreement with the Soviets during strategic arms limitation talks. Nixon and Brezhnev had agreed to meet later in the Fall. Kissinger asked me if I wanted him to push ahead with those plans. 'Yes, of course,' I replied. Anything that would bring the arms race under control would be a plus for the entire world."[129] Hours after Ford took the oath of office, Soviet ambassador Dobrynin was invited into the Oval Office and became the new president's first foreign visitor.[130] Soon thereafter Ford received Soviet foreign minister Andrei Gromyko, who "hinted that his colleagues might be more 'responsive' to the Ford administration" and that "they just might be willing to make the sort of concessions that would enable us to agree on a new arms limitation pact."[131] But this was not to be.

In November 1975 Ronald Reagan told President Ford he was going to challenge him for the Republican nomination.[132] Within a few months, President Ford was in deep political trouble. A January 1976 poll showed that his performance had a 46 percent disapproval rating. The president attributed much of the dissatisfaction to "an image and not a substance problem" and resolved "to remain on the course [he] had set."[133] Early in January 1976 President Ford defended the policy of detente he had inherited and said in an NBC News interview: "I think it would be very unwise for a President—me or anyone else—to abandon detente. I think detente is in the best interest of this country. It is in the best interest of world stability, world peace."[134]

In January President Ford also decided to authorize Kissinger to make one more attempt ("our last chance," as Ford later put it) to negotiate a SALT agreement, to salvage the principal foreign policy achievement of the Ford administration (the Vladivostok Accord [see the next chapter]), and to provide a basis for defending the policy of detente.[135] However, while Kissinger was in Moscow, the new secretary of defense, Donald Rumsfeld, engineered

128. Ford, *Time to Heal*, 21.
129. Ibid., 33.
130. Dobrynin, *In Confidence*, 319.
131. Ford, *Time to Heal*, 183–84.
132. Ibid., 333.
133. Ibid., 347.
134. NBC News interview, quoted in Garthoff, *Detente and Confrontation*, 548.
135. Ibid., 540; Ford, *Time to Heal*, 353.

a secret rump meeting of the National Security Council behind Kissinger's back. Adm. James L. Holloway III, representing the Joint Chiefs of Staff, joined with the Defense Department and Fred Ikle, the director of the Arms Control and Disarmament Agency, to express serious reservations about the Moscow negotiations. In a private meeting with President Ford, Ikle argued against the agreement shaping up in Moscow. Ford was persuaded that with the upcoming election the SALT process should be shelved.[136]

In the February 24 New Hampshire primary President Ford nosed out challenger Ronald Reagan by only one percentage point. Reagan began to step up his attacks on the "Ford-Kissinger" foreign policy, claiming that the United States had been permitted to slide into second place and that the Soviet Union was taking advantage of detente at the expense of American prestige and security. Reagan charged that President Ford had fired Secretary of Defense James Schlesinger because he was "afraid to tell the American people the truth about our military status."[137] The heart of Reagan's challenge to the Ford-Kissinger foreign policy was a broad attack on detente, which Reagan denounced as a "one-way street." He cited every overseas setback—Vietnam, Angola, Portugal—as evidence that detente had failed. At each stop he would assail the treatment of Solzhenitsyn—"a true moral hero snubbed by Kissinger and Ford"—and the so-called Sonnenfeldt Doctrine (see the next chapter). The Helsinki conference, Reagan charged, was a sellout of the "captive nations" of Eastern Europe, which Ford and Kissinger felt should "give up any claim of national sovereignty and simply become part of the Soviet Union."[138]

In March, Reagan won the North Carolina primary, only the third time in U.S. history that a challenger defeated an incumbent president in a primary state.[139] Abruptly President Ford banished the word "detente" from his political vocabulary, much to the surprise of the White House staff. "We are going to forget the use of the word detente," the president said in an interview in Florida. "What happens in the negotiations . . . are the things that are of consequence."[140]

Reagan went on to win the Nebraska and Texas primaries as well. A panic

136. Isaacson, *Kissinger*, 629; Garthoff, *Detente and Confrontation*, 543.

137. Ford, *Time to Heal*, 346.

138. Isaacson, *Kissinger*, 695.

139. Anne Hessing Cahn, "Team B: The Trillion-Dollar Experiment," *Bulletin of Atomic Scientists* 49, no. 3 (1993): 22–27; Ford, *Time to Heal*, 375.

140. President's remarks and a question-and-answer session, Peoria, Ill., quoted in Garthoff, *Detente and Confrontation*, 548; Hyland, *Mortal Rivals*, 163.

reaction to the Nebraska loss caused even a ceremonial Rose Garden signing
of the Peaceful Nuclear Explosives Treaty (PNET) to be delayed because
Ford's domestic advisers thought a loss to Reagan in Ford's home state of
Michigan would be fatal. According to former Soviet ambassador Dobrynin,
"Ford's domestic policy advisers pleaded with him to postpone signing the
agreement, while his foreign policy advisers, headed by Kissinger, believed
that the agreement might enhance his chances." According to Dobrynin,
National Security Adviser Brent Scowcroft, an air force lieutenant general,
remarked, "It seems that our foreign policy and our relations with you won't
amount to anything worthwhile until August"—after the Republican convention.[141] The treaty was finally signed May 28.

With the Florida primary in early March, Reagan began to reiterate a
major campaign theme in words like these: "Under Kissinger and Ford, this
nation has become Number Two in a world where it is dangerous—if not
fatal—to be second best. All I can see is what other nations the world over
see: collapse of the American will and the retreat of American power. There
is little doubt in my mind that the Soviet Union will not stop taking advantage of detente until it sees that the American people have elected a new
President and appointed a new Secretary of State."[142]

By the time the Republican convention convened in August, the delegate
count was 1,035 for Reagan and 1,115 for the president, with 1,130 needed
for nomination. On the third day of the convention, Ford finally had enough
delegates to win. The administration's policy of detente was in full retreat.
Ford accepted a "morality-in-foreign-policy" plank in the party platform,
which commended Solzhenitsyn for "his human courage and morality,"
characterized the Helsinki agreement as "taking from those who do not have
freedom the hope of one day getting it," and committed the Republican
Party to a foreign policy "in which secret agreements, hidden from our people, will have no part."[143] Thus an incumbent president was forced to accept
a platform that was, in his words, "nothing less than a slick denunciation of
Administration foreign policy."[144]

Many domestic factors contributed to the end of detente. The Nixon and
Ford administrations attempted to inform the American public about detente and other foreign policy objectives by means of annual foreign policy

141. Dobrynin, In Confidence, 367.
142. Quoted in Ford, Time to Heal, 373–74.
143. Ibid., 398.
144. Ibid., 385.

reports, speeches, and interviews. But the public and, more important, the Congress never fully supported the administration's aims and remained skeptical of our policy toward the Soviet Union. Thus the Jackson amendment to the SALT I Treaty, the Jackson-Vanik amendment to the trade bill, and the Stevenson amendment limiting credits for the Soviet Union were significant congressionally imposed obstacles to the implementation of the Nixon-Kissinger policy of detente.

The arrival in the United States of the exiled Soviet writer Aleksandr Solzhenitsyn, with his inflammatory denunciations of the Soviet prison state, played a part. So did increases in food prices after the Soviet grain purchases. So did the overselling of detente. In their efforts to change U.S. foreign policy Nixon and Kissinger tended to distort and oversimplify. The China trip was "the week that changed the world"; the SALT and Vladivostok agreements "were breakthroughs"; and the Agreement on the Prevention of Nuclear War marked "the end of the cold war."[145] With the benefit of hindsight, Nixon wrote in 1980: "Creation of a willowy euphoria is one of the dangers of summitry. During my administration excessive euphoria built up around the 1972 Beijing and Moscow summit meetings. I must assume a substantial part of the responsibility for this. It was an election year and I wanted the political credit for what I believed were genuinely major advances toward a stable peace."[146]

In any case, detente was short-lived. By the 1980 presidential election, the choice in foreign and defense policy was between that of the Carter administration, which favored the MX missile, the Trident submarine, a Rapid Deployment Force, a "stealth" bomber, cruise missiles, counterforce targeting leading to a first-strike capability, and a 5 percent increase in defense spending, and that of the Republicans under Ronald Reagan, who favored all of these *plus* the neutron bomb, antiballistic missiles, the B-1 bomber, civil defense, and an 8 percent increase in defense spending.

---

145. Caldwell, *American-Soviet Relations*, 256.
146. Richard M. Nixon, *The Real War* (New York: Warner Books/Random House, 1980), 266, quoted in Caldwell, *American-Soviet Relations*, 97.

3

The Demise of Detente:
International Causes

Background

The Nixon administration formally ushered in detente with the president's historic visit to Moscow in May 1972 and the signing of the Strategic Arms Limitation Talks (SALT) and Anti-Ballistic Missile (ABM) Treaties. The two treaties limited two new weapons systems whose deployment threatened to escalate into a major new arms race: The ABM system the Soviets had deployed around Moscow in the late 1960s, and the other, developed to overcome this defensive system, was the MIRV (rhymes with "nerve"), the multiple independently targetable reentry vehicle. A MIRVed missile was able to carry several warheads on the end of one missile, with each warhead capable of being guided to separate and even widely dispersed targets. The two systems were seen to be linked: if one side had an effective defense, the other country would feel compelled to counter with a more powerful offense.

As discussed in the last chapter, the SALT Treaty limited the number of offensive intercontinental ballistic missiles to 1,410 land-based missiles and 950 submarine-launched missiles on the Soviet side, and 1,000 land-based missiles and 710 submarine-launched weapons on the U.S. side. The Americans more than made up the gap with the allies' nuclear deterrents in Western Europe, the greatly superior fleet of U.S. bombers (450 to 150 Soviet planes), and especially MIRV technology. The ABM Treaty limited each side to two defensive sites.

The third agreement signed at the momentous first U.S.-Soviet Summit in 1972 was the Basic Principles of Relations Between the United States of America and the Union of Soviet Socialist Republics. This contained a pledge to refrain "from efforts to obtain unilateral advantage at the expense of the other, directly or indirectly." The context in which it was signed undoubtedly fueled American public perceptions that the Soviets had adopted a more benign, less competitive stance toward the United States. When this proved not to be so, disenchantment with detente quickly followed.

This document was an attempt to set up ground rules to make the superpower competition less dangerous. Detente was to be about more than strategic weapons. To the Soviets, this agreement and one signed the following year, the Agreement on Prevention of Nuclear War, were the most important products of detente. Both were declaratory and executive agreements rather than treaties.

Right from the beginning, the United States and the Soviet Union interpreted these executive agreements differently. In an editorial on May 30, 1972, the *New York Times* described the Basic Principles agreement as "an approximation to a set of Marquis of Queensbury rules for peaceful coexistence in an era of mixed cooperation and competition."[1] The Soviet interpretation of "peaceful coexistence" never was the same as that of the United States. *Pravda*, on August 22, 1973, stated in the typical Soviet prose of that era, "From the class and sociopolitical angle the implementation of the principles of peaceful coexistence means: securing the conditions for the peaceful development of the socialist countries; curbing the imperialist policy of aggression and the conquest and annexation of other people's territory; preventing imperialist interference in other countries' internal affairs, particularly for the purpose of suppressing the peoples' liberation struggle—that is, preventing imperialist 'export of counterrevolution'; and preventing the use of force to resolve conflicts between states."[2]

In their attempt to sell detente to the American public, President Nixon

1. "Rules for Coexistence," *New York Times*, May 30, 1972, 36.
2. Quoted in Foy Kohler, "Soviet 'Peaceful Coexistence' Is Not Western 'Detente,' " Testimony before Subcommittee for Europe, House Committee on Foreign Affairs, May 15, 1974, 6–7 (also in Box 63/10, Henry M. Jackson Papers, Acc. 3560-6, University of Washington Libraries, 30).

and Secretary of State Kissinger vastly exaggerated its purported benefits for U.S. foreign relations. In 1974 Kissinger stated, "The biggest problem American foreign policy confronts right now is not how to regulate competition with its enemies . . . but how to bring our friends to a realization there are greater common interests than simple self-assertiveness."[3]

U.S. Foreign Policy

During the 1970s, the heyday of detente, foreign affairs in general were not going well for the United States. In the single month of March 1975, the final North Vietnamese offensive began, and the imperial city of Hue fell. The Khmer Rouge assaulted the American-backed government in Cambodia. In Portugal a coup against the left-leaning government supported by the Soviet Union failed. As Third World revolutions swept the globe from Saigon to Managua, Soviet actions in the Third World and in the strategic arms arena fueled American suspicions about Soviet intentions and capabilities.

Nor were things going well in Europe. Portugal, a NATO country, contemplated granting port facilities to the Soviet navy. According to President Ford, "The new left-wing leaders of Portugal posed a danger of a different kind. Suppose Communists joined or, worse yet, dominated the Lisbon government. How could the West share military secrets with them? What would happen if the Soviets won access to Portuguese airfields or naval bases? Would we have to strip Portugal of its NATO membership?"[4]

The clash between Greece and Turkey, both NATO members, over Cyprus left Greece with a grudge against the United States and a less-than-wholehearted commitment to NATO. There were fears that after General Franco's death in 1975, Spain might turn to the Left. As with Portugal, this turned out not to be so. Italy's political and economic stability was suspect; elections were scheduled in June, and it was feared that the Communists would score heavy gains. Communist parties in Western Europe, which had condemned the Soviet-led invasion of Czechoslovakia in 1968, increasingly asserted their independence from Moscow. This development came to be

3. Quoted in Mary Kaldor, *The Disintegrating West* (London: Allen Lane, Penguin Books, 1978), 25.
4. Gerald Ford, *A Time to Heal: The Autobiography of Gerald R. Ford* (New York: Harper & Row, 1979), 285–86.

known as Eurocommunism, and these parties grew in popularity and acquired substantial followings in Italy and France.[5]

Leo Cherne, a member of the President's Foreign Intelligence Advisory
Board (PFIAB), summarized in testimony to the House Intelligence Committee on December 11, 1975, the conservatives' pessimistic view of where
the Soviet Union and the United States were going:

> The Soviet Union has already made it clear that it does not inter-
> pret the Helsinki agreement as in any way moderating the urgency
> of its ideological efforts. Indeed, leaders of the Soviet Union have
> been remarkably candid in observing that they think the tide is
> running in their favor. There *is* no monolithic Communist move-
> ment, but there *are* Communist parties in most countries which are
> more or less available to advance the interests of one of the centers
> of Communist power. I am doing no more than describing the
> events which occurred in Portugal, which presently exist in Angola,
> which hopefully will not threaten a Spain in transition. The Italian
> Communist Party may be closer to achieving its purposes in Italy
> today than it was when we were so fearful of that prospect in the
> late 1940s. . . . Whatever danger may lie before us from the Soviet
> Union or any other foreign source cannot be readily corrected by
> the American people. No ballot box will diminish that danger, no
> burst of renewed faith among us can altogether deflect that danger—
> not here, not in Angola, or Portugal, or Central Europe. . . . Intelli-
> gence cannot help a nation find its soul. It is indispensable, however,
> to help preserve that nation's safety while it continues the search.[6]

This testimony elicited a handwritten congratulatory letter from George
Bush, who was just leaving Beijing to assume the directorship of the CIA.[7]
Fellow PFIAB member Clare Boothe Luce gushed, "What a noble balance
there is between heart and mind, passion and reason there is in all that you
say and write—and *are*" (emphasis in original).[8] Senator Hubert Humphrey

5. S. R. Ashton, *In Search of Detente: The Politics of East-West Relations Since 1945* (New
York: St. Martin's Press, 1989), 134–35.

6. Leo Cherne, *U.S. Intelligence Agencies and Activities: Risks and Control of Foreign Intelli-*
gence, hearings before the House Select Committee on Intelligence, 94th Cong., 1st sess.,
December 12, 1975, 1882–91.

7. George Bush, letter to Leo Cherne, December 31, 1975 (provided by Leo Cherne).

8. Clare Boothe Luce, letter to Leo Cherne, December 29, 1975 (provided by Leo
Cherne).

"felt [the testimony] was extremely worthwhile,"[9] while Secretary of Defense Rumsfeld wrote, "It was excellent."[10] George Shultz, then president of the Bechtel Corporation, called the testimony "a fine statement."[11]

While conservatives dwelt exclusively on what the Soviets were doing to destroy detente, the United States was pursuing its own unilateral interpretation of detente. On their way back from the Moscow summit in 1972, Nixon and Kissinger stopped in Teheran and pledged support to the shah in his efforts to use Kurdish guerrillas to destabilize Iraq, an ally of Moscow. In 1973 the administration waged economic warfare against the government of Salvadore Allende in Chile in an attempt to overthrow it. The administration also denied the Soviets a role in the Middle East after the October 1973 Yom Kippur War. To the Soviets, these maneuvers seemed a direct repudiation of the Basic Principles of Relations of 1972, which in their eyes granted the Soviet Union coequal status in international relations.

Third World Revolutions and Interventions

Much of the criticism of detente came because of Soviet actions, particularly in the Third World. All during this period of detente, the Soviet Union continued to intervene in a succession of Third World countries, and the tide seemed to be turning against the United States. The first setback came in February 1974 with a revolution in Ethiopia, the third most populous nation in Africa and the recipient of two-thirds of U.S. military aid to the sub-Saharan region since 1945. In September 1974, after the overthrow of longtime emperor Haile Selassie by a radical but ineffectual regime, the Soviets and Cubans intervened on behalf of Haile-Mariam Mengistu, and the United States began to back Somalia in its attempt to change international borders by force.

Two months after the beginning of the Ethiopian revolution, a coup succeeded in overthrowing Portugal's military dictatorship, and independence for its colonies became a certainty. In all five—Angola, Cape Verde, Guinea-Bissau, Mozambique, and São Tomé—guerrilla movements soon seized power.

9. Hubert H. Humphrey, letter to Leo Cherne, February 10, 1976 (provided by Leo Cherne).
10. Donald H. Rumsfeld, letter to Leo Cherne, January 5, 1976 (provided by Leo Cherne).
11. George P. Shultz, letter to Leo Cherne, December 22, 1975 (provided by Leo Cherne).

A three-way contest for power in Angola quickly developed, but the fight only acquired strong international overtones in 1975, when Cuba began sending, with Soviet financing and protection, military advisers and then combat units to support the Marxist-oriented Popular Movement for the Liberation of Angola (MPLA, or Movimento Popular de Libertação de Angola), which comprised about 15–20 percent of the population. Between March 1975 and February 1976, eleven thousand Cuban combat troops and $300 million in Soviet military equipment were introduced into Angola.[12] South Africa soon invaded Angola in cooperation with the two other contending groups, UNITA (National Union for the Total Independence of Angola, or União Nacional para a Independência Total de Angola), which held the allegiance of about 40 percent of the Angolans, and the FNLA (National Front for the Liberation of Angola, or Frente Nacional de Libertação de Angola), containing about 20 percent of the population.[13] The FNLA was also backed by China, Romania, India, Algeria, Zaire, the AFL-CIO, and the Ford Foundation. UNITA, headed by Jonas Savimbi, who denounced "American interests" and the "notorious agents of imperialism," was backed by North Vietnam, China, and North Korea. Many years later, Savimbi ended up allied with South Africa and loosely with the United States, where he was cast as one of the Reagan Doctrine's deserving "freedom fighters."[14] In his memoirs many years later, the longtime Soviet ambassador to the United States, Anatoly Dobrynin, wrote about these Angolan factions: "Such ideological or other fundamental differences as may have existed among them had to be left to the trained observer, a point that might easily be discerned from the similarity of their names."[15]

Angola became a festering sore in bilateral superpower relations. In March 1975 the administration announced that meetings of the three cabinet-level joint U.S.-Soviet commissions on trade, housing, and energy set up in 1972 would be postponed as a signal of American displeasure over Soviet activities in Angola.[16]

---

12. Richard J. Barnet, *The Giants: Russia and America* (New York: Simon & Schuster, 1977), 41.

13. H. W. Brands, *The Devil We Knew: Americans and the Cold War* (New York: Oxford University Press, 1993), 135; Constantine C. Menges, *The Twilight Struggle: The Soviet Union v. the United States Today* (Washington, D.C.: AEI Press, 1990), 103.

14. Walter Isaacson, *Kissinger: A Biography* (New York: Simon & Schuster, 1992), 675.

15. Anatoly Dobrynin, *In Confidence: Moscow's Ambassador to America's Six Cold War Presidents (1962–1986)* (New York: Times Books, 1995), 360.

16. Raymond Garthoff, *Detente and Confrontation: American-Soviet Relations from Nixon to Reagan* (Washington, D.C.: Brookings Institution, 1985), 549.

In July 1975 President Ford approved a significant increase in the CIA's covert paramilitary operations, which had been going on since the 1960s.[17] As this became known, opposition to the policy was quickly energized. In December 1975, the U.S. Senate voted 54 to 22 to block any new funds for support of military or paramilitary operations in Angola. The following month the House of Representatives voted 323 to 99 in favor of a similar measure. The congressional votes on Angola were the culmination of a series of attempts to check presidential military actions abroad. The Cooper-Church amendment of 1970 prohibited U.S. combat forces in Cambodia; in 1973 Congress voted to ban all U.S. involvement in Indo-China after August 15 of that year; and the Hughes-Ryan amendment of 1974 limited the powers of the CIA.

Henry Kissinger warned, "Angola represents the first time that the Soviets have moved militarily at long distance to impose a regime of their choice. It is the first time that the United States has failed to respond to Soviet military moves outside the immediate Soviet orbit. And it is the first time that Congress has halted national action in the middle of a crisis. . . . An ominous precedent has been set. . . . If the pattern is not broken now, we will face harder choices and harder costs in the future."[18]

Kissinger went to Moscow in January 1976 in a last ditch effort to complete a SALT II treaty before the fall election. He insisted that Angola should be discussed, while Brezhnev and Gromyko said they, at least, would not discuss it.[19] According to Soviet ambassador Dobrynin, when an American journalist asked Brezhnev about the agenda, Brezhnev snapped, "If Kissinger wants to talk about Angola, he has Sonnenfeldt [counselor at the State Department and very close to Kissinger] to talk with."[20] Kissinger argued that "the impact of the Soviet and Cuban action in the U.S., even if it did not lead to American counteraction in Angola, was seriously affecting the American perception of Soviet policy and was thus harming the overall relationship. It could have an impact on trade relations and other aspects of bilateral relations and on detente as a whole. The Soviet leaders, however, continued to object to discussing Angola."[21]

In their vision of detente, Nixon and Kissinger sought to create rules of

17. Peter Kornbluh and James G. Blight, "Dialogue with Castro: A Hidden History," *New York Review of Books,* October 6, 1994, 1–4.

18. Quoted in Menges, *The Twilight Struggle,* 111.

19. Garthoff, *Detente and Confrontation,* 546.

20. Dobrynin, *In Confidence,* 363.

21. Garthoff, *Detente and Confrontation,* 547.

conduct, rules and procedures to define the limits of acceptable behavior in international relations. Clearly Soviet actions in Angola violated this vision. As Moscow proclaimed it would continue aiding "wars of national liberation," six new pro-Soviet dictatorships took power around the world in 1975, including Guinea-Bissau, Mozambique, Vietnam, Cambodia, Laos, and Angola.

From the Soviet perspective, their actions in the Third World were not inconsistent with detente. In Moscow's eyes, detente did not mean an end to competition between capitalism and socialism. The Soviet Union was not prepared to abandon all global roles for a few paragraphs of the SALT I Treaty and the benefits of U.S.-Soviet trade. If the United States considered it self-interest to maintain close political economic and military ties with right-wing regimes in Latin and Central America, southern Africa, and southern Asia, then, by the same token, the Soviet Union considered that it was in its interests to support national liberation movements wherever the opportunity arose. But the very success of these Soviet projections of power, coupled with a perceived erosion of U.S. strategic superiority, contributed to a reawakening of Cold War fever.

CSCE and the Helsinki Accords

In July 1975, President Ford and General Secretary Brezhnev met in Helsinki, Finland, to cap a two-year-long series of meetings of the Conference on Security and Cooperation in Europe. The Soviets had long wanted such a conference to ratify their postwar borders. The Europeans were keen for the conference because this would be their entrée into the "big-time" international scene. It would enable them to exert pressure on both the United States and the Soviet Union. The conference eventually produced three "baskets" of agreements that came to be known as the Helsinki Final Act.

The first basket, "Security in Europe," confirmed the postwar borders, tacitly accepted the incorporation of the Baltic states into the Soviet Union, and required "nonintervention in the internal affairs" of sovereign nations. It included confidence-building measures such as giving advance notice of military exercises. This part of the agreement was essentially a de facto World War II peace treaty.

The second portion dealt with science, technology, the environment, tourism, and trade, and committed East and West to promote freer transnational trade, joint manufacturing ventures, technology transfers, transportation, tourism, and labor migration. The final basket, "Humanitarian and Other Fields," pledged greater educational and cultural exchanges and endorsed the free movement of people and ideas as well as respect for human rights. This soon led dissidents in the Warsaw Pact countries to begin testing the outer limits of the agreement.

The conference proved to be extremely unpopular in the United States. Americans of Eastern European descent and conservatives excoriated President Ford for going. The vice-president of the Latvian Press Society opined that "President Ford will sign his name on a miserable and un-American treaty—a treaty which buries the hopes of millions of Eastern European peoples in ever securing freedom and independence, a treaty which buries the principles of the Atlantic Charter, the ideals of which kept hope in the hearts of the Latvians, Lithuanians, Estonians, Ukrainians, Poles, etc."[22]

Senator Henry Jackson issued a press release stating, "There are times in international diplomacy when the President of the United States ought to stay home. By cooperating with Brezhnev at the Helsinki summit in fostering the illusion that substantive progress toward greater security in Europe has been made, President Ford is taking us backward not forward, in the search for a genuine peace."[23] Even the New York Times, generally supportive of detente and improved relations with the Soviets, called it "the Helsinki carnival" and saw the conference as "a regrettable, unilateral gain for the Soviet Union without any corresponding advantage for the United States."[24] In his memoirs, President Ford wrote: "No journey I made during my Presidency was so widely misunderstood. 'Jerry, don't go,' the Wall Street Journal implored, and the New York Times called the trip 'misguided and empty.' " And most important, Ronald Reagan said, "I am against it and I think all Americans should be against it."[25]

The Soviet Nobelist and Gulag survivor Aleksandr Solzhenitsyn, smarting over President Ford's decision not to receive him at the White House, accused Ford of "participating in the betrayal of Eastern Europe by planning to attend the 35-nation European summit meeting."[26] Ford, in office less

22. Osvalds Akmentine, "A 'Miserable' Treaty," letter, New York Times, July 25, 1975, 30.
23. Henry M. Jackson press release, July 22, 1975, Legislation Department, Records, 1906–78, Box 0079, Folder 68, The George Meany Memorial Archives.
24. "European Security and Real Detente," New York Times, July 21, 1975, 20; "Symbolic Journey . . . ," New York Times, July 27, 1975, 16.
25. Ford, Time to Heal, 300.
26. Bernard Gwertzman, "Solzhenitsyn Says Ford Joins in Eastern Europe's Betrayal," New York Times, July 22, 1975, 1.

than a year, went largely because he seemed unable to escape it. Before leaving for Helsinki, he pointed out that "[t]he document I will sign is neither a treaty nor is it legally binding on any participating state."[27] The Helsinki Conference was billed by some as a kind of Munich.[28]

Immediately after the conference, Kissinger and his close aide Helmut Sonnenfeldt briefed American diplomats in London. Sonnenfeldt's briefing was later summarized in a State Department cable, which was promptly leaked to journalists Rowland Evans and Robert Novak. It became infamous as the "Sonnenfeldt Doctrine," which "supposedly urged the United States to consign the East Europeans to the Soviet sphere, indeed, to assist in forming an 'organic' link between Moscow and its satellites."[29] Sonnenfeldt's point was that an "organic" relationship was better than the present "inorganic, unnatural relationship," which was based entirely on "the presence of sheer Soviet military power."[30] But the Sonnenfeldt Doctrine, as it was discussed in the media, resembled the conservatives' worst nightmare of a secret Yalta-like sellout—an admission by the United States that the "captive nations" of Eastern Europe were naturally part of Moscow's sphere of influence. "Whatever was actually meant by Mr. Sonnenfeldt, the latest mini-Metternich of Foggy Bottom, the idea sent shivers up the spine," C. L. Sulzberger wrote in the New York Times. "It would seem to be an invitation to the Kremlin to assert fuller control of Eastern Europe, perhaps even absorbing it into the U.S.S.R."[31]

Ronald Reagan, getting ready to challenge Ford for the Republican nomination, blasted the Sonnenfeldt Doctrine for saying that "slaves should accept their fate," and he linked it to other cases where the Kissinger-Ford team had abandoned human rights concerns.[32]

To make matters worse, the Soviets tried to invoke the Helsinki principles to complain about the European countries' unwillingness to provide economic and financial assistance to the Communist military clique in Portugal, which had seized power in defiance of the overwhelmingly anti-Communist vote in the last election. James Reston, in a scathing article, blistered the

27. Kevin Klose, "Bearing Witness in a New Europe," Washington Post, November 25, 1990, C1.

28. Joseph Kraft, "The Limits of Detente," Washington Post, August 7, 1975, 15.

29. William G. Hyland, Mortal Rivals: Superpower Relations from Nixon to Reagan (New York: Random House, 1987), 120.

30. "State Dept. Summary of Remarks by Sonnenfeldt," New York Times, April 6, 1976, 14.

31. Quoted in Isaacson, Kissinger, 664.

32. Ibid.

Soviets for invoking "the Helsinki principles of liberty in order to help destroy liberty in Portugal" and pointed out that the weakness of the Helsinki agreement was the lack of agreement on what detente means.[33]

Vladivostok

In November 1974, President Ford and General Secretary Brezhnev met at Vladivostok to sign a follow-on agreement to the SALT Treaty. The meeting gave the two leaders their first opportunity to size each other up. A cable from the U.S. embassy in Moscow just before the summit opined that "perhaps the most important message the President can leave with Brezhnev is that progress in SALT will be a critical element in determining the American people's continued support for economic cooperation and other aspects of detente."[34]

The two leaders agreed to a "framework" for an agreement that would limit each side's missiles and bombers to 2,400, of which not more than 1,320 missiles could be MIRVed, thus ratifying the equal-aggregates approach. A final treaty was to be negotiated and signed in the United States within months. The administration put on a full-court press to hype the accord. For President Ford, "the results of the trip had exceeded my expectations. There was, of course, no way for me to know at that time that this would be a high-water mark and that the next five and a half months would be the most difficult of my Presidency—if not my life."[35] Secretary of State Kissinger described the agreement as "a breakthrough." Ron Nessen, White House press secretary, said, "[T]he President will return home in triumph."[36]

The Soviet press called the meeting a "new major step" in U.S.-Soviet relations. According to the U.S. embassy in Moscow, "[T]he tone and language used in describing the results of the meeting are warmer than those used in a similar evaluation of the July summit."[37]

But the reaction in the United States was generally negative. For decades

33. James Reston, "Soviets Invoke Helsinki," *New York Times,* August 13, 1975, 33.

34. "The Soviets Look at the Vladivostok Summit," Department of State cable, November 1974, obtained through FOIA and made available by the National Security Archive.

35. Ford, *Time to Heal,* 219.

36. John Herbers, "Ford, Brezhnev Agree to Curb Offensive Nuclear Weapons; Final Pact Would Run to 1985," *New York Times,* November 25, 1974, 1.

37. "Politburo Approval of Summit: Warmer Than July," Department of State cable, November 1974, obtained through FOIA and made available by the National Security Archive.

Americans had been used to the idea that we had nuclear superiority. Now news that Ford had agreed to nuclear parity raised concern and worry. Despite the fact that Senator Jackson's principle of equality was accepted at Vladivostok, he called the agreement "a severe disappointment." In a memo shortly after the summit, he wrote: "Far from 'putting a cap on the arms race,' as Administration spokesmen have argued, it provides the basis for a sustained 10-year arms build-up, authorizes astonishingly high MIRV levels, and legitimizes a continuation of the Soviets' massive strategic arms expenditures."[38]

The *New York Times* critiqued the accord in several editorials. One pointed out that "it would authorize both sides to go ahead with their planned buildups. Costs and instabilities are likely to increase."[39] Another stated, "[M]ore and more, the Vladivostok accord appears to be an agreement between the military on both sides—achieved through the intermediaries of the chiefs of government—to permit the buildups each desired. . . . If this is 'putting a cap on the arms race,' then a shrimp can whistle—as a former Soviet leader, Nikita Khrushchev, was fond of saying."[40]

Howard Flieger, in a *U.S. News and World Report* editorial, diagnosed: "[T]he uneasiness that lurks around the arms agreement stems in large part from a feeling that maybe the U.S. is paying too high a price to preserve detente. Perhaps less haste and more confidence in America's real power could have produced a tighter and less costly 'cap' for the arms race."[41]

President Ford felt that the "Soviets achieved a propaganda victory. No sooner had I returned to Washington than I saw evidence of this. The first sampling of White House mail showed 122 letters condemning the accords; only eleven letters approved of what I had done, and I dropped several percentage points in the polls. The well-meaning ethnic groups in this country simply didn't understand our accomplishment. This was not a failure in substance. It was a failure in public relations, and I will have to accept a large share of the blame."[42] (Shades of Bill Clinton twenty years later!)

Surprisingly, one of the supporters of the agreement was Edward Teller, the "father of the H-bomb" and a member of the President's Foreign Intelli-

38. Henry M. Jackson, memorandum, "On the Vladivostok Strategic Arms Agreement," December 1974, Henry M. Jackson Papers, Accession Number 3560-6, Box 11, Folder 50, University of Washington Libraries.

39. "Vladivostok Arms Pact," *New York Times*, November 29, 1974, 38.

40. "Spurring the Arms Race," *New York Times*, December 4, 1974, 42.

41. Howard Flieger, "Loose-Fitting Cap," *U.S. News and World Report*, December 23, 1974, 76.

42. Ford, *Time to Heal*, 306.

gence Advisory Board, who generally opposed any arms control treaty. In a response to Flieger's editorial, Teller pointed out that under the terms of the agreement, the United States would be permitted to build up to the ceiling, while the Soviets might have to dismantle existing equipment. Teller wrote, "[A]s a result of Vladivostok, there may emerge a thorough shift in the development of arms: quality rather than quantity will be emphasized"; and Teller praised the agreement for "making this fact obvious to all of us."[43]

Other scientists gave the agreement lukewarm support. Writing in the *Bulletin of Atomic Scientists,* Frank Long, a professor at Cornell University, opined that 1,320 MIRVed missiles "seems needlessly—almost foolishly—high for either the United States or the Soviet Union." On balance, Long gave qualified approval to the agreement.[44]

But the agreement reached at Vladivostok soon collapsed as President Ford began to retreat from his policy of detente with the Soviet Union under the pressure of the challenge from Ronald Reagan.

Strategic Arms and the Soviets: Were the Soviets Cheating?

Questions about Soviet compliance with the arms control treaties they had signed began to surface soon after the ink dried on the agreements. Members of the administration were adamant in maintaining that there was no Soviet cheating. Even the hawkish secretary of defense James Schlesinger, in a December 1974 news conference, stated, "[T]here is no conclusive evidence of any violations." In June 1975 he reiterated "that we cannot state that the Soviets have violated the Interim Agreement." And the next month, he repeated, "[W]e have no firm evidence of proof that the Soviets have indeed violated the SALT I agreement . . . as yet, we have no demonstrated case of violation by the Soviet Union."[45] President Ford and Secretary of State Kissinger and even hard-line ACDA director Fred Ikle repeatedly denied that the Soviets were cheating.

43. Edward Teller, "Arms Deal: A Defense," *U.S. News and World Report,* December 30, 1974, 68.

44. Frank A. Long, "Should We Buy the Vladivostok Agreement?" *Bulletin of Atomic Scientists* 31, no. 2 (1975): 5–6.

45. "Summary of U.S. Official Statements," n.d., National Security, SALT Treaties Folder, Box 32, Presidential Handwriting Files, Gerald R. Ford Library, Ann Arbor, Mich.

Nonetheless, in July 1975, former secretary of defense Melvin Laird, now a senior counselor for national and international affairs at the *Reader's Digest*, in a widely quoted story, accused the Soviets of repeatedly committing deliberate acts that mocked detente and threatened the free world. Laird alleged that the Soviet Union violated the SALT and ABM Treaties, assisted North Vietnam in making a shambles of the Paris peace accords and overrunning South Vietnam, sponsored a massive campaign in Portugal to impose a Communist regime there, and was engaging in a relentless effort to attain military supremacy.[46] President Ford was sufficiently upset by this article, written by his former congressional colleague, to ask his National Security Adviser, Henry Kissinger, for a point-by-point analysis prior to meeting with Laird.

Kissinger, of course, was determined to defend the integrity of the agreements he had negotiated. In his eight-page memo Kissinger concluded: "The Soviet Union has complied with both the strategic arms agreements and the Quadripartite Agreement on Berlin; the Soviet Union is pursuing a very active strategic program, but one that cannot secure for it a margin of strategic advantage unless we let down our guard; developments troublesome to us in Portugal are due primarily to internal Portuguese considerations rather than to Soviet interference, although the Soviets undoubtedly have given financial support to the Portuguese communists."[47]

On the question of Soviet compliance with arms control treaties, President Ford stated:

> I have investigated the allegations that the Soviet Union has violated the SALT agreements, that they have used loopholes to do certain things that were intended not to be done under the agreement. I have found that they have not violated the SALT agreement, they have not used any loopholes. And in order to determine whether they have or they have not, there is a standing consultative group that is an organization for the purpose of deciding after investigation whether there have been any violations. And that group, after looking into the allegations, came to the conclusion there had been no violation.[48]

46. Melvin Laird, "Is This Detente?" *Reader's Digest* 107, no. 639 (1975): 54–57.
47. Henry Kissinger, memorandum to President Ford, n.d., Folder Melvin Laird, Box B 2, Kissinger-Scowcroft Name File, Gerald R. Ford Library, Ann Arbor, Mich.
48. "Summary of U.S. Official Statements," Gerald R. Ford Library.

Why did accusations of Soviet cheating persist?

Negotiations on the SALT I and ABM Treaties lasted two and one-half years. In addition to the text, the completed treaties also contained "Agreed Statements" initialed by the heads of the delegations and "Common Understandings" agreed to by both sides. But each treaty also contained "Unilateral Statements." These were subjects, such as what constituted testing "in an ABM mode" or the definition of a "heavy missile," about which no agreement had been reached. Many of the later accusations of Soviet noncompliance with the treaties dealt with those items, items the Soviets had never agreed to. Even in the agreed areas, both the United States and the Soviet Union soon began to push the treaty to the outer edges of the permissible.

Who's Ahead?

Throughout the Cold War, Americans were preoccupied with the question, "Who's ahead?" Long used to the notion of U.S. superiority, we were never comfortable with the idea of parity. Back in 1963, during congressional hearings on the Partial Nuclear Test Ban Treaty, Senator Jackson had asked every key administration witness exactly the same question: "Can the U.S. afford a position of parity or equality with the Soviet Union in nuclear weapons technology and systems?" The answers were uniformly in the negative. Air force chief of staff Curtis LeMay's response was most succinct: "I would never be happy with a situation where we had parity with our enemies."[49]

In 1976 the debate turned not so much on the question of parity as on whether the Soviets were attempting to achieve military superiority. Of course, the affirmative contention would be easier to prove if the United States were disarming, while the Soviets were arming. This is just what Albert Wohlstetter set out to demonstrate in an article in the *Wall Street Journal* in 1974, a few months after his address at the Los Angeles meeting of "strategic thinkers and worriers." In this article, titled "Clocking the Strategic Arms Race," Wohlstetter conveniently ended three of his four charts in 1972, just before the MIRV technology came "on-line" in the American arsenal. Wohlstetter's charts showed U.S. megatonnage, the number of warheads, "equivalent megatonnage" (a technical term used to compare differ-

49. Both quoted in Michael Krepon, *Strategic Stalemate: Nuclear Weapons and Arms Control in American Politics* (New York: St. Martin's Press, 1984), 31.

ent forces by estimating the total area on which they could inflict structural damage), and strategic spending all decreasing.[50] However, by the time of Wohlstetter's writing, the U.S. trend had already started to climb upward steeply again.

The refrain of the United States' standing still while the Soviets pressed ahead was widely disseminated. The syndicated columnist Joseph Alsop wrote, "[I]n recent years, however, our strategic weapons programs have stayed almost stock-still, while the Soviets have forged ahead with fearful rapidity. Thus American superiority has been transformed into a slight edge for the Soviets; and if we continue to stay stock-still, while the Soviets go on forging ahead—as is now the realistic prospect—the Soviet edge will turn into a significant Soviet strategic superiority."[51]

Former defense secretary Schlesinger echoed the same refrain: "Since the Vietnam peak, U.S. military spending has been reduced by some 40%. In the same period, the Soviet effort has grown by 25%. Today in crude dollar estimates, the Soviet effort exceeds the American by 45%." According to Schlesinger, "[T]he Soviets outproduce us in all major categories of military hardware, save helicopters. The pace, the dynamism, the momentum of the Soviet effort vastly exceeds that of the U.S., which has (at best) leveled off."[52]

An example of the increasingly hysterical scare tactics used to inflate Soviet military prowess was a *Time* cover story on the new secretary of defense James Schlesinger in early 1974. It depicted "the Great Caspian Sea Monster," purporting to be the largest aircraft in the world, weighing five hundred tons. Like the hovercraft, the ship was to ride on an air cushion at speeds up to 350 miles per hour. Flying only twenty-five to fifty feet above the water would make radar detection difficult if not impossible. The Sea Monster would give "the Russians a new and ominous means of hunting the U.S. Polaris/Poseidon and Trident submarines as they cruise in the silent depths of the seven seas."[53] The Great Caspian Sea Monster, a huge experimental hovercraft that never became operational, turned out to be as elusive as the Loch Ness monster.

50. Albert Wohlstetter, "Clocking the Strategic Arms Race," *Wall Street Journal*, September 24, 1974, 24.

51. Joseph Alsop, "The Challenge America Must Meet," *Reader's Digest* 107, no. 640 (1975): 49–55.

52. James R. Schlesinger, "The Continuing Challenge to America," *Reader's Digest* 108, no. 648 (1976): 61–66.

53. "Arming to Disarm in the Age of Detente," *Time*, February 11, 1974, 15–24.

The redoubtable longtime labor leader George Meany asked, "[W]hat are the Soviet Union's intentions? Are they seeking superiority? The United States can never accept military inferiority to the Soviet Union. Yet this may be precisely what the Russians hope to achieve in the next round of SALT."[54]

Paul Nitze, too, raised the specter of Soviet supremacy in his influential article that appeared in the January 1976 issue of *Foreign Affairs*. In "Assuring Strategic Stability in the Era of Detente," Nitze concluded:

> [T]here is every prospect that under the terms of the SALT agreements the Soviet Union will continue to pursue a nuclear superiority that is not merely quantitative but designed to produce a theoretical war-winning capability. Further, there is a major risk that, if such a condition were achieved, the Soviet Union would adjust its policies and actions in ways that would undermine the present detente situation, with results that could only resurrect the danger of nuclear confrontation or, alternatively, increase the prospect of Soviet expansion through other means of pressure.[55]

The speed with which the Soviets MIRVed their missiles, putting up to ten miniaturized warheads where a single one had been, startled the Pentagon. So did the introduction of four new models of Soviet strategic missiles in 1974. Henry Kissinger tried to deal with the question of superiority at a press briefing that year. Reporters badgered him about the failure to get a SALT agreement, and Peter Lisagor of the *Chicago Daily News* implied that the Joint Chiefs of Staff had vetoed a new SALT agreement because it would concede military superiority to the Soviets. Kissinger's response was, "[O]ne of the questions we have to ask ourselves as a country is: what, in the name of God, is strategic superiority? What is the significance of it, politically, militarily, operationally, at these levels of numbers? What do you do with it?" According to William Hyland, "these were remarks that he would always regret."[56]

Of course, even within the Pentagon, there was not complete unanimity on who was ahead. Air force general Samuel C. Phillips, chief of the Air Force System Command, the service's research arm, stated that the United

54. George Meany, "How Much Is Enough?" June 8, 1974, Legislation Department, Records, 1906–78, Box 0034, Folder 024, The George Meany Memorial Archives.

55. Paul H. Nitze, "Assuring Strategic Stability in an Era of Detente," *Foreign Affairs* 54, no. 2 (1976): 207–32.

56. Hyland, *Mortal Rivals*, 72.

States is still "at least a few years ahead" in such modern weapons as missiles and warplanes. Phillips, in a farewell interview upon his retirement, did worry about "the will of the country to continue to maintain a sufficient defense to keep the peace."[57]

At the beginning of 1976, a Library of Congress study identified "a strong shift in the quantitative military balance toward the Soviet Union over the past ten years. . . . This country's numerical superiority in strategic nuclear weapons . . . has dissolved."[58] The report examined only static measures, such as numbers of men, tanks, and planes, and entirely excluded such dynamic factors as the accuracy of the weapons, or the leadership, training, and morale of the men. Nevertheless, the report, by John Collins, became very influential and was widely quoted.

Nearly all the Soviet-superiority arguments were specious. Soviet nuclear yields were cited with no reference to overall accuracy. Warhead tabulations excluded categories of U.S. advantage. Soviet systems were dated from their final configuration, while U.S. systems were dated from their first appearance (thus the Soviet SS-18s and SS-19s were said to be fifteen years newer than the American Minutemen, even though many were older than the newest Minuteman III missiles). Naval computations equated aircraft carriers with coastal patrol boats, turning a two-to-one U.S. tonnage advantage into a Soviet lead. Tank numbers incorporated Warsaw Pact reserves but excluded NATO's, and did not mention that NATO's average firing rate was twice that of the Soviets or that Soviet tank guns tended to spear crew members on recoil.

The question of who was ahead in strategic weapons depended on what one was counting. Whereas the Russians' missiles were bigger and heavier, the Americans never had fewer and most of the time had more missile warheads, bombers, nuclear-powered surface ships, and antisubmarine warfare capabilities. During the 1970s the United States increased its strategic arsenal, in round numbers, from seventeen hundred missile warheads to ten thousand, about the same figure the Soviets eventually reached.

Nevertheless, the "decade-of-neglect" argument was resurrected by the Reagan administration in the 1980s, with the president saying that "America had unilaterally disarmed." While that was far from the truth, the fact that the Soviets were attaining parity in some aspects of the arms race galled

57. Quoted in George C. Wilson, "U.S. Said to Lead Soviets in Arms," *Washington Post*, August 17, 1975, 12.
58. "United States/Soviet Military Balance: A Frame of Reference for Congress," Library of Congress, Congressional Research Service, 94th Cong., 2d sess., January 1976, vii, 3.

many Americans. Long used to being the unchallenged "number one" in everything related to nuclear weapons, Americans began to lose confidence in the ability of their government to conduct an effective foreign policy. Soon, according to Hyland, "there was scarcely a national security issue that was not immediately challenged from all sides—right and left—and subjected to the most vicious debate."[59]

When the expected benefits of peace and detente did not materialize, disillusion set in, and the imperatives of domestic politics and a presidential election year took over. Detente ultimately died for many reasons. One was the "equal-aggregates" approach mandated by the Jackson amendment to the SALT Treaty. The inventories of the two sides were quite different, with the Soviets relying on big, heavy land-based missiles and the Americans more on bombers, submarines, and smaller, more accurate missiles with multiple warheads. Neither side was willing to make major cuts in their own weapons, so this approach ensured a new treaty that permitted each side to build up and match the strong points of its adversary. This mutual buildup contributed to the perception on each side that the other side was "not serious" about detente.

Two longtime Sovietologists sum up the decline of detente quite similarly: Raymond Garthoff writes, "[F]rom the American viewpoint, particular issues were Soviet behavior in Angola and earlier in the October 1973 war in the Middle East and concern over a possible gain for communism in southwestern Europe. From the Soviet standpoint, they were the American policy of excluding the Soviet Union from the Middle East, the attempt to use detente to intervene in Soviet domestic affairs, and the collapse of American economic normalization and facilitation of trade between the two countries."[60]

According to Seweryn Bialer:

> In the 1970s, the United States and the Soviet Union were out of phase in their basic attitudes towards the international system, in their fears and ambitions, and in their ability to mobilize internal resources for international purposes. The Soviet Union was still in a rising phase as an international power. Having only recently acquired its global status, it was still flexing its muscles, eager to translate its military status into influence. In America detente found

59. Hyland, Mortal Rivals, 17.
60. Garthoff, Detente and Confrontation, 538.

fertile soil and was understood as a promise of peace and non-involvement to be attained, so to speak, on the cheap. For the Soviet Union, detente proffered temptations to grasp the opportunities of the moment.[61]

Former Soviet ambassador Dobrynin admits forthrightly: "So the crucial difference in the Soviet and American approaches to the issue was that while the Americans wanted to export to the Soviet Union its free humanitarian and commercial values, the Soviet government simply wanted the commercial benefits of trade, but not the political values."[62] The astute Soviet dissident Andrei Amalrik had pointed out the misperceptions already in 1970: "Americans apparently also believe that the gradual improvement in the standard of living, as well as the spread of Western culture and ways of life, will gradually transform Soviet society—that the foreign tourists, jazz records, and miniskirts will help to create a 'humane socialism.' It is possible that we will indeed have a 'socialism' with bare knees someday, but not likely one with a human face."[63]

Before detente totally collapsed following the 1979 Soviet invasion of Afghanistan and the 1981 Soviet-inspired Polish military crackdown on Solidarity and its leader, Lech Walesa, its coffin was measured, as it were, by an intelligence estimate, prepared by people outside the government, in competition with the annual assessment of Soviet strategic strengths by the intelligence community, that portrayed the Soviet Union in the most frightening terms possible.

61. Seweryn Bialer, *The Soviet Paradox: External Expansion, Internal Decline* (New York: Knopf, 1986), quoted in Ashton, *In Search of Detente*, 140.

62. Dobrynin, *In Confidence*, 268.

63. Andrei Amalrik, *Will the Soviet Union Survive Until 1984?* (New York: Harper & Row, 1970), 29.

4

The CIA as a
Vulnerable Institution

An institutionalized intelligence agency came into being late in U.S. history. In contrast, formalized reporting organizations existed in the sixteenth century in Great Britain, in the eighteenth century in Czarist Russia, and by the nineteenth century in France. It was only during the Second World War that the United States implicitly rejected Secretary of State Henry Stimson's statement, "[G]entlemen do not read each other's mail," and created the Office of Strategic Services (OSS). After the war ended, President Truman disbanded the OSS, and the Central Intelligence Agency was created in its stead in 1947.

During the Cold War and the Soviet occupation of Eastern Europe, the Korean War, the building of the Berlin Wall, and even the abortive Bay of Pigs invasion, foreign policy ends, to contain Soviet expansion, were congruent with the means, to build strong defense and intelligence establishments. For the first twenty years of its existence, the CIA enjoyed broad acceptance by the American public, sympathetic reporting from most journalists, benign oversight by congressional committees, and favorable portrayals in the spy literature.

The Consensus Evaporates

But by the end of the 1960s the consensus that had supported and protected the CIA began to evaporate. In the 1970s the CIA became an agency under siege. First there was the CIA's involvement in the increasingly unpopular war in Vietnam. That war dealt a double whammy to the CIA. For those who were opposed to U.S. involvement, the CIA, with its heavy engagement in that country, became the enemy. It has been estimated that the CIA's Phoenix program to identify the members of the Vietcong infrastructure was responsible for the deaths of at least twenty-one thousand supposed enemy civilians who worked in the villages of South Vietnam.[1] Colleges across the country forbade the CIA to recruit on their campuses. Marchers and demonstrators spewed their venom and hatred at the agency and its recruiters.

To compound the agency's woes, not only opponents to the Vietnam War railed against the CIA. For many hard-liners as well, the CIA became the enemy because of its realistic assessments—assessments that failed to see light at the end of the tunnel. According to the last director of the agency's Board of National Estimates,[2] John Huizenga, "[W]e didn't offer sufficient enthusiastic support for the Vietnam War. Most of the staff thought Vietnam was a bad idea. Our line was that the policies of the U.S. Government were premised on underestimation of North Vietnamese military and political capacity and overestimation of the willingness of South Vietnam to fight."[3]

When the CIA was being attacked from the Left in Congress and the press, the onslaught was parried by letting it be known—quite truthfully— that the CIA's Vietnam projections had always been the most pessimistic of those made in the government. For example, in a December 1967 exhaustive analysis, the CIA said no amount of bombing would deter North Vietnam from its objective of winning the South and that a U.S. withdrawal would not undermine the nation's overall security interests.[4]

Another factor contributing to the disparagement of the CIA's analytical

1. Walter LaFeber, *The American Age: United States Foreign Policy at Home and Abroad Since 1750* (New York: W. W. Norton, 1989), 606.

2. From 1950 to 1973 NIEs were produced by the Board of National Estimates. Originally the membership of the board included active and retired military officers, former ambassadors, and so forth. Over the years, the number of outsiders decreased, and promotions from within the agency and from the Office of National Estimates became more frequent, so the board came to be seen by some as too inbred and parochial.

3. Interview with John Huizenga, November 27, 1990.

4. Thomas W. Lippman, "McNamara Writes Vietnam Mea Culpa," *Washington Post*, April 9, 1995, 1.

branches was their manner of thinking about, analyzing, and conceptualizing the Soviet threat. Nearly twenty years after his forced retirement, Huizenga, now white-haired and living in a retirement village in Maryland, recalled vividly:

> In the late 1960s the numbers of Soviet ICBMs were approaching our own and were estimated to surpass our own. There had been an assumption that the Soviets wouldn't exceed us in numbers, because that would spur us to increase our numbers. Beginning in 1969, the estimates were very contentious. The Office of National Estimates[5] took the view that there was no cause for hysteria. There were lots of reasons for the Soviets to push the numbers up: bureaucratic inertia; the military always wants an edge; they may have felt they needed to compensate in quantity for the qualitative edge the U.S. had. But the phenomenon did provoke hysteria.

Huizenga continued, "There were two classes of people: those with an apocalyptical view of the Soviets, that the Soviets would use their military might to strike at the U.S.; and [those with] our view, [that] this would be out of character for the Soviets, [that] it is not in their mode to launch high-risk attacks. We thought of it as a lava flow; they went where they could without high risk."[6]

Such views, no doubt, were on his mind when former CIA director[7] and former secretary of defense James Schlesinger testified before the Senate Select Committee to Study Governmental Operations with Respect to Intelligence Activities that CIA analysts were viewed in some quarters as being inclined to provide intelligence estimates supporting the "preferences of the arms control community." Schlesinger went on: "There developed an institutional bias amongst the analytic fraternity. . . . There was an assumption that the Soviets had the same kind of arms control objectives that they wished to ascribe or persuade American leaders to adopt."[8] Such flashes of candor helped earn Schlesinger a reputation for independent thinking and credibility.

5. The Office of National Estimates was the support staff of the Board of National Estimates. It was formally created in 1950 and abolished in 1973.

6. Interview with John Huizenga, November 27, 1990.

7. See the Appendix for a list of CIA directors and their tenures.

8. Quoted in Cecil Brownlow, "CIA Threat-Juggling Confirmed," *Aviation Week and Space Technology*, May 3, 1976, 14.

Of course, the CIA had its defenders too. Former secretary of defense Melvin Laird titled an article in the *Reader's Digest* "Let's Stop Undermining the CIA." Laird pointed out, *"[D]uring the past 25 years, the Soviet Union has not developed a single major new weapon without our knowing it well in advance"* (emphasis in original). Laird continued, "[C]urrent efforts to negotiate curtailment of the nuclear arms race are possible only because our precise intelligence enables us to count every Soviet missile, submarine and bomber and to monitor Soviet compliance with the treaties achieved."[9]

In June 1972 came Watergate, the biggest scandal in U.S. history, which began with a break-in at the Democratic Party's national headquarters in the Watergate complex of apartments and office buildings in Washington, D.C. James McCord, a former high-level security officer at the CIA, and Eugenio Martinez, a Cuban exile, who was then employed at the CIA, were among those arrested, and the name of E. Howard Hunt, a longtime CIA operative, turned up in the pocket notebooks of two of the Watergate burglars. The ensuing revelations of wiretapping, burglary, violations of campaign financing laws, and the attempted use of government agencies to harm political opponents resulted in the resignation of President Richard Nixon in 1974. Both the Vietnam War and Watergate were watershed events that led to a breakdown of public confidence in all government institutions and especially in the CIA.

Other factors that contributed to the far-reaching change in the CIA's fortunes during the 1970s included President Nixon's distrust of the agency and congressional reassertion of its oversight prerogatives following Watergate. Disclosure of a host of illegal CIA activities played a role, as did conservative suspicions about detente and the perception that the CIA was pushing the "detente line." There was also bureaucratic resentment that the CIA had not been a "team player" during the Vietnam War, and the antagonism that developed between the operational and analytical sides of the agency undermined it from within. The final straw, perhaps, was the rapid turnover in directors from 1973 to 1977 (see the Appendix).

Nixon's Animosity Toward the CIA

Distrust and displeasure with the CIA and its intelligence products in the 1970s started right at the top with President Nixon. Nixon considered the

9. Melvin R. Laird, "Let's Stop Undermining the CIA," *Reader's Digest* 108, no. 649 (1976): 101–5.

CIA "a refuge of Ivy League intellectuals opposed to him," and referred to the CIA as "those clowns out at Langley."[10] Nixon was abetted by National Security Adviser Kissinger, who created his own intelligence staff within the National Security Council. Both Nixon and Kissinger preferred working with small, tightly managed staffs, and both expressed unhappiness with the quality of the intelligence they were receiving from the CIA.

President Nixon had no confidence in either the CIA or CIA director Richard Helms. Helms's biographer, Thomas Powers, reports that "Helms had often been reduced to leaving him [Nixon] notes at National Security Council meetings. He would arrive early. There was a yellow legal pad and sharpened pencil before every chair. Helms would go to Nixon's chair at the head of the table and write him a note on the yellow pad, asking to see him."[11] In his memoirs, Kissinger writes that "Nixon felt ill at ease with Helms personally, since he suspected that Helms was well liked by the liberal Georgetown social set to which Nixon ascribed many of his difficulties."[12]

Nixon's opinion of the CIA is also revealed in notes kept by White House chief of staff H. R. Haldeman of an 11 A.M. White House budget meeting on July 23, 1971. President Nixon stated, "[T]he CIA tells [me] nothing I didn't read three days earlier in the *New York Times*." He went on to say, "Intelligence is a sacred cow. We've done nothing [about reducing its budget] since we've been here. [The] CIA isn't worth a damn. We have to get at the symbolism." He suggested a "25% cut across the board" and getting "rid of the disloyal types." Later, at the same meeting, the president again raised the subject of intelligence and described it as "how to spend $5 billion and learn nothing." Returning to the topic one last time that morning, Nixon said, "Intelligence reform won't save a lot of money but will do a helluva lot for my morale."[13] Nearly a decade later, Nixon's animus toward the CIA was still apparent as he wrote: "American presidents were being supplied by the CIA with figures on Russian military spending that were only half of what the Agency later decided spending had been. Thanks in part to this intelligence blunder, we will find ourselves looking down the nuclear barrel in the 1980s."[14]

10. Rhodri Jeffreys-Jones, *The CIA and American Democracy* (New Haven, Conn.: Yale University Press, 1989), 177.

11. Thomas Powers, *The Man Who Kept the Secrets: Richard Helms and the CIA* (New York: Knopf, 1979), 15.

12. Henry Kissinger, *The White House Years* (Boston: Little, Brown, 1979), 36.

13. Richard Nixon Presidential Papers, White House Special Files: H. R. Haldeman notes, July 23, 1971, National Archives.

14. Richard M. Nixon, *The Real War* (New York: Warner Books/Random House, 1980), 261–62.

Much of Nixon's hostility toward the CIA was ironic. Under the leadership of successive presidents, the CIA had clandestinely funneled support to centrist democratic parties and political forces in Chile since 1963.[15] In the 1970 Chilean presidential campaign, the CIA directed propaganda attacks in a "spoiling campaign" against Salvador Allende, who advocated an alliance with Cuba's Fidel Castro. When Allende won the election, "Nixon was furious . . . and gave [CIA director Richard] Helms a very clear order to block Allende from assuming office."[16] When this failed, Nixon and Kissinger blamed Helms for Allende's electoral victory. As the full story of the CIA's involvement in Chile and Allende's assassination became known, it fed the public's and the Congress's disenchantment with and wariness of the agency.

Kissinger and the CIA

In his autobiography, Henry Kissinger describes his objections to the CIA's "Eastern Establishment" bias and overly guarded judgments. "CIA analyses were not . . . infallible. Far from being the hawkish band of international adventurers so facilely portrayed by its critics, the Agency usually erred on the side of the interpretation fashionable in the Washington Establishment. In my experience, the CIA developed rationales for inaction much more frequently than for daring thrusts."[17] Kissinger strongly objected to the analytic caution of the papers he got from the CIA. "He didn't like its literary style; he didn't like the burial of opposing views in one- or two-sentence footnotes of dissent, and as often as not he didn't like the conclusions. Kissinger was confident in his own abilities, and he demanded paper crisper in style backed up by appendices filled with raw data. He'd make up his own mind."[18]

Former CIA director William Colby reported that Kissinger told him, "[G]ive me things that make me think."[19] While the intelligence community tried hard to arrive at consensus, Kissinger sought to encourage competition

15. William Colby and Peter Forbath, *Honorable Men: My Life in the CIA* (New York: Simon & Schuster, 1978), 191, 302.

16. Ibid., 303.

17. Henry Kissinger, *White House Years*, 208.

18. Powers, *The Man Who Kept the Secrets*, 204.

19. William Colby, memorandum for the record, January 27, 1976, cited in Harold P. Ford, "Estimative Intelligence: The Purposes and Problems of National Intelligence Estimating" (Defense Intelligence College, Washington, D.C., 1989), 177.

within it. Kissinger was especially critical of the CIA's annual survey of Soviet intentions and capabilities. "He wanted more and he wanted it better."[20] Director of Central Intelligence[21] (DCI) Helms took Kissinger's criticism seriously and initiated a major effort to rework the survey from a single slim report to three volumes with extensive appendices, charts, and graphs.[22]

Notwithstanding Helms's efforts, at the end of 1970 the White House assigned James Schlesinger, assistant director of the Office of Management and Budget, to conduct a major review of the intelligence community. The Schlesinger working group completed its assignment by March 1971 and found, among other things, "that the Director of Central Intelligence's theoretical control of the community was an impolite fiction; that the total cost of intelligence, obscured by various techniques of financial sleight of hand, was at least twice the figure formally submitted to Congress; that intelligence estimates too often hid differing judgments in bland compromise; that the CIA's policy of no lateral entry of personnel had rendered the Agency almost claustrophobically insular, and that technical intelligence far surpassed political intelligence in quality."[23]

In November 1971, Nixon announced a major reorganization of the intelligence community. The new plan gave CIA director Richard Helms sweeping authority over the whole intelligence community and established a National Security Intelligence Committee. Helms, whose CIA career was in the operations side of the agency until he became DCI, was not very interested in the management of the agency. One colleague stated, "During his term as Director, Helms ran the Directorate for Plans [the clandestine or spy part of the agency] out of his hip pocket."[24] Helms convened one thirty-minute session of the newly created National Security Intelligence Committee and then waited for two and a half years to call another meeting. This time the committee met for a little over an hour. But Helms's major problems stemmed from Nixon's inherent distrust of the agency and his preference for working within his White House staff.

20. Powers, The Man Who Kept the Secrets, 204.

21. The director of the CIA is both the chief executive officer of the CIA and, as the director of Central Intelligence, the chairman of the board of the entire intelligence community.

22. Powers, The Man Who Kept the Secrets, 205.

23. Ibid., 207.

24. "Supplementary Detailed Staff Reports on Foreign and Military Intelligence," bk. 4, Final Report of the Senate Select Committee to Study Governmental Operations with Respect to Intelligence Activities, April 23, 1976, 66; hereafter referred to as the Karalekas Report, after Ann Karalekas, the principal author.

Immediately after his 1972 reelection, Nixon called for the resignation of every presidential appointee. Helms, a career intelligence officer, did not consider himself a political appointee and thus did not offer his resignation.[25] On November 20, Helms was summoned to Camp David and was told that the president intended to name a new director of the CIA. Although it was very abrupt, Helms said, "All right, perhaps a good time for a changeover would be the following March, since [he] was turning sixty and that was the Agency's mandatory retirement age."[26] But Nixon demurred. After serving in the CIA for more than thirty years and as DCI for more than six years, Helms, the first intelligence professional to work his way up through the ranks to the top, was asked to leave a few months short of retirement age. On the spur of the moment Nixon asked Helms if he wanted another job, perhaps an ambassadorship. Helms suggested possibly Iran, and Nixon appointed him ambassador soon thereafter.[27] In the middle of January, Helms was abruptly informed that he would not be leaving on February 14, as originally planned, but nearly two weeks earlier, on February 2.[28]

White House aide Charles Colson "began spreading rumors around town that Helms was being let go because he couldn't run the Agency, he couldn't take hold of the Intelligence Community and run it the way the President wanted." Helms was convinced that he was fired because "he had refused to go the extra mile and help the President on Watergate."[29] Helms's successor as DCI was James Schlesinger, the author of the reorganization plan for the intelligence community.

When James Schlesinger became, at forty-three, the youngest-ever DCI, he came with a mandate from Nixon to turn the place upside down. To all outward appearances Schlesinger seemed like an academic, with his craggy good looks, tweed jackets, and ever-present pipe. But upon arriving at the CIA, he allegedly said, "[T]his is a gentleman's club, and I am no gentleman."[30] And as far as the CIA was concerned, he most certainly was not. Early in February, at a meeting of the Directorate for Plans staff (the spies or operatives) in the agency's main auditorium, Schlesinger stated, "[F]rom now on intelligence is going to be a 20 year career. It's time to give way to young blood."[31] During his four-month tenure as DCI, the shortest in the agency's

25. Powers, *The Man Who Kept the Secrets*, 242.
26. Ibid., 243.
27. Ibid.
28. Ibid., 271.
29. Ibid., 244.
30. Ibid., 57.
31. Ibid., 278.

history, about 7 percent of the CIA's staff were either fired or forced to resign or retire. Most of the reductions came from the Directorate for Plans.[32] Schlesinger changed the name of the clandestine service from the Director-ate for Plans to the Directorate for Operations.

The "Family Jewels"

It was during Schlesinger's brief reign that the Watergate scandal exposed the agency to charges of involvement with Howard Hunt, a former CIA employee. As a result of repeated allegations that the agency acquiesced to White House demands to cover up official involvement in the break-in at the Watergate, Schlesinger turned to William Colby, the ramrod-postured, no-nonsense career CIA official newly promoted to the number-three job in the agency, executive director–comptroller.

Colby was committed to reconciling the agency's priorities with the changing public attitudes and expectations. He "suggested that Schlesinger issue a directive to every CIA employee instructing him to come forward with *anything* the CIA might have done which exceeded the limits of the Agency's charter. Schlesinger thought this a good idea. Colby wrote the order, Schlesinger signed it, and copies were distributed within the CIA on May 9."[33] By coincidence, this was the same day that Nixon named Schle-singer secretary of defense, replacing Elliot Richardson, who became attor-ney general, and appointed Colby as the new director of Central Intelligence (see the Appendix).

As the report resulting from the order was being compiled, a deluge of suspected and real misdeeds emerged. By the end of May, a twenty-six-page preliminary summary had been prepared and forwarded to new DCI Colby under the title "Potential Flap Activities." And so they were. The full report, completed later, came to 693 pages in all, and it quickly acquired the *nom de scandale* of the "family jewels." It covered just about every serious charge brought against the CIA. These included Operation Chaos, whose purpose was to determine whether domestic dissidents, including students, were re-ceiving foreign support, and resulted in the agency's collecting information on thousands of Americans; a sketchy account of CIA drug-testing programs;

---

32. Karalekas Report, 85, and Colby and Forbath, *Honorable Men,* 333.
33. Powers, *The Man Who Kept the Secrets,* 286.

surveillance and bugging of American journalists; the connections with the Watergate conspirators and White House "plumbers"; training programs for local police departments; and a mail interception program. Most startling of all was a special annex summarizing the Inspector General's Report of 1967 on the CIA's involvement in assassination plots against foreign leaders such as Rafael Trujillo of the Dominican Republic, Ngo Dinh Diem of Vietnam, and Fidel Castro of Cuba.[34]

From the very beginning of his directorship, Colby had decided that the best way to avoid wrecking the agency for which he had worked most of his adult life was to "fess up" to past misdeeds and to tighten internal controls to make sure they wouldn't recur in the future. Colby's strategy was "to be guided by the Constitution, and to apply its principles. This meant that I had to cooperate with the investigations and try to educate the Congress, press, and public, as well as I could, about American intelligence, its importance, its successes and its failings."[35] In essence, whenever a congressional committee asked for more information, Colby handed it over—postmortems, inspector general reports, cables to the field, internal memos, and draft studies—being careful, however, to protect the names of agents and staff.[36] In April of 1974 Colby testified before the House Armed Services Committee and outlined CIA efforts to "destabilize" Allende's regime. This caused Helms to complain to a friend, "Colby's not only telling all, he's telling more than all."[37] Colby quotes Kissinger as having once said to him, "Bill, you know what you do when you go to the Hill? You go to confession!"[38]

In August 1974, Nixon was forced to resign, and Gerald Ford, whom Nixon had appointed vice-president following the revelations of corruption that had forced Vice President Spiro Agnew to resign in October 1973, became president. In December, Pulitzer Prize–winning journalist Seymour Hersh called Colby and told him "he had a story bigger than My-Lai." Hersh had won the Pulitzer award for his reporting about a civilian massacre at My-Lai in Vietnam. Colby agreed to meet with Hersh and realized that Hersh "had come upon some disjointed and distorted accounts of several items on our highly secret 'family jewels' list." Colby did not deny the allegations but

34. Karalekas Report, 89; Powers, *The Man Who Kept the Secrets*, 287; and Colby and Forbath, *Honorable Men*, 340.

35. Colby and Forbath, *Honorable Men*, 15.

36. Ibid., 405.

37. Powers, *The Man Who Kept the Secrets*, 14.

38. Quoted in George Bush, with Victor Gold, *Looking Forward* (Garden City, N.Y.: Doubleday, 1987), 160.

tried to allay the damage by saying that the illegal activities "had been few and far between, had occurred years before, and had been stopped many months ago."[39] But on Sunday, December 22, 1974, the CIA's worst nightmares became a reality. The *New York Times* published a story by Seymour Hersh on the front page under a three-column headline titled "Huge CIA Operation Reported in U.S. Against Anti-War Forces, Other Dissidents in Nixon Years." That headline seemed to crystallize much of the public's worst fears of an agency run amok, a "rogue elephant."

Public and journalistic concern was widespread. Starting from the Left, editors at the *Progressive* wondered why everyone else had taken so long to catch on to what they had known and been telling their readers for decades. "The problem that confronts us," Theodore Draper declared, "is not just that the CIA occasionally lapses into illegal activities, but that it is, inherently, an illegitimate enterprise. No institution cloaked in secrecy, immune to scrutiny, and empowered to spend vast sums of public money without accounting to the taxpayers or even to their elected representatives can constitute anything but a threat to democracy."[40]

In the middle of the American political spectrum, *Newsweek* titled its piece on the CIA "Abolish the CIA." Even William F. Buckley's conservative *National Review* carried an article by James Burnham in which he confessed, "[H]ubris does come before a fall. I would have boasted myself one of the last persons on earth who could have been snowed by the CIA. And I've just learned that those rascals hornswoggled me as neatly as if I'd been a college president."[41]

Within two weeks, on January 4, 1975, President Ford signed an executive order creating the Commission on CIA Activities Within the U.S., usually referred to as the Rockefeller Commission, after its chairman, Vice President Nelson Rockefeller. Commission members included former secretary of commerce John T. Connor; former secretary of the treasury C. Douglas Dillon; former solicitor general and dean of Harvard Law School Erwin N. Griswold; Secretary-Treasurer Lane Kirkland of the AFL-CIO; former chairman of the Joint Chiefs of Staff Gen. Lyman L. Lemnitzer; just-retired eight-year governor of California Ronald Reagan; and former president of the University of

---

39. Colby and Forbath, *Honorable Men*, 389, 390, 15.

40. Theodore Draper, "The Enemy Within," *Progressive*, February 1975, quoted in H. W. Brands, *The Devil We Knew: Americans and the Cold War* (New York: Oxford University Press, 1993), 138–39.

41. James Burnham, "Too Much Intelligence," *National Review*, July 4, 1975, quoted in Brands, *The Devil We Knew*, 141.

Virginia Edgar F. Shannon Jr. Its charge was to investigate alleged domestic spying by the CIA. (Reagan skipped most meetings and asked to be excused from the commission because he was so busy campaigning for Republicans.) When the Rockefeller Commission submitted its final report to President Ford in June 1975, it basically exonerated the agency but acknowledged the assassination plots. The report found that the CIA had engaged in several activities that violated its charter, such as domestic spying and illegal mail intercepts, and, as expected, laid down prescriptions for future CIA actions.

During this trying time, Colby sought assurance that the president retained confidence in him. Such was given to Colby in June 1974, and he gratefully wrote to President Ford: "You have many times extended yourself to defend the Agency in this time of trial. We professionals deeply appreciate this confidence and take from it renewed energy to justify it."[42] Yet within four months, Colby was fired.

On February 28, 1975, Daniel Schorr went on CBS *Evening News* at seven o'clock to break the biggest CIA story of all: "President Ford has reportedly warned associates that if current investigations go too far they could uncover several assassinations of foreign officials in which the CIA was involved."[43] Given the nature of these serious charges, it was inevitable that Congress would now rise out of its somnolent oversight of the intelligence agencies.

Congressional Concerns

In its early years the CIA was largely exempt from public and congressional examination. Senator Richard Russell (D-Ga.), chairman of the Senate Armed Services Committee, one of two Senate committees that had oversight authority for the CIA, had great power, "which he exercised to preserve the security and the autonomy of the CIA. He trusted the CIA not to do anything he wouldn't do, and didn't pay attention to the details."[44]

When Senator Mike Mansfield (D-Mont.) introduced a bill in 1955 to create a congressional oversight committee, he queried Senator Leverett Saltonstall (R-Mass.), a ranking member of the Senate Armed Services and Appropriations Committees, "How many times does the CIA request a

42. William Colby, letter to President Gerald Ford, June 24, 1975, Folder Colby, Box B1, Kissinger-Scowcroft Names File, Gerald R. Ford Library, Ann Arbor, Mich.
43. Quoted in Powers, *The Man Who Kept the Secrets,* 291–92.
44. Ibid., 276.

meeting with particular subcommittees of the Appropriations Committee and the Armed Services Committee, and how many times does the Senator from Massachusetts request the CIA to brief him in regard to existing affairs?" Saltonstall's reply was, "It is not a question of reluctance on the part of the CIA officials to speak to us. Instead, it is a question of our reluctance, if you will, to seek information and knowledge on subjects which I personally, as a Member of Congress and as a citizen, would rather not have, unless I believed it to be my responsibility to have it because it might involve the lives of American citizens."[45]

Mansfield's oversight resolution was defeated, as was a later attempt in 1961 by Senator Eugene McCarthy (D-Minn.), following the abortive Bay of Pigs invasion in Cuba, to establish a CIA oversight committee.[46] In 1971, the CIA subcommittee of the Senate Armed Services Committee did not hold one formal meeting to discuss CIA activity. It met only once in 1972 and 1973.[47] But this changed dramatically. In January 1975, the Senate voted to create a Select Committee to Study Governmental Operations with Respect to Intelligence Activities, and the House of Representatives did likewise. By 1975 there were eight congressional committees, four from each house, that DCI Colby had to brief and keep informed: the Appropriations, Armed Services, Foreign Affairs, and Select Intelligence Committees.[48] The revelations before the Rockefeller Commission and the Congress undermined the consensus of trust under which the CIA had operated for so long. In short, the CIA had become subject to scrutiny and vulnerable to attack.

The Analysts' Turn to Come Under Attack

The operational side of the CIA committed all of the acts disclosed by Colby. Within the CIA, the Directorate for Intelligence (the analysts) and the Directorate for Operations (the spies, or "spooks") evolved out of separate independent organizations serving different policy needs, and essentially, the two directorates still function as separate organizations. Anne Karalekas, author of the definitive Senate Select Committee on Intelligence

45. Karalekas Report, 53, 54.
46. Ibid., 54–55.
47. Ibid., 88.
48. Colby and Forbath, *Honorable Men*, 423.

report on the agency, writes that the two directorates "maintain totally independent career tracks and once recruited into one, individuals are rarely posted to the other."[49]

The Directorate of Operations relies on secrecy, hierarchy, and strict enforcement of need-to-know constraints on the dissemination of information. The Directorate of Intelligence, which is devoted to analysis, needs free exchange of information. Some have argued for separating the two branches into different agencies.[50] As for relations between the two branches, according to Thomas Powers, "for the most part, they have been cool toward one another, skeptical within the bounds of politeness; but occasionally civility is strained, differences grow acerbic, and conflicts of style and outlook erupt into something very like open warfare, with all the incestuous bitterness of an argument in the family."[51] This proved to be the case as the agency was reeling from Schlesinger's "reign of terror" and the seemingly unending presidential and congressional investigations.

Almost as soon as Schlesinger was sworn in as DCI on February 2, 1973, newspaper stories indicated that he was going to revamp both the analytical and the operations side of the CIA. According to pundit Joseph Alsop, Schlesinger would "sweep out the old time estimating hierarchy [the analysts] which has long had a line of its own, which might even be called a marked historical bias." Alsop also stated that Schlesinger was "even bringing in from the Defense Department the most pungent and persistent single critic of the CIA's estimating-analyzing hierarchy."[52]

The individual Alsop was referring to was Lt. Gen. Daniel Graham, who had "been talking to Alsop for years."[53] Graham had previously worked at the CIA in the Office of National Estimates from 1964 to 1966 and again from 1968 to 1970. Graham transferred to the Defense Intelligence Agency (DIA) and became deputy director for estimates in 1970.

Graham disagreed most strongly with the CIA's premise, summarized in a paragraph of the executive summary of the National Intelligence Estimate (NIE) on Soviet strategic forces, that the USSR was not seeking strategic

49. Karalekas Report, 94.

50. Melvin A. Goodman, "We Need Two C.I.A.'s," New York Times, July 21, 1994, 15.

51. Powers, The Man Who Kept the Secrets, 35.

52. Joseph Alsop, "The CIA Analysts: Changes at the Top," Washington Post, February 23, 1973, 23.

53. Memorandum from Acting Chief, Office of Strategic Research (OSR), to Chief, Congressional Support Staff Center for Policy Support, March 14, 1977, obtained through FOIA.

superiority or a first-strike capability. Graham called this "the pablum statement" and began footnoting, or registering his disagreement with, "the basic tone of the NIEs."[54]

A final reason for the CIA's institutional vulnerability in the 1970s was a rapid turnover in directors: between 1973 and 1976 there were four different CIA directors, the same number that had led the agency for the preceding twenty years. Richard Helms, the last of the DCIs to serve for more than four years until the six-year reign of William J. Casey in the 1980s, was replaced by James Schlesinger, who headed the agency for four months. William Colby was DCI for a little more than two years, and George Bush ran the CIA for just one year (see the Appendix).

President Ford's nomination of George Bush to head the CIA marked the first time that partisan politics played a part in naming the DCI. Although President Ford promised that George Bush would not be on the 1976 ticket, Senators Thomas McIntryre (D-N.H.), Gary Hart (D-Colo.), and Patrick Leahy (D-Vt.) voted not to confirm Bush. They stated their reasons: "Rightly or wrongly the public will be understandably suspicious of the potential for political abuse of the agency by a Director who once chaired one of the major political parties. . . . We are also concerned that Mr. Bush's nomination sets a precedent of political appointments to a post that should be completely insulated from political considerations."[55]

The Senate Armed Services Committee as a whole wanted some "measure of confidence that Mr. Bush, if confirmed, would remain in the post of Director of Central Intelligence for a sufficiently long period to make a constructive contribution to the intelligence community. Particularly at this difficult and complicated time for the intelligence community, it is essential that there be as much continuity as possible in the directorship of Central Intelligence."[56]

Apparently Bush wanted to stay on as DCI for some months after Jimmy Carter's election in 1976 to maintain the principle that the office should be above party politics. John Ranelagh writes that Bush "promised to renounce his own political ambitions in exchange. Carter refused, not believing such a senior Republican would be politically loyal to him."[57]

54. Victoria S. Price, "The DCI's Role in Producing Strategic Intelligence Estimates" (Naval War College Center for Advanced Research, January 1980), 84.

55. Senate Armed Services Committee, Nomination of George Bush to Become Director of Central Intelligence, 94th Cong., 1st sess., January 6, 1976, S. Rept. 94-21, 4–5.

56. Ibid., 4.

57. John Ranelagh, The Agency: The Rise and Decline of the CIA (New York: Simon & Schuster, 1986), 633.

By the end of 1974 the "agency's vulnerability was indicative of the degree to which American foreign policy and the institutional framework that supported that policy were undergoing redefinition. The closed system that had defined and controlled U.S. intelligence activities and that had left decisions in the hands of a small group of individuals began to break down."[58]

When those who thought detente was heretical cast about for ways to bury it, the Wohlstetter charges of persistent underestimation of Soviet deployments pointed to one approach. If the National Intelligence Estimates could be called into question or, better, rewritten to give credence to "the growing Soviet threat," then perhaps the United States would pursue a more aggressive stance vis-à-vis the Soviets, and detente would wither away. Two things were needed to deliver the coup de grâce. One was to select the most vulnerable CIA product, and the other was to choose the most powerful vehicle to spearhead the attack.

58. Karalekas Report, 90.

5

National Intelligence Estimates

Throughout the Cold War and the rise and demise of detente, the most influential and most talked-about analytical products of the national intelligence community were the dozen or so yearly National Intelligence Estimates (NIEs). By far the most important of these, the "creme de la creme" of analysis, was the series that dealt with Soviet strategic forces, a series known as NIE 11-3/8 followed by the year for which it was issued, such as 11-3/8-76.[1]

Not only did these estimates provide guidance for the size and shape of the defense budget, but they also helped to determine the strategic stance the military would assume, as well as the government's overall approach to East-West relations, including arms negotiations. This is not to say that other things, such as the secretary of defense's annual posture statement or special reports such as the Gaither Report during the Eisenhower administration and the Scowcroft Commission Report during the Reagan administration, didn't play important roles in defining U.S. national security policies. Of course they did. But of the analytical products prepared by the intelligence community, the series of NIE 11–3/8s were the most important.

1. From 1959 through 1973, it was labeled NIE 11-8. After 1973, it became 11-3/8.

About NIEs in General

Estimating is what you do when you don't *know*. Estimating is a process that both precedes and follows a written estimate. National Intelligence Estimates present both current *knowledge* and *predictions* on what will happen within a given future period, usually five or sometimes ten years. Each NIE is reviewed by the National Foreign Intelligence Board (NFIB), a senior interagency body chaired by the director of Central Intelligence. Representatives from the CIA, Defense Intelligence Agency, the army, navy, and air force intelligence branches, the State Department, the Federal Bureau of Investigation, the Department of Energy, and the National Security Agency (an independent agency within the Defense Department responsible for monitoring foreign radio and phone transmissions and for decoding foreign communications) all sit on the National Foreign Intelligence Board.

The final product of this process is a paperbound monograph, some quite brief and others very extensive. In the case of the National Intelligence Estimates on Soviet strategic military forces in the 1970s, they usually ranged in size from just under one hundred to over four hundred pages. They normally included two main volumes: an executive summary, sometimes called "Key Judgments," and the backup factual and analytical data. Jeffrey Richelson writes: "NIE 11-3/8 reads as a systematic, blow-by-blow description of Soviet weapons military doctrine. Each chapter deals with a different category of Soviet weaponry. . . . Along with the description of current Soviet forces, parts of the text will also summarize the intelligence community's projection for future Soviet force levels in a given year and the time at which the Soviets are expected to be able to deploy a weapon incorporating a certain type of technology."[2]

These NIEs take months to prepare and involve dozens of analysts from each component of the National Foreign Intelligence Board and tend not to vary much from one year to the next. A longtime intelligence analyst described the NIE 11-3/8 series as being "like the George Washington Bridge, constantly painted. Everyone knows what the estimate will look like. The annual NIE process does not admit to a sea change, and NIEs are not the place to make startling predictions."[3] Walter Slocombe, who held high posi-

2. Jeffrey Richelson, *The U.S. Intelligence Agency* (Cambridge, Mass.: Ballinger, 1985), 244–45.
3. Interview with Mark Lowenthal, February 8, 1989.

tions in both the Carter and Clinton administrations, has said that "NIEs are always pablum. NIE 11-3/8 is a magisterial overview."[4]

Throughout the process, any member agency of the intelligence community can insert a footnote in the estimate to indicate where it disagrees with a particular passage and to explain why it disagrees, and in some cases this footnote includes an alternative paragraph to insert in place of the original passage. But most analysts feel that footnotes do not carry the same weight as the body of the text. So there are built-in incentives to arrive at a consensus document, and agencies find it worthwhile to moderate their position at least a little in order to have their opinion incorporated as part of the estimate rather than as a footnoted dissent.[5]

The CIA wants to keep the number of footnotes to a minimum. In the past some critics even accused the agency of trying to suppress dissenting views by putting the footnotes in small type. But accommodation of numerous and disparate views frequently leads to conclusions that are hedged judgments rather than firm predictions. To obtain the broadest possible consensus, the sharp distinctions between alternate evaluations are often compromised. This limits the NIE's utility for policymakers. And this is what bothered National Security Adviser Henry Kissinger. Kissinger rejected NIEs that "waffle on sharp judgments by containing trade-off paragraphs reflecting different departmental or agency views."[6] Kissinger and many of his key staffers preferred to get the raw intelligence information. He wanted to see the disagreements in a disputed intelligence estimate spelled out in black and white and then to draw his own conclusions.

It is important to understand that uncertainty is inherent in the estimating process. Particularly when the NIE deals with possible future events in other countries, the estimate must predict the outcome of debates probably still underway. In his *Foreign Policy* article Wohlstetter admitted that "[p]redicting the size and exact mixture of a potential adversary's weapon deployments several years hence is a hard line of work. It is intrinsically uncertain, reversible by the adversary himself between the time of prediction and the actual deployment."[7]

4. Interview with Walter Slocombe, October 4, 1989.

5. Bruce D. Berkowitz, *American Security: Dilemmas for a Modern Democracy* (New Haven, Conn.: Yale University Press, 1986), 233.

6. William Colby, memorandum for the record, January 27, 1976, cited in Harold P. Ford, "Estimative Intelligence: The Purposes and Problems of National Intelligence Estimating" (Defense Intelligence College, Washington, D.C., 1989), 177.

7. Albert Wohlstetter, "Is There a Strategic Arms Race?" *Foreign Policy* 15 (summer 1974): 3–20.

The writers of estimates try to reduce the uncertainty to a minimum, but invariably a large area of ambiguity remains in which the available evidence could support a variety of more or less reasonable interpretations. Ray Cline, short, squat, an intelligence officer for more than thirty years, described the process:

> In a sense these NIEs are the dry bones, almost the archeological remains, of a big debate with real intellectual conflicts and attempts by many hundreds of people to express themselves in ways which were circulating in Washington at that time. And in the last analysis, a formal estimate is just a racetrack bettor's book on what he thinks is going to happen: "It's six to five this way." If it is six-to-five this way—and that is pretty much what the estimates said—remember it is five-to-six the other way. So it is not always an egregious error not to be able to predict which side of a close bet is going to pay off.[8]

As soon as Albert Wohlstetter published his findings of alleged consistent underestimation of Soviet deployments, even though his data were carefully selected to stop just before the planned U.S. buildup, the NIEs dealing with Soviet forces became vulnerable and soon were the focus of a concerted attack by conservative opponents of detente. The end result was an alternative assessment, produced by outsiders, that came to be known as the Team B report.

Bureaucratic Politics in the NIE Process

The intelligence community is far from monolithic, and producing an NIE, particularly one perceived to have special importance for policymakers, illustrates the old Washington adage "Where you stand depends on where you sit." During the 1970s, the standing insider joke about the intelligence community went like this: The State Department's Bureau of Intelligence and Research felt the Russians were not coming; the CIA thought the Russians were coming but couldn't get here; the Defense Intelligence Agency believed

8. Ray Cline, discussion in *Intelligence Requirements for the 1980s: Analysis and Estimates*, ed. Roy Godson (New Brunswick, N.J.: Transaction Books, 1980), 78.

the Russians were coming and were almost here; and the air force felt the Russians were already here and working in the State Department!

Such differences are not surprising, because estimators do not work in ivory towers but in different intelligence agencies, each with its own political structure, mores, and belief structures. Within that agency, they are likely to work with colleagues who share a particular worldview. The interagency clearance procedure often becomes a "them-against-us" situation.

Bruce Berkowitz describes the process aptly:

> Intelligence analysts usually are objective seekers of truth when conducting their own analysis. But, once they have made their own professional judgment on an issue and have to defend these views against other viewpoints in the intelligence community, they can become fierce political animals. Each believes—and defends—his or her point of view. As a result, the action in a coordination meeting is at least as much bargaining as it is arguing fine points of analysis. The analysts try, if they are unable to make the estimate match their original view to the letter, to at least make sure that it comes close.[9]

Some of the tension in the NIE process comes from the civilian-military bifurcation. The three military services often have been charged with basing excessive estimates of Soviet weaponry on their own budgetary priorities. Presidents Truman and Eisenhower expressed concern about NIEs on that account.[10] Thomas Powers cites the example of De Forrest Van Slyck, an early member of the Board of National Estimates, who concluded that the Soviet Union would not attack Western Europe. "We can't accept this paper," stated Gen. Charles Pease Cabell, then chief of Air Force Intelligence, "We'll never get any budgets through."[11]

The well-known bomber and missile "gaps" of the 1950s, later proved false, firmly implanted in the public's mind the intelligence community's penchant for overestimation. Humorous exchanges such as the following letter, dated January 19, 1961, from George Kistiakowsky, President Eisenhower's science adviser, to Herbert (Pete) Scoville, CIA director of science and technology, were common. "Dear Pete: Thank you for your very kind,

9. Berkowitz, *American Security*, 238.

10. Victoria S. Price, "The DCI's Role in Producing Strategic Intelligence Estimates" (Naval War College Center for Advance Research, January 1980), 4.

11. Thomas Powers, *The Man Who Kept the Secrets: Richard Helms and the CIA* (New York: Knopf, 1979), 404.

but misinformed letter. Firstly, you highly overestimate (must be a habit acquired from NIE activities) my contributions hereabout."[12]

The military's distrust of the CIA estimators was also widespread. According to former CIA director of strategic research Noel Firth, "When Elmo Zumwalt was chief of naval operations, he sent a lieutenant commander or commander over to CIA for six months to check on our [supposed] 'underestimation.' When the six months were over, the naval officer said the problem for him was how to write his report to Zumwalt explaining that everything was okay with the CIA's estimating process and not ruin his own career in the process."[13]

The bureaucratic politics involved in NIEs also sometimes produced military underestimates of the opponent's capabilities. For example, for many years, Air Force Intelligence under Gen. George Keegan maximized assessments of all Soviet capabilities except their missile accuracy. That was because very accurate Soviet missiles would diminish the survivability and hence the value of the air force's Minuteman missiles.[14]

NIEs and the Policymaker

NIEs are produced for multiple audiences, who, according to a longtime CIA official, "will have different interests, backgrounds, perspectives and concerns. It is fairly easy to produce an intelligence product which satisfies none of these audiences, and impossible to produce a single product which will satisfy them all simultaneously. Almost by definition, a level of detail and mode of treatment which one senior consumer finds right for his needs, will be regarded as less than satisfactory by many other consumers—usually including the staff of the consumer who is himself satisfied."[15]

If the National Intelligence Estimate is in agreement with the decision maker's views, it is likely to be seen as objective and useful in bolstering

12. Kistiakowsky General Correspondence Box 29, Folder "Miscellaneous Correspondence from Washington," George Kistiakowsky Archives, Harvard University Library. Courtesy of the Harvard University Archives.

13. Interview with Noel Firth, January 11, 1990.

14. Angelo Codevilla, "Comparative Historical Experience of Doctrine and Organization," in *Intelligence Requirements for the 1980s*, ed. Godson, 30; interview with Daniel Graham, September 30, 1990.

15. George A. Carver, memorandum for the record, June 30, 1976, obtained through FOIA.

policy decisions. As former CIA director Robert Gates writes, "In my 21 years in intelligence, I have never heard a policy maker (or anyone else for that matter) characterize as biased or cooked a CIA assessment with which he agreed."[16] Gates also asserts that policymakers in the past have not had time to read NIEs, and he advocates discontinuing them except in special cases.[17] This is corroborated by Lt. Gen. William Odom, director of the National Security Agency from 1985 to 1988, who states, "I can think of almost no time when the findings of an NIE caused any policymaker to change his mind on anything or caused a policy to move in one direction or another. . . . You could close down the DDI [intelligence analysis directorate] tomorrow and nobody would miss it."[18] Estimative intelligence is, of course, conveyed to policymakers through conversations or briefings as well as through intelligence documents.

However, even the best possible intelligence is not likely to convince the policymaker with firmly held contrary views. For example, in the mid-1970s, it is unlikely that strongly held views of the Iranian shah's strengths and survivability would have been swayed by intelligence community warnings that there was a great deal of political unrest in Iran and that the shah might fall. And even if such intelligence reporting had been offered and accepted, it is doubtful whether it would have drastically changed events in Iran. Former CIA director Stansfield Turner stunned a conference of present and former CIA analysts by asserting that the agency had shortchanged President Jimmy Carter in the late 1970s. Turner claimed that the lengthy NIEs were simply "irrelevant" to the president in making policy and that the agency should have told Carter, "There was no need to build more weapons, except for purely political reasons."[19]

While National Intelligence Estimates are important, no single intelligence document is so important that it is ever accepted as holy writ. As one former intelligence official has said, "No one ever brought a meeting to a halt by waving the NIE in the air and declaring 'but this is what the estimate

16. Robert Gates, "The CIA and American Foreign Policy," *Foreign Affairs* 66, no. 2 (1987–88): 215–30.

17. Walter Pincus, "Ex-CIA Chief Backs Smaller Spy Agency," *Washington Post*, December 10, 1994, A4.

18. Kirsten Lundberg, "CIA and the Fall of the Soviet Empire: The Politics of 'Getting It Right' " (C16-94-1251.0, case study of the Kennedy School of Government, Harvard University, 1994), 2.

19. Christopher B. Daly, "Ex-Director Faults CIA of Carter Era," *Washington Post*, December 3, 1994, A11.

says!' "[20] Nevertheless, the National Intelligence Estimates that dealt with the strategic forces of the Soviet Union, together with the estimating office of the CIA that oversaw their production, became one of the battlegrounds of the war over the Nixon-Ford policy of detente. The following discussion of the estimates concerning the Soviets' SS-9 missile illustrates the NIE process and outlines the beginnings of the assault on the CIA estimates.

The SS-9 Controversy

In the summer of 1968, the United States observed the first test of a Soviet intercontinental ballistic missile (ICBM) with three five-megaton warheads.[21] This missile, the SS-9, was mammoth. It weighed 450,000 pounds, stood ten stories high, and could carry 10,000–15,000 pounds of weapons and penetration aids (commonly referred to as the payload) a distance of seven thousand nautical miles. In contrast, the mainstay of the U.S. ICBM force, the Minuteman, had only a one-megaton warhead and could carry a payload only one-tenth that of the SS-9.

The question was whether the SS-9 was "MIRVed" (armed as a multiple independently targetable reentry vehicle) or "MRVed" (armed as a multiple reentry vehicle). In both cases multiple warheads are carried on a single intercontinental ballistic missile. But in the first instance they are individually released one after the other with sufficient accuracy to hit separate targets; in the latter instance the MRV releases its warheads almost simultaneously, so they fall on or near the same target in a shotgun pattern. If the gigantic SS-9 was MIRVed, the Soviets would need fewer of them to pose a mortal threat to the U.S. ICBM force of one thousand Minuteman missiles.

The CIA was convinced that the SS-9 was MRVed and estimated "that accurate MIRVs suitable for use against Minuteman missiles could not be operational until 1972 at the earliest."[22] When NIE 11-3/8-68 was published in October 1968, it concluded that the SS-9 was a MRV and very inaccurate, with a circular error probability (CEP) of more than one nautical mile. CEP

20. Berkowitz, *American Security*, 248.
21. A one-megaton nuclear warhead has the explosive power of one million tons of TNT but weighs only a few hundred pounds.
22. Kirsten Lundberg, "The SS-9 Controversy: Intelligence as Political Football" (case study of the Kennedy School of Government, Harvard University, 1989), 5.

is a measure of missile accuracy and refers to the radius of the circle around the target within which 50 percent of the warheads aimed at that target will fall. (The smaller the CEP, the more accurate the missile.) At the time, there were 228 SS-9s in place or under construction.

In December 1968, the Soviets readied six new silos for the SS-9 in an entirely new field. Moreover, the holes were started in midwinter, an unusual time for construction in the Soviet Union. The Air Force Systems Command engaged its Foreign Technologies Division to analyze the SS-9. But before their report was available, Secretary of Defense Clark Clifford gave his farewell defense posture statement to Congress in January 1969. He stated unequivocally that the SS-9 was not MIRVed. Soon thereafter, from the telemetry of the SS-9 Mod (model) 4 tests, the air force's Foreign Technologies Division deduced that the Mod 4 might be a primitive MIRV.[23] This split within the intelligence community, with the CIA maintaining the SS-9 was *not* MIRVed and the air force saying it might be, of course became known to the Nixon administration when it took office later that month.

In 1964 the Soviets had begun to deploy a primitive antiballistic missile (ABM) around Moscow. Soon thereafter conservative senators and congressmen struck the tocsin about the need for a U.S. ABM system to protect the American people. President Lyndon Johnson did not want to run against charges of an "ABM gap" in 1968, so in September 1967 he instructed Secretary of Defense Robert McNamara to announce the deployment of a "light" ABM defense of fifteen major cities against an attack by the kind of force China might assemble and against an accidental launch. The system was named Sentinel.

A strong stimulus for an ABM was the army's unhappiness about being left out of the nuclear business. The air force had its ICBMs, the navy had its nuclear submarines, and the army wanted ABMs under its control. For quite some time the army declined to identify which cities would be defended, because they feared an outcry from citizens in undefended cities. But to their great surprise, as each city—Boston, Chicago, Seattle—was announced as the site for an ABM, citizens arose in vehement protest. They did not want those missiles in their backyards.[24]

In 1968 President Johnson decided not to run for reelection, and Richard Nixon beat Senator Hubert Humphrey (D-Minn.) to become the thirty-

23. Ibid., 5, 7.
24. Anne Hessing Cahn, "Eggheads and Warheads: Scientists and the ABM" (Ph.D. diss., Center for International Studies, Massachusetts Institute of Technology, Cambridge, Mass., 1971).

seventh president of the United States. Nixon had campaigned on charges of a "security gap." He was not about to cancel deployment of the ABM system approved by President Johnson. But to negate the public protests, Nixon announced that the United States would change the mission of the antiballistic missile system to defend Minuteman silos. Not coincidentally, Minuteman silos were mostly located in sparsely populated areas of North Dakota and Montana.

If the public and Congress could be made to see the SS-9 missiles as threatening the Minuteman silos, it would be easier to sell the ABM system, renamed the Safeguard. The principal salesman for the Safeguard system was Dr. John Foster, a former director of the Livermore Laboratory and in 1969 director of Defense Research and Engineering (DDR&E) in the Department of Defense. Based on the analysis of the Foreign Technologies Division, Foster adopted the view that the SS-9 was a MIRV and convinced not only his boss, Secretary of Defense Melvin Laird, but also for a critical time National Security Adviser Henry Kissinger.[25]

Within one week of President Nixon's March 1969 ABM deployment decision, DOD Secretary Laird testified before the Disarmament Subcommittee of the Senate Foreign Relations Committee that the Soviets were "going for a first-strike capability" aimed at wiping out U.S. defenses in a single blow. He supported his assertion with hitherto secret information about the SS-9. Laird stated that the Soviets had deployed two hundred SS-9s and predicted five hundred would be in silos by 1975. This turned out to be a gross exaggeration. Laird also credited the SS-9 missile with an accuracy of .6 mile or better, which would qualify it for use against "hard" targets, such as the U.S. Minuteman, which were protected against the blast, heat, and radiation effects of nuclear weapons.[26] Laird argued that the SS-9 threat could be countered only with an ABM system.

Three days after Laird's testimony, the *New York Times* carried a story by John Finney saying that the CIA disagreed with Laird's testimony regarding the SS-9. Finney wrote that the CIA and DOD disagreed about the size of the SS-9's warhead, the rate of its deployment, its accuracy, and its purpose.[27] The Finney article set off alarm bells in the White House. Not only did the story portray disarray within the administration on the all-important ques-

25. Lundberg, "SS-9," 7.

26. Ibid., 5–6; Marvin Kalb and Bernard Kalb, *Kissinger* (Boston: Little, Brown, 1974), 109.

27. John W. Finney, "SS-9 Helps Administration Score Points in Missile Debate," *New York Times*, March 24, 1969, 30.

tion of Soviet capabilities, but the CIA's disagreement with the DOD threw a monkey wrench into administration efforts to persuade Congress to approve funds for the Safeguard ABM. What the Finney story didn't cover were the many arguments between Henry Kissinger, who believed Laird, and the analytical side of the CIA. Kissinger appointed one of his National Security Council staffers, Laurence Lynn, a Ph.D. from Yale in his early thirties, to head a working group that would report to a senior "MIRV Panel," which Kissinger chaired, to clarify the differences between the Defense Department and the CIA over the SS-9.[28] Later, a Verification Panel was formed in July 1969 to analyze whether compliance with various arms control proposals could be verified by U.S. intelligence. Soon it took charge of managing all arms negotiations.[29]

In the meantime, between the beginning of April and the middle of May, the Soviets conducted three more tests of their SS-9, each with three warheads. This time the telemetry results were sent to TRW, an aerospace company, for analysis. Their report claimed that the three warheads from each missile were landing in a triangular pattern, forming a "footprint" that resembled the deployment of Minuteman missiles.[30]

This footprint theory was originally developed by the staff of DDR&E during the pre–Nixon administration debates on the early triplet tests.[31] Now repeated in the TRW analysis, it provided the administration fresh ammunition in its selling of the ABM. And so dire predictions about the SS-9 continued. At a press conference on April 18, President Nixon stated, "[E]ver since the decision to deploy the ABM system called Sentinel in 1967, . . . the intelligence estimates indicated that the Soviet capability with regard to their SS-9s, their nuclear missiles, was 60% higher than we thought then."[32]

By May, the Kissinger-appointed MIRV panel concluded that the possibility the Soviets were testing a MIRV could not be ruled out. That conclusion supported Defense Secretary Laird and John Foster rather than the Central Intelligence Agency on the MIRV issue. Publicly, however, the administration was trying hard to downplay or deny any internal disagreements about the Soviet missile. For example, in May, DDR&E director John Foster

28. Lundberg, "SS-9," 12.

29. Walter Isaacson, *Kissinger: A Biography* (New York: Simon & Schuster, 1992), 204.

30. Lundberg, "SS-9," 13.

31. Lawrence Freedman, *U.S. Intelligence and the Soviet Strategic Threat*, 2d ed. (Princeton: Princeton University Press, 1986), 139.

32. "Transcript of the President's News Conference on Foreign and Domestic Affairs," *New York Times*, April 19, 1969, 14.

stated, "I would like to say that I have no disagreements with the CIA nor has [Deputy] Secretary Packard or Secretary Laird."[33]

But differences of opinion did exist, and the disagreement between Kissinger and the CIA came to a head at an important meeting of the U.S. Intelligence Board (USIB, which later became the National Foreign Intelligence Board). At a June 12 meeting, the board approved a "memorandum to holders." This was an update of the 1968 NIE 11-3/8 and restated that the SS-9 was *not* a MIRV and that Soviets neither could nor wanted to launch a first strike against the United States. The following day, Kissinger summoned DCI Helms and the chairman of the Board of National Estimates, Abbot Smith, to an NSC meeting.[34] Kissinger and the NSC staff made clear their view that the new SS-9 might be MIRVed and asked that Helms's draft NIE be rewritten to provide more information supporting the DCI's judgment that the SS-9 had not demonstrated a MIRV capability. Smith rewrote the draft, but did not change the conclusion: *All seven tests of the SS-9 showed MRVs.*[35]

Smith wrote a memo about the June 13 meeting: "Out of this meeting came requests for (a) some reordering of the paper; (b) clarification of some points; and (c) additional arguments pro and con about the MRV-MIRV problem. We have accordingly redrafted the paper with these requests in mind. No changes in the estimates were asked nor (we think) have been made."[36]

The following week, at a press conference on June 19, President Nixon referred to the SS-9, saying, "Its footprints indicate that it just happens to fall in somewhat the precise area in which our Minuteman silos are located."[37] One day before the Senate was to vote on whether to proceed with deploying an ABM, DDR&E director John Foster told a House subcommittee in a closed hearing, "I believe the evidence indicates that [the triplet] is a MIRV. It doesn't prove without question that it is a MIRV, but to me, it very strongly indicates that it is a MIRV. I believe it is a MIRV."[38]

33. Quoted in Lundberg, "SS-9," 10.

34. Ibid., 14.

35. Cecil Brownlow, "CIA Threat-Juggling Confirmed," *Aviation Week and Space Technology,* May 3, 1976, 14.

36. Senate Select Committee to Study Governmental Operations with Respect to Intelligence Activities, final report, bk. 1, "Foreign and Military Intelligence," 94th Cong., 2d sess., 1976, 78 n. 24.

37. Lundberg, "SS-9," 14.

38. John Prados, *The Soviet Estimate: U.S. Intelligence Analysis and Soviet Strategic Forces* (Princeton: Princeton University Press, 1986), 216.

The next day, on August 6, Vice-President Spiro Agnew had to break a fifty-fifty tie vote in the Senate to proceed with the Safeguard deployment. Shortly thereafter Carl Duckett, deputy director for science and technology at the CIA, convinced Kissinger that the SS-9 was not MIRVed.[39]

By the end of August, the draft NIE 11-3/8-69 was scheduled to go before the USIB for approval. The Board of National Estimates had drafted a paragraph stating, "We consider it highly unlikely that they (the Soviet Union) will attempt within the period of this estimate to achieve a first strike capability."[40] But Defense Secretary Laird had publicly raised the SS-9's threat to Minuteman in open congressional testimony. Laird's special assistant, William Baroody, went to DCI Helms and asked him to delete the paragraph from the 1969 NIE, saying that it "contradicted the public position of the Secretary."[41] Helms must have felt under terrific pressure because he decided to delete the paragraph and so informed the USIB members. But when the NIE was published in final form, the outgoing director of the Bureau of Intelligence and Research in the State Department, Thomas Hughes, reinstated that paragraph as a footnote.[42]

Four postscripts are pertinent. First, the CIA view that the Soviets did not have a MIRV capability in 1969 and would not have one for five years was borne out in 1974, when the USSR tested its first MIRV. What the Soviets tested in 1969 was a MRV, like those the United States had been deploying on its Polaris submarines since 1963.

Second, whereas the Defense Intelligence Agency projected that 420 SS-9s would be deployed and the air force expected 700, the Soviets eventually deployed 280.[43]

Third, a decade later, former DDR&E director John Foster admitted that he was wrong "in believing the Mod 4 was a MIRV, but believe[d] he was correct in pushing this view."[44] What a telling remark. For Foster and others, pushing an aggressive view vis-à-vis the Soviet Union was paramount. If the data didn't support their conclusions, so what! Within a few years, Foster became a member of the President's Foreign Intelligence Advisory Board. From that vantage point, he was instrumental in setting up competing teams

39. Lundberg, "SS-9," 14.

40. Price, "The DCI's Role," 67.

41. Les Aspin, "Debate over U.S. Strategic Forecasts: A Mixed Record," *Strategic Review* 8 (summer 1980): 38, and Brownlow, "CIA Threat-Juggling Confirmed."

42. Lundberg, "SS-9," 20.

43. Aspin, "Debate over U.S. Forecasts."

44. Memorandum for the record, March 10, 1976, obtained through FOIA. Name of author withheld by CIA.

of outside experts to second-guess the CIA about Soviet missile accuracy, air defense, and strategic objectives. John Foster was to play a vital role in the formation of these "B" teams.

Last, in 1996 Senator Jesse Helms (R-N.C.) denounced a current intelligence estimate as skewed to fit the administration's position on the need to deploy a national missile defense system. "I must say I was stunned when I noted the politicization of the most recent National Intelligence Estimate to support the administration's position in this regard," said Helms, the chairman of the Senate Foreign Relations Committee.[45]

45. Quoted in Thomas W. Lippman and Bradley Graham, "Helms Offers Bill to Force U.S. out of ABM Treaty," *Washington Post*, February 8, 1996, 20.

6

PFIAB into the Fray

Once the right-wingers convinced themselves that National Intelligence Estimates were underestimating the Soviet threat, they cast about for an entry point to challenge the official estimates. They found a ready-made vehicle: the President's Foreign Intelligence Advisory Board, PFIAB, pronounced "piffy-ab."

A Brief History of PFIAB

On February 6, 1956, President Dwight D. Eisenhower signed an executive order establishing a Board of Consultants on Foreign Intelligence Activities to conduct independent evaluations of U.S. foreign intelligence programs. It was created primarily in response to the second Hoover Commission on the Reorganization of the Government, which called for the president to appoint such a committee. A secondary purpose for establishing the board was to

preempt a congressional move by Senator Mike Mansfield (D-Mont.) to create a Joint Congressional Committee on Intelligence.[1]

In his charge to James Killian, president of the Massachusetts Institute of
Technology and the first chairman of this Board of Consultants, Eisenhower
wrote: "While the review of your group would be concerned with all governmental foreign intelligence activities, I would expect particular, detailed attention to be concentrated on the work of the CIA and of those intelligence
elements of key importance in other departments and agencies. I am particularly anxious to obtain your views as to the overall progress that is being
made, the quality of training and personnel, security, progress in research,
effectiveness of special projects and of the handling of funds and general
competence in carrying out the assigned intelligence task."[2]

Other original board members, all recommended by CIA director Allen
Dulles (who was not a member), were retired admiral Richard L. Conolly,
president of Long Island University; World War II hero Lt. Gen. James H.
"Jimmy" Doolittle; Benjamin F. Fairless, chairman of U.S. Steel; retired general
John E. Hull; former ambassador Joseph P. Kennedy; former secretary of defense
Robert Lovett; and Edward Ryerson, former chairman of Inland Steel.[3] This
first board, like others to follow, had a decidedly conservative tinge.

When Eisenhower left office in 1961, the board ceased to function.
Within a month of the failed Bay of Pigs invasion, however, President John
F. Kennedy reactivated it and changed its name to the President's Foreign
Intelligence Advisory Board. Kennedy reappointed Killian as chairman and
also reappointed Doolittle, then chairman of the board of Space Technologies, Inc., and William O. Baker, vice-president for research at Bell Labora-
tories, who had joined the board in 1959. Clark Clifford and later Gen.
Maxwell Taylor became PFIAB chairmen in the 1960s. During the time of
the CIA's declining fortunes in the 1970s, the chairmen were Adm. George
W. Anderson Jr., former chief of naval operations and ambassador to Portugal, appointed in 1970, and Leo Cherne, chairman of Freedom House and
the International Rescue Commission, who followed Anderson in 1976.

In 1969 President Nixon directed the board to make "an annual study of

1. Senate Select Committee to Study Governmental Operations with Respect to Intelligence Activities, final report, bk. 1, "Foreign and Military Intelligence," 94th Cong., 2d sess.,
1976, 63; hereafter referred to as Church Committee Report.
2. Quoted in Albert Wheelon, "History of PFIAB" (Flag Day luncheon address to former
intelligence officers), *Periscope* 10, no. 3 (1985).
3. List of PFIAB members furnished to the author by PFIAB, August 18, 1993.

the level of the threat to supplement the analysis in the National Intelligence Estimates."[4] When the Anti-Ballistic Missile Treaty was signed in Moscow in 1972, Nixon publicly stated that PFIAB would conduct an annual threat assessment to assure him that the intelligence on Soviet strategic forces was adequate.[5]

The Rockefeller Commission, established in 1975 in response to the revelations of illegal CIA activities, observed that PFIAB "does not exert control over the CIA. In fact, the CIA is the Board's only source of information about CIA activities."[6] The commission recommended that PFIAB be expanded and given a more specific mandate, including assessing the compliance by the CIA with its statutory authority and the quality of foreign intelligence estimates and collection. In addition, the commission recommended that the board's chairman be made "full-time."[7]

In its 1976 report, the Senate Select Committee on Intelligence credited the board with significant contributions to the government's intelligence programs, such as "reorganizing Defense intelligence[,] applying science and technology to the National Security Agency, and rewriting the National Security Council Intelligence Directives."[8] However, PFIAB never uncovered any of the CIA's assassination schemes that were detailed in the annex to the "family jewels" report.[9]

William Miller, staff director of the Senate Select Committee on Intelligence for many years, found PFIAB useful, "especially senior people like William Baker." When President Carter abolished PFIAB, the Senate committee continued using PFIAB members as consultants.[10] President Reagan reestablished PFIAB in 1981 and Presidents Bush and Clinton continued it.

4. John Prados, *The Soviet Estimate: U.S. Intelligence Analysis and Soviet Strategic Forces* (Princeton: Princeton University Press, 1986), 209; John Steven Chwat, "The President's Foreign Intelligence Advisory Board: An Historical and Contemporary Analysis (1955–1975)," Library of Congress, Congressional Research Service, November 13, 1975, 14.

5. Lionel Olmer, "Watchdogging Intelligence," in "Seminar on Command, Control, Communications, and Intelligence" (Center for Information Policy Research, Harvard University, 1980), 165.

6. Report to the President by the Commission on CIA Activities Within the U.S., 299, cited in Chwat, "President's Foreign Intelligence Advisory Board," 7.

7. Stephen Flanagan, "Managing the Intelligence Community," *International Security* 10, no. 1 (1985): 70; Chwat, "President's Foreign Intelligence Advisory Board," 18.

8. Church Committee Report, 63; Scott D. Breckinridge, *The CIA and the U.S. Intelligence System* (Boulder, Colo.: Westview Press, 1986), 20.

9. Loch K. Johnson, *America's Secret Power* (New York: Oxford University Press, 1989), 137.

10. Interview with William Miller, July 25, 1989.

PFIAB has had a checkered life, being abolished and reconstituted by various presidents. During most of its existence, PFIAB has met formally two days every other month, with ad hoc committee meetings as required, in the Old Executive Office Building. PFIAB meetings generally begin with a briefing by the director of Central Intelligence. After the director's presentation, the board may meet with other intelligence principals, cabinet officers, and other officials as necessary. The board reports directly to the president and on occasion requests a meeting with him, or he with them. These then occur in the Cabinet Room in the White House.[11]

PFIAB members are eligible to receive, but not all accept, the current government consultant's fee plus per diem and travel expenses. Leo Cherne, when he was chairman of PFIAB, submitted time logs estimating he spent about 750 hours, or 94 days, annually on PFIAB business.[12]

PFIAB's estimated budget for the last nine months of 1976 was $178,300.[13] PFIAB then had a small staff headed by an executive secretary. From June 1973 to 1976 the executive secretary was Wheaton Byers, a former diplomat. Byers had been a special assistant to his predecessor and in turn was succeeded by his deputy, Lionel Olmer, a career naval officer and specialist in cryptology and Soviet strategic forces communications. Olmer became executive secretary in March 1976.

In the 1970s, PFIAB's assessments of the threat posed by the Soviet Union began to take a view decidedly more conservative than that taken by the National Intelligence Estimates. This change was largely due to the composition of the board. Adm. George Anderson, who was PFIAB chairman from 1969 to 1976, thought that an ideal board should be "composed of no more than 12 members selected on a politically nonpartisan basis. . . . The diversity in expertise might be represented as follows: retired senior military officer; former senior career Foreign Service Officer; former Cabinet-level official; distinguished lawyer or jurist; media specialist; scientist; academician; economist; former Congressman; industrialist or prominent businessman."[14]

11. Interview with Leo Cherne, August 2, 1990.
12. Time log, Leo Cherne, July 12, 1976, PFIAB Time Logs, Box 2, Leo Cherne Papers, Gerald R. Ford Library, Ann Arbor, Mich.
13. "PFIAB Budget," Paper, n.d., Folder PFIAB Budget, Box 4, Leo Cherne Papers, Gerald R. Ford Library, Ann Arbor, Mich.
14. George Anderson, letter to Donald Rumsfeld, November 5, 1974, James Connor Collection, Box 54, Gerald R. Ford Library, Ann Arbor, Mich.

PFIAB Composition

In November 1974, PFIAB members were, indeed, a diverse group. Four were scientists: William Baker, who by then had been on the board nearly fifteen years; John Foster, former director of the Livermore Weapons Laboratory and former director of Defense Research and Engineering; Edwin Land, founder and chairman of the Polaroid Corporation and a member of the National Academy of Sciences; and Edward Teller, often referred to as "the father of the H-bomb." In addition, there were three members with governmental experience: former Texas governor John Connally; former secretary of the army and special assistant to President Eisenhower for national security affairs Gordon Gray; and Vice President Nelson Rockefeller, former governor of New York. Other members included Robert Galvin, chairman and CEO of Motorola and a director and past president of the Electronic Industries Association, and George Shultz, who met several of Anderson's criteria. He was an economist who had been chairman of the Council of Economic Advisers, secretary of labor, and director of the Office of Management and Budget.

Diplomacy was represented by Clare Boothe Luce, the former ambassador to Italy, who had also been a Connecticut congresswoman. Seventeen years after its formation, Luce became the first woman appointed to PFIAB. One of her more noteworthy accomplishments was to introduce Henry Kissinger to Richard Nixon in 1967. "It was my idea," she reminisced. "I wanted to introduce Henry to Nixon, and I more or less arranged it."[15]

Leo Cherne straddled several of Anderson's categories. He had a law degree, was executive secretary of the Research Institute of America, which primarily published business and legislative reports, and was also chairman of the International Rescue Committee. Chairman Anderson was himself a senior military officer.

The majority of these PFIAB members in 1975 were openly skeptical about detente, viewed the Soviet Union as an expansionist totalitarian state that posed a great threat to world peace and freedom, and believed that the survival of free institutions around the world depended on a resurgence of American military power. Most of them had held these views for a long time. For example, Gordon Gray had been the first director of the Psychological Strategy Board, created by President Harry S. Truman in the spring of 1951

15. Quoted in Marvin Kalb and Bernard Kalb, *Kissinger* (Boston: Little, Brown, 1974), 14. Also Walter Isaacson, *Kissinger: A Biography* (New York: Simon & Schuster, 1992), 134.

to coordinate secret efforts to win the ideological struggle for the hearts and minds of people living under Communist domination. In the early 1950s this board promoted covert psychological and political warfare against Moscow to pave the way for liberating the "captive peoples."[16] Clare Boothe Luce was convinced that the Soviets had "*both* the capability and the intention to defeat the West" (emphasis in original) and called the policy of detente "fatal."[17]

The right-wing disposition of most board members was well known. They were described by one State Department official as "amateurish" and "dreadful."[18] One former NSC staffer said, "We ignored PFIAB. . . . [They were] hard-core permanent right-wing. Teller was kept at bay through PFIAB. They were shown secrets in hopes of keeping them [the PFIAB members, not the secrets!] quiet."[19] Other common critiques of PFIAB have been that its members were alleged to have close ties to the Defense Department and defense contractors and were therefore not likely to be entirely objective, and that it was considered a safe "in-house" presidential investigative unit not taken seriously by the intelligence community.[20]

PFIAB and Directors of Central Intelligence

When each was director of Central Intelligence, James Schlesinger (briefly in 1973) and William Colby (from 1973 to 1976) were well aware of PFIAB's unhappiness with some National Intelligence Estimates and took remedial steps. Schlesinger first tried an incremental approach and promoted the use of "Interagency Intelligence Memoranda" to deal in depth with technical issues, such as Soviet civil defense and defense spending. These memoranda were coordinated informally with the Pentagon and other intelligence agencies and did not require formal approval by the whole intelligence community. Their conclusions could then be summarized in the appropriate NIEs.[21]

16. James Hershberg, *James B. Conant: Harvard to Hiroshima and the Making of the Nuclear Age* (New York: Knopf, 1993), 511.

17. Clare Boothe Luce, letter to Frank R. Barnett, June 10, 1976, Papers of Clare Boothe Luce, Manuscript Division, Library of Congress.

18. Lawrence Freedman, *U.S. Intelligence and the Soviet Strategic Threat*, 2d ed. (Princeton: Princeton University Press, 1986), 29.

19. Telephone interview with Jan Lodal, October 23, 1989.

20. Chwat, "President's Foreign Intelligence Advisory Board," 18.

21. Victoria S. Price, "The DCI's Role in Producing Strategic Intelligence Estimates" (Naval War College Center for Advance Research, January 1980), 44.

But Schlesinger soon decided more drastic action was needed and, with White House approval, started the process of eliminating the Board of National Estimates and the Office of National Estimates. However, this process had not been completed when Schlesinger became secretary of defense and Colby became director of the CIA.

Colby immediately became "troubled over how badly the machinery was organized to serve me. If I wanted to know what was happening in China, for example, I would have to assemble individual experts in China's politics, its economics, its military, its personalities, as well as the clandestine operators who would tell me things they would tell no one else. Or I could commission a study that would, after weeks of debate, deliver a broad set of generalizations that might be accurate but would be neither timely nor sharp."[22]

Fortuitously, at the time that Colby became DCI, there were six vacancies on the twelve-member Board of National Estimates (BNE). Colby abolished it, and thereby created twelve positions he could fill. Colby decided that these new intelligence officers would report directly to him. BNE chairman John Huizenga retired rather than accept this change, and Colby selected eleven men and one woman as the first National Intelligence Officers (NIOs).[23] Colby decreed each NIO was to have only one assistant and a secretary as staff, and they were to be the director's eyes and ears on the world and provide him with prompt, up-to-date intelligence answers and survey broad intelligence requirements.[24] They were also to act as his principal representatives in policy meetings—such as meetings of the administration's interagency or senior working groups.[25] The new NIOs were directed to get away from their CIA headquarters desks and "mix it up with their policy-making opposite numbers, face-to-face, so that both producers and consumers of intelligence would profit from heightened knowledge of each other's needs and problems."[26]

In interview, Colby indicated that he told the new NIOs: "I think you will have the best job in the bureaucracy. All substance and no bureau-

22. William Colby and Peter Forbath, *Honorable Men: My Life in the CIA* (New York: Simon & Schuster, 1978), 352.

23. Ibid.

24. Price, "The DCI's Role," 45.

25. Gregory F. Treverton, "Estimating Beyond the Cold War," *Defense Intelligence Journal* 3, no. 2 (1994): 5–20.

26. Harold P. Ford, "The U.S. Government's Experience with Intelligence Analysis: Pluses and Minuses" (August 1994), 12.

cracy."[27] Some NIOs had geographic responsibilities such as China, the Soviet Union, Europe, or Latin America, while several had functional tasks
such as strategic weaponry, conventional forces, and economics.[28] To the
cognoscenti they came to be known as the "twelve apostles," in contrast to
the previous BNE, which had been labeled the "College of Cardinals."[29]

One of Colby's rationales for the change was to respond to criticisms by
PFIAB and others that the CIA dominated the estimating process. Colby
wanted to create a NIE drafting system that relied more heavily on the direct
input of intelligence agencies other than the CIA.[30] Thus, in 1975, the Defense Intelligence Agency prepared the first drafts of two chapters of the NIE
on Soviet offensive and defensive strategic forces.[31] Colby contended that,
as a consequence, analysts throughout the intelligence community felt more
involved.[32] As another innovation military and civilian analysts were paired
on specific tasks: if the NIO for Soviet strategic forces was a civilian, the
deputy would be from the military; and if the NIO on Soviet conventional
forces was a military officer, the deputy would be a civilian.[33]

CIA Response to Wohlstetter Articles

Early in his regime, Colby sent the Wohlstetter article that had appeared in
the summer 1974 issue of *Foreign Policy* (discussed in Chapter 1) to his staff
and asked them to answer the charges of perennial underestimation of Soviet
deployments. He was not impressed with their responses: "I got back pretty
vague and defensive stuff. It didn't go into the nuts and bolts of what we
said, and what he said. They said that the Defense Intelligence Agency had
also underestimated! I thought the Wohlstetter critique was devastating."[34]

General Graham, who was then deputy director for the national intelligence community and who later became a member of Team B, also commented on the Wohlstetter article. He wrote to Colby:

27. Interview with William Colby, August 9, 1989.
28. Colby and Forbath, *Honorable Men*, 353.
29. Ford, "The U.S. Government's Experience."
30. Price, "The DCI's Role," 45.
31. Tyrus G. Fain, *The Intelligence Community: History, Organization, and Issues* (New York:
R. R. Bowker, 1977), 44, and Freedman, *U.S. Intelligence and the Soviet Strategic Threat*, 55.
32. Church Committee Report, 75.
33. Interview with George A. Carver, January 17, 1990.
34. Interviews with William Colby, August 9, 1989, and September 17, 1990.

I don't know how your NIOs are going to answer to the Wohlstetter article. In my view, his criticisms should be taken *very* seriously. A case can be made that the projections in national and Pentagon estimates can appear either too low or too high depending on how the data [are] selected. Pick the right estimates and the right number of years in the forecasts and you can "prove" that estimates erred on the high side.

Where Wohlstetter misses the boat from time to time is in his failure to understand some of the reasons for bad projections. After the [Intelligence] Community had gotten over the missile gap syndrome it tended to look for rationales that would prevent another gross overestimate. In the mid-60s, the Soviets had essentially stopped deployment and seemed to have no chance of reaching a *militarily significant* numerical advantage . . . the only logical Soviet force level that anyone could prognosticate was a numerical equality with the U.S. (based on political urges), or a minimum deterrent of some 350 Inter-Continental Ballistic Missiles (ICBM) plus Sea-Launched Ballistic Missiles and bombers.

This bracket was too low . . . [because] long before we did, the Soviets recognized a need for ICBMs directed against China (or at least ICBMs usable in either or both directions). Also, we did not expect that the Soviets would replace lesser range missiles directed at Europe with ICBMs that could go, if necessary, to North America. . . .

This rationale and a number of others are better explanations for the low estimates made by the Community from about 1964 to 1970 than those put forward by Wohlstetter. However, the fact remains that neither national estimates nor the estimates of the Pentagon were "consistently high." The reverse is true, as Wohlstetter indicates. (Emphasis in original)[35]

Another CIA response to Wohlstetter appeared in the classified internal CIA quarterly *Studies in Intelligence*. The author was a CIA analyst who had drafted some of the early NIEs he or she now reexamined. Going back to 1960, the author wanted to see whether the Wohlstetter critique was valid for the estimates of the whole U.S. intelligence community. Remember that the Wohlstetter article was based on data released by the Defense Depart-

35. Daniel Graham, memorandum to DCI Colby, July 1, 1974, obtained through FOIA.

ment. The analyst concluded "that Dr. Wohlstetter is essentially correct in the case of ICBMs during the 1960s" and suspected "that part of the reason for the repeated underestimation of the growth of Soviet ICBM forces was a subconscious (or maybe even conscious) overreaction by the Intelligence Community to the gross *over*estimation of Soviet ICBM growth during the days of the 'missile gap' " (emphasis in original).[36]

The following issue of the same journal carried a rebuttal to this review of Wohlstetter's article. This author had also drafted some of the NIEs under discussion, and quite defensively pointed out that the NIE

> estimates were right with respect to a number of important, non-quantitative judgments made over the years about Soviet forces. Perhaps the most significant of these was the repeated judgment throughout the Sixties that the Soviets could not expect to achieve strategic capabilities which would make rational the deliberate initiation of general war.
>
> Any review of the Estimates written since about 1962—i.e., since the advent of improved collection systems—would also show that the Intelligence Community has been able to provide warning of the introduction of every major Soviet strategic weapon system well before its initial operational capability.[37]

Colby's First National Intelligence Estimate as Director

Responding to Wohlstetter's critique was not a major undertaking for Colby and other CIA officials. They had the yearly NIEs to prepare, and in January 1974, DCI Colby submitted his first NIE on "Soviet Forces for Intercontinental Attack" (NIE 11-8-73). (From 1974 on, the series came to be known as 11-3/8 because the previously separate series on strategic defense and strategic offense were merged and the title of the series changed from "strategic attack" to "intercontinental conflict," and later to "strategic nuclear con-

36. "Wohlstetter, Soviet Strategic Forces, and National Intelligence Estimates," *Studies in Intelligence* 19, no. 1 (1975), obtained through FOIA. Author's name withheld by CIA.

37. "More on the Military Estimates," *Studies in Intelligence* 19, no. 2 (1975), obtained through FOIA. Author's name withheld by CIA.

flict.") It claimed that despite substantial improvements in the USSR's strategic attack forces, the Soviets "are *not* likely to be able to negate the U.S. deterrent under any circumstances we can foresee over the next ten years" (emphasis in original).[38]

When PFIAB chairman Anderson sent PFIAB's annual assessment of the strategic threat to President Nixon three months later, he objected to that statement in the NIE. In PFIAB's view, the Soviets believed they were approaching overall superiority in strategic power.[39] PFIAB was also concerned about the need to improve intelligence in three areas of significant Soviet research and development: accuracies of Soviet missiles, prospects for detecting U.S. ballistic missile submarines, and Soviet laser developments.

In good bureaucratic fashion, Colby then issued his comments on PFIAB's assessment. Colby wrote, "How far they [the Soviets] will press any attempt to achieve superiority will depend to a considerable degree on U.S. negotiating and defense policies, in particular on our ability to persuade the Soviets that: they cannot continue indefinitely to have both substantially improving strategic capabilities and the benefits of detente; non-restraint on their part will produce offsetting U.S. reactions; restraint on their part will be reciprocated."[40]

As for the three research areas PFIAB had noted, Colby assured the president, "These three subjects are listed among the Key Intelligence Questions toward which I have directed the entire Intelligence Community to focus its attention."[41] Concerns over Soviet superiority in missile accuracy, antisubmarine warfare capabilities, and laser developments continued to be recurrent worries of PFIAB and of some in the intelligence community for years.

Throughout his tenure as director of Central Intelligence, Colby had to deal with PFIAB's increasing unhappiness with CIA estimates concerning the Soviets. Under the best of conditions, the relationship between the DCI and PFIAB can be prickly. In interview, the ebullient Leo Cherne, who became PFIAB chairman in 1976, commented, "It would be a remarkable person who would welcome evaluation of the enterprise they are working so hard to direct."[42] Colby, however, claimed that he considered PFIAB "very valuable. I thought of it as a Board of Directors. I rather welcomed going

38. William Colby, letter to President Gerald Ford, May 18, 1974, obtained through FOIA.

39. Ibid.

40. Ibid.

41. Ibid.

42. Interview with Leo Cherne, August 2, 1990.

down there."[43] When Colby left the intelligence community in January 1976, he wrote to Cherne, "I have found our bi-monthly PFIAB conferences most useful. . . . In my view, the PFIAB is an important element of the Intelligence Community."[44]

Up to a point, Colby tried to placate PFIAB. "When they worried that the estimates were 'soft,' I arranged for Gen. George Keegan, air force chief of intelligence, to brief the Intelligence Board on lasers and particle beams," Colby said in interview.[45] Keegan was well known for his extreme views concerning Soviet prowess in exotic technologies. Like Schlesinger before him, Colby focused on procedural changes in the estimating business. Colby told PFIAB, "I accept your criticisms. Let's set up this year's process so it will have an adversarial element." Colby "sought to make sure the NIE came out to be a procedurally tough estimate." He tried to make the NIE "competitive within the [intelligence] community."[46]

Colby arranged a series of debates among the different representatives of the intelligence community where they "took up some of big issues," such as lasers, missile accuracy, and the Soviet Backfire bomber. About fifty intelligence officers attended these meetings. In interviews at his Georgetown home, Colby stated, "I charged people to stand up and give their positions." Colby claims he briefed PFIAB on what he was doing and "they said okay."[47] But several PFIAB members complained to Colby about the suggestion in NIE 11/3-8-74 that the Soviets were seeking only "rough parity" with the United States. Colby defended the NIE on the grounds it represented the best combined judgment of the intelligence community, and appeared reluctant to go further.[48] PFIAB continued to be dissatisfied with the tone and substance of the NIEs dealing with the Soviet Union.

The Birth of an Idea

One of the most outspoken critics of the National Intelligence Estimates was John Foster, who figured in the SS-9 story in the previous chapter and who

43. Interview with William Colby, September 17, 1990.

44. William Colby, letter to Leo Cherne, January 27, 1976, Folder "William E. Colby," Box 2, Leo Cherne Papers, Gerald R. Ford Library, Ann Arbor, Mich.

45. Interview with William Colby, August 9, 1989.

46. Colby interviews.

47. Ibid.

48. Price, "The DCI's Role," 102.

joined PFIAB in September 1973. Because of his past position as director of Defense Research and Engineering, Foster was quite conversant with intelligence and the Defense Department's assessment of it. In an interview, slight, trim, outspoken Foster opined that "the others on PFIAB were weekend warriors" and that he began to "read the NIEs seriously." According to Foster, "It soon became clear to me that in a number of cases the NIE overstated the situation. They stated as facts things for which they didn't have the sources to defend the statement. After I bitched for about a year, Chairman Anderson said, 'Why don't you, Teller [Edward Teller] and Galvin [Robert Galvin], form a Committee on NIE Evaluation?'"[49]

Before doing so, Foster met with Teller and Richard Latter to brainstorm how this PFIAB Committee on NIE Evaluation should proceed. Latter, also a physicist, had known both Foster and Teller for decades. When the Lawrence Livermore Laboratory had opened, Latter had taken a leave from RAND to become the acting head of the new laboratory's Theoretical Division. Foster was the chief of the Small Weapons Group at the same laboratory. Later, Foster and Latter were allies in the SS-9 missile accuracy controversy and together with Teller were united in opposing the Limited Test Ban Treaty in 1963 and the Anti-Ballistic Missile Treaty in 1972. When Foster was director of Defense Research and Engineering, Latter served on the Defense Science Board, an advisory committee to the Defense Department. Teller and Foster had a long association as well. Foster was a former director of the Lawrence Livermore Laboratory, sometimes referred to as Teller Tech because of Teller's instrumental role in its establishment and later its management.

Latter has said in interview that he suggested that what was needed was a second CIA, an alternative source of information. To Latter's surprise, Teller reacted negatively to this idea. Latter pointed out that Teller had formed a second weapons laboratory for much the same reason. Foster, however, liked the concept but thought it would be too difficult bureaucratically, and came up with a less grandiose notion—a small group of outside experts should perform an alternative threat assessment. Teller agreed with this plan. Latter, Teller, and Foster then discussed what issues such a group might examine and decided on Soviet missile accuracy, Soviet air defense, and Soviet antisubmarine warfare capabilities, the same topics about which PFIAB had continuously expressed concern.[50] Foster wanted to include "the strategy of the

49. Interview with John Foster, May 9, 1990.
50. Telephone interview with Richard Latter, February 28, 1990.

Soviet Union presumed by the CIA" and Soviet passive defenses as well.[51] It was clear from the beginning that the outsiders would need both access to all the data available to the intelligence community in making its yearly assessments and an official imprimatur to make their assessment legitimate.

Foster returned to Washington and reported to Chairman Anderson and PFIAB member Galvin the idea of setting up an independent team consisting of knowledgeable people, exposing them to the same data base as used by the intelligence community, and seeing if they would come up with different results.[52] It is important to remember that such an exercise did not stem from a complaint by the users, that is, the policymakers, but was an initiative from PFIAB.[53]

Planning the Experiment

Edward Teller had a long history of grossly overestimating the technological prowess of the Soviet Union. Asked in the early 1960s what we would find if we landed on the moon, Teller answered simply, "Russians."[54] Now, in 1975, Teller quickly prepared a draft "alternative NIE" and gave it to State Department counselor Helmut Sonnenfeldt to pass on to Secretary of State Kissinger. Teller explained to Sonnenfeldt that current NIEs didn't deal with worst-case scenarios but his draft did. Teller introduced three propositions: Soviet missile accuracies might be better than estimated and would continue to improve; U.S. submarines would become increasingly vulnerable due to breakthroughs in Soviet antisubmarine warfare; and U.S. bombers might be destroyed before reaching the Soviet Union.[55] Sonnenfeldt effectively discounted Teller's NIE by commenting, "Teller's technique is to take propositions that can neither be proved nor disproved at this time. Nevertheless, his consistent suggestion that every proposition will unfold in a worst case situation for the U.S. undermines the over-all credibility of his 'alternative' NIE."[56]

51. Interviews with John Foster, May 9, 1990, and September 1, 1990.

52. Ibid.

53. Interview with Robert Galvin, September 24, 1990.

54. Joel Achenbach, "So It Was a Fair Race . . . and We Won," *Washington Post*, July 1, 1994, D5.

55. "An Alternative NIE," June 18, 1975, obtained under Mandatory Review, Gerald R. Ford Library, Ann Arbor, Mich.

56. Helmut Sonnenfeldt, memorandum for Secretary of State Kissinger, July 22, 1975, obtained through FOIA.

Next came a meeting on August 6, 1975, at CIA headquarters in Langley, Virginia, between PFIAB members Foster and Teller and the NIO for Soviet strategic programs, Howard Stoertz, and his assistant, Col. Henson R. De-Bruler. Foster and Teller expressed their disagreement with key judgments in NIE 11-3/8-74 concerning the Soviet threat to each leg of the U.S. triad (strategic bombers, land-based intercontinental missiles, and submarine-launched ballistic missiles). For each they thought Soviet developments "held some prospect for a serious threat to [the] U.S."[57]

Foster and Teller also disagreed with what they called the "net assessment of the estimate." A net assessment is an overall comparison of the relative military postures of two opponents, in this case, the United States and the USSR, that draws conclusions about their current or future relative capabilities and compares them according to the same identified criteria. Foster and Teller disagreed with the statement "that it is extremely unlikely that during the next ten years the Soviets will conclude that they could launch an attack which would prevent devastating U.S. retaliation."[58]

Stoertz explained that NIE 11-3/8-75, then underway, would pay particular attention to key factors "affecting estimated Soviet capabilities; whether, when and by what means the Soviets may be able to overcome these key limitations; [and] likely lead-times required for the Soviets to develop improved capabilities and to incorporate the improvements into their operational forces."[59]

Foster told the CIA officials that he was drafting a memorandum for PFIAB's consideration. It would establish an organization, responsible to the DCI, that would prepare analyses to compete with those of the CIA for the most critical intelligence issues. He cited the success of the Livermore Laboratory in developing the H-bomb in competition with Los Alamos Laboratory and also Soviet successes in establishing competing research and design institutes.[60]

At the meeting Teller opined that "intelligence was not adept in the adversary process while planners and policy-makers are schooled in adversarial relationships." Stoertz pointed out that the national estimating process involves "advocates of different views and backgrounds" and thereby "does surface adversary positions."[61]

57. Henson DeBruler, memorandum for the record, August 8, 1975, obtained through FOIA.
    58. Ibid.
    59. Ibid., 3.
    60. Ibid.
    61. Ibid.

But the PFIAB members were unconvinced by these CIA protestations. Foster spent the afternoon with intelligence agency representatives involved in the preparation of NIE 11-3/8-75 to give them "an opportunity to propose changes to his draft memorandum." These included representatives from Naval Intelligence, the National Security Agency, and the Defense Intelligence Agency.[62]

Foster's draft memo contained three suggestions: first, that "an organization responsible to the DCI [be established] to prepare analyses of the most critical intelligence issues to compete with analyses currently performed"; second, that the consumers of intelligence, the policymakers, "ask the DCI to organize intelligence material in ways which will best assist him in making a decision, for example, to examine case[s] A, B, and C, present the evidence supporting each case, and give the probability of each case eventuating"; and third, that "the NIE should not contain 'net assessments.' "[63] It is interesting to note that when Foster was director of Defense Research and Engineering in 1971, he established a Net Technical Assessment Group that provided him with an "in-house" capability to challenge intelligence community assessments.[64]

PFIAB's Discontent

When President Nixon resigned in August 1974 as a result of the Watergate break-in and subsequent cover-up, Gerald Ford became president. Two days after Foster drafted his memo, PFIAB chairman Anderson sent a letter to President Ford stating "that NIE 11-3/8-74 (Soviet Forces for Intercontinental Conflict Through 1985) is seriously misleading in the presentation of a number of key judgments and in projecting a sense of complacency unsupported by the facts; as a consequence it is deficient for the purpose it should serve."[65] If Wohlstetter's articles were the opening salvo in the conservative assault on the CIA's Soviet estimates, Anderson's letter to President Ford began the second round.

Anderson accused the NIE of many sins: for example, of presenting the

62. Ibid., 5.
63. Ibid.
64. Freedman, U.S. Intelligence and the Soviet Strategic Threat, 51.
65. Attachment to Henson DeBruler briefing memorandum for the DCI, June 2, 1976, obtained through FOIA.

assessment "that for the next ten years it is extremely unlikely that the Soviets will conclude they could launch an attack which would prevent devastating U.S. retaliation . . . confidently, with the force of fact, although the cumulative evidence on which it is based is conflicting, often flimsy, and in certain cases does not exist."[66]

Colby's response was tart: "The estimative words 'extremely unlikely' are not intended to mean it is fact. It is our *estimate* supported by the evidence and discussion in the body of the NIE" (emphasis in original).[67]

With respect to Soviet ICBM accuracy and the survivability of the U.S. Minuteman force, Anderson faulted the NIE for "averaging the worst and best cases when the data could really support either interpretation." Colby replied, "In no case has any 'averaging of worst and best cases' taken place." Anderson contended that "the NIE . . . accepts optimistic and unproven data regarding U.S. silo hardness," to which Colby answered, "The data used were provided by the CINCSAC—the operational commander of the Minuteman force—a source we would expect to be best informed on this subject."[68]

Turning to the survivability of the U.S. sea-based deterrent, Anderson objected to the NIE's assertion "there should be little worry . . . now or in the next ten years." Colby explained that

> the basis for the conclusion is spelled out in some detail in the body of the Estimate, so it is something more than an assertion . . . there is strong positive evidence of a current lack of Soviet ASW [antisubmarine warfare] capability against the U.S. SSBN [strategic nuclear ballistic missile submarine force]. . . . The Estimate also addressed Soviet capability to impair the effectiveness of the SSBN *force* in the next ten years. . . . Our principal reason for projecting a future lack of Soviet capability to meet this goal is our inability to identify any Soviet approach, either "classical" or non-conventional, for detection of deployed SSBNs which could meet either the numerical or time criteria. (Emphasis in original)[69]

On the subject of bomber penetration, Anderson accused the NIE of making assumptions about Soviet deficiencies, and Colby responded, "The as-

66. Comments on George Anderson's August 8, 1975, letter to President Ford, appended to letter from William Colby to George Anderson, December 2, 1975, obtained through FOIA.

67. Ibid., 1.

68. Ibid., 2.

69. Ibid., 4–5.

sessed capabilities . . . are based on exhaustive analysis of Soviet air defenses—they were not merely assumed."[70] Here again, PFIAB was voicing its concern about the recurring three subjects: whether Soviet missiles had counterforce accuracy, whether our sea-based deterrent might become vulnerable, and whether our bombers had the ability to penetrate Soviet air defenses.

The NSC Chimes In

By September 1975, the National Security Council (NSC) had entered the melee. Colby received a memorandum from National Security Adviser Kissinger claiming that PFIAB had recommended "the current NIE process be converted to a new three-step process" that entailed "production of a purely intelligence document which avoids net assessments[,] a detailed net assessment and a thorough critique of the new assessment by an independent entity."[71] A draft presidential directive to conduct and evaluate an experiment in competitive estimates in two specific areas—antisubmarine warfare and the accuracy of Soviet ICBMs—was attached. Kissinger's memo envisioned changes much more sweeping than what PFIAB was actually recommending and, not surprisingly, was the subject of a meeting between the staffs of the CIA, PFIAB, and the NSC. Attendees were George Carver, CIA deputy director for NIOs; Colonel DeBruler, deputy NIO for Soviet programs; Richard Ober, director for intelligence coordination at the NSC; Wheaton Byers, executive secretary of PFIAB; his assistant, Commander Lionel Olmer; and Roger Molander of the NSC staff.

That meeting occurred on September 11, 1975. While the "memorandum for the record" is written in the obligatory dry and detached bureaucratic manner, one can imagine that, at times, it was a testy meeting. Byers and Olmer repeated Foster's complaint that adversarial positions "were not exposed to the President and other consumers." When the PFIAB representatives said that differences over such technical issues as "the data processing system for netting low altitude surveillance radars" were what Dr. Foster had in mind, DeBruler and Molander answered that "exposing details about differing interpretations about biases in accelerometer quality measurements

70. Ibid., 7.
71. Henry Kissinger, memorandum to DCI Colby, September 8, 1975, obtained through FOIA.

would hardly be an appropriate communication to Dr. Kissinger and the President."[72]

Carver noted "that since Dr. Foster and Dr. Teller disagreed with some of the judgments we [the intelligence community] are making, the PFIAB proposal could be construed as recommending the establishment of another organization which might reach conclusions more compatible with their thinking." Byers "denied emphatically that this was Dr. Foster's and Dr. Teller's intent."[73] But of course, that was precisely the case!

When pressed to identify which high-level consumers were dissatisfied with the NIE, Byers named Kissinger and the president. Molander pointed out that neither Kissinger nor the president read the entire NIE, and Byers "admitted that he had not read NIE 11-3/8-74." Carver reported that Secretary of Defense Schlesinger "had praised it [NIE 11-3/8-74] as a useful and most impressive document." About the only thing on which there was general agreement was that "the experiment could not be conducted until after the current NIE 11-3/8 is completed."[74]

Colby's Response

Two eventful months elapsed before Colby, in a five-page letter to President Ford dated November 21, 1975, officially responded to the Kissinger memo. The letter was reviewed, discussed, and unanimously endorsed by the U.S. Intelligence Board. Colby wrote:

> I certainly share the PFIAB's view that "National Intelligence Estimates should be among the most important documents issued by the Intelligence Community." NIE 11-3/8-74 was the product of a still-continuing evolutionary process through which the Intelligence Community is endeavoring to make each of these major annual assessments of Soviet strategic capabilities better than those of preceding years. While I would not contend that NIE 11-3/8-74 was a perfect document, I cannot agree with the PFIAB's contention that

72. Henson DeBruler, memorandum for the record, September 15, 1975, 3, obtained through FOIA.

73. Ibid.

74. Ibid., 6.

it errs by "projecting a sense of complacency" or for that matter, in offering any judgments "unsupported by the facts."[75]

After paying the mandatory obeisance to "any suggestions on how those products [intelligence] can be made more informative and enlightening to the policy officials for whom they are written" and welcoming "any improvements in the U.S. Government's procedures for developing net assessments of U.S. capabilities with respect to those of potential or putative adversaries," Colby strongly opposed the estimating experiment:

> Our annual estimates on Soviet strategic capabilities . . . utilize all the information known by and the best analysis available to the U.S. Government. Undergirding the production of the actual estimate itself . . . is an extensive research program examining specific aspects of Soviet capabilities in considerable detail, a research program involving not only all concerned elements of the Intelligence Community but also drawing on the views and talents of knowledgeable experts in specific fields outside the government. *It is hard for me to envisage how an ad hoc "independent" group of government and non-government analysts could prepare a more thorough, comprehensive assessment of Soviet strategic capabilities—even in two specific areas—than the Intelligence Community can prepare.* (Emphasis added)[76]

Colby ended by noting that NIE 11-3/8-75 would "be in the hands of concerned consumers, including the PFIAB, within the next few days." He suggested that the "consumers—especially the PFIAB—scrutinize NIE 11-3/8-75 and ascertain the extent to which it overcomes or rectifies what they may have perceived as deficiencies in NIE 11-3/8-74. After this process of review has been completed . . . [we] can then sit down with members of the PFIAB and the NSC Staff to discuss specific courses of action most likely to be of value in our joint, continuing quest for a better national intelligence product."[77] Colby was strongly supported by NIO Howard Stoertz, who argued that a parallel NIE would put intolerable pressures on the CIA's regular analysts.[78]

75. William Colby, letter to President Gerald Ford, November 21, 1975, 3, obtained through FOIA.

76. Ibid., 4.

77. Ibid., 5.

78. Thomas Powers, "Choosing a Strategy for World War III," *Atlantic Monthly,* November 1982, 82–110.

And so one might expect the story to end there. PFIAB had asked the CIA to conduct an experiment in alternative threat assessment, and the entire intelligence community, as represented by the U.S. Intelligence Board, had turned the request aside. Even such a consistent critic of NIE 11-3/8 as air force chief of intelligence Gen. George Keegan "fully supported" Colby's opposition to "preparation of an experimental estimate by an independent analysis group."[79] Yet . . .

---

79. George Keegan, letter to William Colby, November 21, 1975, obtained through FOIA.

7

Team B Is Born (or How Did We Get Here from There?)

On October 20, 1976, readers of the *Boston Globe* learned that "a presidential advisory group has commissioned an independent analysis [of intelligence estimates] by outside experts." The study responded to concerns "that the intelligence community may have significantly understated the threat of the Soviet military buildup in recent years." The group "is charged with coming up, by November 7, with a parallel National Intelligence Estimate executive summary for 1976 and recommendations for ways to minimize institutional bias in the existing analytical process."[1]

What happened in the eleven months between the end of November 1975, when Director of Central Intelligence William Colby and the entire intelligence community rejected just such an experiment rather forcefully, and this first public indication that such a study was, in fact, occurring? Several factors contributed to the turnaround. First came the requested resignation of CIA director William Colby and the unabated insistence by the President's Foreign Intelligence Advisory Board (PFIAB) that such an experiment take place. Then came a "track record" study conducted by the CIA

---

1. William Beecher, "Special Unit Analyzing U.S. Spy Data," *Boston Globe*, October 20, 1976, 1.

to assess the accuracy of past National Intelligence Estimates, and new revelations and public debate about the level of Soviet defense spending. Finally, the selection of George Bush as Colby's successor as director of the CIA and the high politics of election year 1976 played a major role. I will look at each of these in turn.

Who's In? Who's Out?

In October 1975 President Ford asked his closest advisers, his "kitchen cabinet," why his approval rating in the Gallup polls had leveled off at 47 percent. Bryce Harlow replied that "public divisions," particularly the growing feud between National Security Adviser and Secretary of State Henry Kissinger and Secretary of Defense James Schlesinger were creating the impression that Ford was not fully in command.[2] The Kissinger-Schlesinger quarrel centered mainly on relations with the Soviet Union and negotiations to achieve a second strategic arms accord.

As vice-president, Ford had already tangled with Schlesinger about the way Schlesinger treated congressional committee chairs.[3] Schlesinger's "aloof, frequently arrogant manner" antagonized the president, and Ford decided to "sever [his] relationship with him at the earliest opportunity."[4]

Ford also decided to change the leadership at the CIA. In his estimation,

> Bill Colby had been director of the CIA at a traumatic period in the agency's history. He had gone through hell and, in my opinion, done a splendid job. In the fall of 1975, many people felt that I was angry at him for disclosing too much about CIA activities in his appearances before Congressional committees. That was not the case. He was on a hot seat before one committee after another. I supported his decision to tell the truth about past agency misdeeds even though both of us recognized that his testimony would be embarrassing. Colby was smart; he possessed both integrity and guts,

2. Gerald Ford, A Time to Heal: The Autobiography of Gerald R. Ford (New York: Harper & Row, 1979), 320.
3. Ibid., 321.
4. Ibid., 324.

and I liked and respected him very much. Yet this did not alter my conviction that the agency needed a change at the top.[5]

The problem was that Colby had been contaminated by events. He had changed procedures, cleaned house, sought to make sure that past abuses wouldn't recur, and yet people focused on the odors lingering from those past abuses and associated them with Colby.

Ford also decreed that "Henry Kissinger should wear only one hat; to expect him to function effectively both as Secretary of State and as National Security Adviser to the President was to ask too much of any one man."[6] These changes necessitated new appointments. Gen. Brent Scowcroft was named national security adviser, with William Hyland as his deputy; Donald Rumsfeld became secretary of defense; Richard Cheney was named chief of staff; and George Bush was recalled from China, where he was the U.S. representative (ambassadors between the United States and the People's Republic of China had not yet been exchanged), to become the new director of the CIA.

At this time Ford also decided to deal with the question of who would be his vice-presidential running mate in the forthcoming election. Ever worried about polls, President Ford suggested to Vice President Nelson Rockefeller that "there are serious problems, and to be brutally frank, some of these difficulties might be eliminated if you were to indicate that you didn't want to be on the ticket in 1976. I'm not *asking* you to do that, I'm just stating the facts" (emphasis in original). Rockefeller agreed to give Ford a letter saying that he did not want to be considered as a vice-presidential nominee.[7] Later, Ford called his treatment of Rockefeller "one of the few cowardly things I did in my life."[8]

When all these personnel changes were announced on November 3, 1975, the press dubbed them the "Halloween Massacre," inviting comparison with the Watergate "Saturday Night Massacre." According to Ford, the personnel changes pleased almost no one. "Conservatives screamed about my dismissal of the supposedly 'hard-line' Schlesinger. Liberals were upset by Rockefeller's

5. Ibid., 324–25.
6. Ibid., 325.
7. Ibid., 328.
8. Quoted in Douglas Brinkley, "The Unexpected President," *Washington Post Book World,* February 6, 1994, 11.

withdrawal as my 1976 running mate. And the press had a field day."[9] What was worse, from Ford's point of view, was that his popularity as measured by the Gallup poll plummeted and Ronald Reagan edged ahead.[10]

PFIAB Perseveres

When Colby, in his capacity as director of Central Intelligence, wrote his November 21, 1975, letter to President Ford, in which he turned aside PFI-AB's request to permit "an ad hoc independent group of government and non-government analysts to prepare an assessment of Soviet strategic capabilities," it had already been announced that George Bush would become the new director of the agency. Colby was only staying on as DCI at President Ford's request, until Bush was confirmed by the Senate. No doubt buoyed by this knowledge, PFIAB proceeded as if its request had never been rejected.

In December 1975, CIA officials met with PFIAB to discuss the "Key Judgments" of NIE 11-3/8-75 and the board's recommendations to the president for changing the process of preparing NIEs on Soviet strategic forces.[11] Much of the ensuing conversation concerned the question of Soviet missile accuracy and therefore U.S. ICBM vulnerability. John Foster, the most vocal and outspoken PFIAB member, maintained that the "Soviets would have high confidence in attacking Minuteman, had demonstrated the ability to trail U.S. submarines, and that all they [the Soviets] need is an AWACS [Airborne Warning and Control System] and they would have high confidence in their air defenses." He also thought that Soviet civil defense was sophisticated enough so that the "leaders could survive if they decided to sacrifice a few million people."[12]

John Foster and George Carver, CIA deputy director for National Intelligence Officers, had a philosophical discussion about the function of intelligence estimates, with Foster opining that "history shows that intelligence has always been conservative in estimating [meaning that we had underestimated] Soviet capabilities." He "does not get the same degree of concern from reading the NIEs as he would if intelligence told him the worst case

9. Ford, A Time to Heal, 330.
10. Ibid., 331.
11. Henson DeBruler, memorandum for the record, December 8, 1975, obtained through FOIA.
12. Ibid., 5.

the data will support and the best case." Carver's response was, "We can't give the policy-maker two extremes and stop there. We are called on to assess the most likely Soviet capabilities, and to judge how the Soviets themselves probably view their capabilities."[13]

PFIAB member Edward Teller continued to feel that the NIE conveyed an "insufficient degree of anxiety," but to Leo Cherne "this year's NIE conveyed a perceptibly greater sense of anxiety than did last year's Estimate," and he "could not believe that this document [NIE 11-3/8-75] would convey to any reader a tranquil view of the Soviet threat."[14] Robert Galvin, the chairman of PFIAB's National Intelligence Estimate Evaluation Committee, "regarded NIE 11-3/8-75 as eminently better than last year's estimate" and told a CIA official privately "he thought NIE 11-3/8-75 was an excellent job."[15]

The next day, Teller met with CIA officials and began by stating that "ten-year intelligence predictions usually have not been very accurate." In typical hyperbole, Teller opined, "Student disturbances and radical administrations at MIT and Stanford have wiped out military R&D. The U.S. is short of human material—except for some old people—which has [sic] the imagination to look into the future. There is no reason to believe that anything similar has happened in Russia. We do not have the experience to chart the course of the Russians, but it is 'practically certain' that they will get ahead of us."[16]

Teller observed that "intelligence had been challenged by Dr. John Foster on three separate matters: the accuracy of Soviet ICBMs, Soviet air defense against low-flying planes, and the Soviet counter to U.S. submarine-based missiles. Between the three of them, the entire U.S. triad could be challenged."[17]

Foster, meeting with intelligence community personnel a week later, stated his view that this year's NIE was a considerable improvement over last year's "because (a) the material in dissenting footnotes . . . in the past was not presented in a coherent way, but it was now coherently presented, especially 'Keegan's stuff' [Gen. George Keegan, air force chief of intelligence,

13. Ibid., 6.
14. Ibid., 4.
15. Ibid., 11.
16. Memorandum for the record, December 11, 1975, 1, obtained through FOIA. Author's name withheld by the CIA. However, the author's designation is shown as A/NIO/SP. In the previous memo DeBruler was identified as "Assistant National Intelligence Office for Strategic Programs," which appears abbreviated as A/NIO/SP.
17. Ibid., 2.

had been dissenting in footnotes for years], and this was 'refreshing' because it was difficult to do; and (b) the general tone of the strategic situation is different, i.e., the situation is portrayed as getting worse because the 'other guy' seems to be doing more than we are."[18]

Foster referred to his "experiment" and noted "that competition results in a better product for the nation." Foster said "a couple of teams—'red' and 'blue'—ought to be selected and they should operate under the same ground rules without ulterior motives. One develops the best, credible, 'optimistic' case and the other the best, credible case on the 'conservative' side. The decision-maker should then make a choice between them."[19]

Foster again raised the issues of Minuteman survival, bomber penetration, and SSBN survival as those the outside group should examine. General Keegan opined, "[W]e need a factual, detailed statement of the conflict objectives which Soviet declarations have made abundantly clear." Foster replied that "there was a big difference between declaratory policy and action policy."[20] In other words, the experiment in Foster's mind was to look at data, not intentions. Up to this point, the three subject areas for the competitive threat assessment seemed certain: Soviet missile accuracy, air defenses, and antisubmarine warfare (ASW) capabilities.

The Navy Enters the Fray

Now, however, the navy stepped in. When Adm. Bobby Inman, director of Naval Intelligence, heard that ASW was on the agenda of an alternative threat assessment, he decided that the CIA was "jockeying for independent access to raw materials on ASW."[21] According to Inman, information about the operational aspects of each submarine patrol, including where they operated and whether they were trailed, is the most closely held information in the government, and the navy refused to share that information with anyone, including the CIA.[22]

---

18. Memorandum for the record, December 17, 1975, obtained through FOIA. Author's name withheld by the CIA. However, the author's designation is shown as A/NIO/SP.

19. Ibid., 2–3.

20. Ibid., 4.

21. Interview with Adm. Bobby Inman, May 4, 1989.

22. Ibid.

Independent verification of the navy's withholding of information about Soviet ASW capabilities is revealed in a memo written by the NIO for strategic programs in 1978: "Data on Soviet ASW capabilities are controlled by the US Navy to the extent that it is difficult to perform a critical, independent assessment elsewhere. Although this may be reasonable, given the security requirements for the data involved, there is a significant cost to the overall estimative process."[23]

Inman informed the secretary of the navy, the secretary of defense, and the chief of naval operations that he opposed sharing operational details with anyone and objected to any reevaluation of the problem of submarine vulnerability, particularly by a group of outsiders. Inman was aided in this effort by Adm. Daniel Murphy, former director of ASW and electronic warfare, who had come back to the Pentagon in 1975. Murphy felt outsiders "didn't know shit about it."[24] Inman was encouraged to take a "hard line" and asked for an appointment with Robert Galvin, chairman of the PFIAB NIE Evaluation Committee. After hearing of the navy's objections, Galvin, with John Foster's concurrence, took ASW vulnerability off the agenda of the alternative threat assessment.[25]

Soon thereafter, Keegan's suggestion that Soviet objectives be included in an alternative assessment was adopted. This was greeted with dismay by many of the very people who had been pushing for an alternative threat assessment. Richard Latter, who had met with Foster and Teller earlier and had suggested that an alternative intelligence agency be formed, stated that he was "terribly opposed" to including Soviet objectives, because "a priori that's a non-technical subject. It is an argumentative subject and conflicted with the intent of the competitive analysis."[26]

While these bureaucratic negotiations were going on, two other events influenced the new director of Central Intelligence, George Bush, to agree to a competitive threat assessment. One was a "track record" study conducted by the CIA itself to see how accurate their past assessments had been, and the other concerned new calculations of how much the Soviets were spending on their military.

23. Howard Stoertz, "Observations on the Content and Accuracy of Recent National Intelligence Estimates on Soviet Strategic Forces (NIE 11-3/8)," memorandum, July 25, 1978, 7, obtained through FOIA.

24. Interview with Adm. Daniel Murphy, November 9, 1989.

25. Interviews with Adm. Bobby Inman, May 4, 1989; Adm. Daniel Murphy, November 9, 1989; Lionel Olmer, November 8, 1990; and Robert Galvin, September 24, 1990.

26. Telephone interview with Richard Latter, February 28, 1990.

The Track Record Study

The idea of a study to look at past National Intelligence Estimates in order to see how well they had predicted Soviet strategic forces was first mentioned to CIA officials in a letter from Robert Galvin, chairman of PFIAB's NIE Evaluation Committee, to George Carver, deputy to the DCI for National Intelligence Officers, dated December 11, 1975. Galvin asked Carver "to undertake an evaluation of the intelligence community's annual assessments and annual predictions of Soviet Strategic Forces for each of the last ten years."[27] General Keegan also proposed the notion at the meeting Foster had with intelligence officials on December 16. Keegan felt such a "postmortem" should be prepared by an outside agency and should go back to 1940. Carver immediately commented "that he did not agree that this had to be done by an outside group, since what intelligence had estimated was a matter of record."[28]

By December 23 the CIA, still headed by lame duck Colby, had agreed to commission a review of the National Intelligence Estimates on Soviet strategic forces and programs over the past ten years, "to determine the accuracy of the estimates made on major topics." The topics would be "those with relevance to the viability of the three 'legs' of the U.S. deterrent 'triad,' namely the survivability and penetrability of our ICBM, SLBM, and strategic bomber weapon systems."[29] The study was to be conducted by three or four people, "qualified in the subject matter but not recently directly involved in intelligence estimating."[30]

The target date for completing and presenting the report to PFIAB was the end of January 1976, only a month away. The three authors of the forty-one-page report were Robert L. Hewitt, recently retired from the CIA; Dr. John Ashton, a Defense Intelligence Agency official formerly with the CIA; and Dr. John H. Milligan of the CIA's Science and Technology Directorate.

Although the track record's main conclusion was that "the intelligence community, as judged by the findings in its national estimates, has a good record of detecting and determining major characteristics and missions of new weapons systems soon after test begins and usually well before IOC

27. Robert Galvin, letter to George A. Carver, December 11, 1975, obtained through FOIA.
28. Memorandum for the record, December 17, 1975, obtained through FOIA.
29. Howard Stoertz, memorandum for Robert Galvin, December 23, 1975, obtained through FOIA.
30. Ibid., attachment.

[Initial Operational Capability]," particular conclusions were mixed. The report pointed out that "the intelligence community has also been generally successful in monitoring the deployment of new weapons systems and the introduction of major modifications in existing ones, despite some initial difficulties in determining the scope and pace of deployment. There have been recurring minor uncertainties and disagreements about how many silos are under construction, how many submarines are in the building shed, and the like." According to the report, "The most obvious shortcoming was the failure of the earlier estimates to foresee the degree to which Soviets would not only catch up to the U.S. in number of ICBMs but keep right on going."[31]

The study also indicated where the estimates had overestimated Soviet systems, such as their ABMs and SA-5s.[32] Among the surprises, the report mentioned that the Soviets "would undertake the very extensive remodeling of silos and construction of new launch control facilities now going on. . . . More important, they failed to foresee that the Soviets would greatly increase the throwweight of their new missiles and introduce new launch techniques with some."[33]

In terms of the triad, the report found that "[t]he threat to Minuteman from Soviet hard target MIRVs has been overestimated in terms of how soon high accuracy would be obtained, if the current estimates are correct, but was underestimated in terms of throw weight and number of RVs . . . [t]he threat to U.S. bombers and ASMs [air-to-surface missiles] penetrating Soviet territory has grown about as the estimates indicated . . . Soviet ABM capabilities . . . have been slower to develop, additional deployment at Moscow or elsewhere failed to take place, [and] Soviet ASW capabilities against U.S. SSBNs have remained very low as was estimated."[34]

To the layperson the report seems to say, "Yeah, the intelligence community goofed on a few things, but overall the record was pretty good." However, to those inside the government who thought the NIEs were underestimating the threat from the Soviet Union, the study was interpreted differently. Lionel Olmer, a tall man with graying hair, an angular face, and the executive secretary of PFIAB, said, "The study was so condemnatory of

31. Robert L. Hewitt, Dr. John Ashton, and Dr. John H. Milligan, "The Track Record in Strategic Estimating: An Evaluation of the Strategic National Intelligence Estimates, 1966–1975," dated February 6, 1976, i, ii, and iii, obtained through FOIA.

32. Ibid., iii–iv.

33. Ibid., v.

34. Ibid., vi–vii.

the performance of the community over a period of ten years on those three issues that it left no room for argument that something ought to be done."[35]

Even as the track record study was being written inside the CIA, conservatives began to press for release of old NIEs to outsiders, that is, giving outsiders access to CIA data and information. A story in the *Washington Star* stated, "The administration has resisted the release of old NIEs to outside examination, which might test the validity of CIA analysis. But a number of voices around Washington, including those of persons who have been close enough to intelligence to know many of the analytical failures, have called for just such a re-examination."[36]

The new DCI, George Bush, was briefed about the track record study before he met with PFIAB subcommittee chairman Robert Galvin to discuss it. Deputy for National Intelligence George Carver wrote, "The Track Record study is a solid piece of work which is both thorough and objective. Not surprisingly, it indicates that the Community's overall record is a mixed picture of successes and errors; but it also indicates—at least to me—that the balance is very much on the plus side of the ledger . . . in no case have the Soviets ever deployed a major weapons system which the Intelligence Community did not spot and assess well before its operational deployment." Carver continued, "I feel the record does not support the view most sharply articulated by Foster and Teller, though clearly held to some extent by other Board members (e.g., Admiral Anderson, the former Chairman, and Mrs. Luce) that the Intelligence Community, over the past two and one half decades, has systematically under-assessed the growing Soviet threat." Carver spelled out for the new CIA director some of the underlying issues: "Foster and Teller believe intelligence officers should deliberately try to shape policy by calling attention to the worst things the Soviets could do in order to stimulate appropriate countermeasure responses by the U.S. Government. This, they believe, is the path of prudence; but is not the view of intelligence held by your predecessors."[37]

At PFIAB's February meeting, Hewitt briefed the members on the study's conclusions and presented a copy of the study to those attending.[38] But for

35. Lionel Olmer, "Watchdogging Intelligence," in "Seminar on Command, Control, Communications, and Intelligence" (Center for Information Policy Research, Harvard University, 1980), 180.

36. Henry S. Bradsher, "Quality Intelligence Analysis: The Key Factor That Ford Ignored," *Washington Star*, February 19, 1976.

37. George A. Carver, memorandum to director of Central Intelligence, April 24, 1976, obtained through FOIA.

38. Henson DeBruler, memorandum for the record, April 28, 1976, obtained through FOIA.

PFIAB the track record study was not enough. At their April meeting, the NIE Evaluation Committee recommended that PFIAB's proposal of August 1975 to create an experimental competitive analysis group be pursued.[39] Not surprisingly, this was not favored within the CIA. In an internal memo Carver wrote:

> In my opinion, it is essential that we not be unduly defensive in reacting to this document or in any way convey the impression that we are loath to consider innovative procedures which might improve the quality of our strategic assessments. On the other hand, some of the concrete proposals advanced by the Board would be extremely difficult to accommodate without prostituting the whole intelligence process. This applies particularly to the proposal (about which the Board feels very strongly) for a "competitive analysis group" which would be tasked with preparing—on certain selected issues—what would in effect be an alternative estimate to 11-3/8-76.
>
> What the Board wants is a national estimate which will set forth all the things—especially the unpleasant things—which the Soviets could or might do, without any estimative judgments about the relative probability of the Soviets achieving these various goals or pursuing these alternative lines of behavior. The real reason (I think) why some members of the Board are pushing for "the competitive estimate" by a group composed of at least some persons outside the Intelligence Community is that they want to be sure that the total package includes all the worst case possibilities that can be thought of. Under the approach the Board is recommending, the President and his senior policy advisors will simply have this range of possibilities laid before them, hence, powerful arguments could be advanced that the only responsible course to follow to protect the nation's interests would be to hedge against the worst case threats, and NIEs developed through the recommended procedure would serve as ammunition supporting such a pitch. If our nation's resources were infinite, this might be an intellectually defensible thesis. They are not, however and, hence, it isn't. This procedure would leave the decision maker at the mercy of technical shamans with no basis for ascertaining which of these shamans' analyses or predictions were more credible than their competitors'.[40]

39. Henson DeBruler, briefing note for the DCI, June 2, 1976, obtained through FOIA.
40. George A. Carver, memorandum for Mr. Knoche, Admiral Murphy, and Mr. Proctor, May 5, 1976, obtained through FOIA.

Notwithstanding this reasoning, events moved the experiment inexorably forward. One factor contributing to the acceptance of an alternative threat assessment group concerned Soviet military expenditures and how they were measured and presented to Congress.

Soviet Military Expenditures

Estimates of Soviet military expenditures were probably the most important factors determining U.S. military policies toward the Soviet Union. For example, in President Reagan's first State of the Union Address on February 18, 1981, he justified his proposed military buildup by asserting: "Since 1970, the Soviet Union has invested $300 billion more in its military forces than we have."[41]

But how did one measure Soviet military expenditures? The Soviet Union presided over a closed and highly secretive society. By the late 1950s it was recognized that the defense budgets proclaimed by the Soviets were not credible. For long periods of time the announced budgets "remained frozen at levels that could not be reconciled with the evidence of a Soviet military buildup. Moreover, the official defense budget was a single number, providing no information on the composition of Soviet defense outlays. Better figures were needed for purposes of analyzing the Soviet economy and planning for U.S. defense requirements."[42] An enormous effort was expended within the U.S. government to figure out how to estimate and forecast Soviet GNP (gross national product) and military expenditures. Nick Eberstadt, organizer of a conference on the Soviet economy in 1990, said, "I believe it may be safe to say that the U.S. government's effort to describe the Soviet economy may be the largest single project in social science research ever undertaken."[43]

Instead of trying to manipulate the Soviet statistics in order to coax some sense out of them, the intelligence community used what was called "the building-block" method because "it relied on costing out a long menu of

41. Franklyn D. Holzman, "Politics and Guesswork," *International Security* 14, no. 2 (1989): 101.
42. James H. Noren, "The Controversy over Western Measures of Soviet Defense Expenditures," *Post-Soviet Affairs* 11 (July–September 1995): 238–76.
43. Quoted in David M. Kennedy, "Sunshine and Shadow: The CIA and the Soviet Economy" (case study of the Intelligence and Policy Program at the Kennedy School of Government, Harvard University, 1991), 1.

goods and services purchased by the Soviet defense establishment."[44] The strategy worked as follows: The Defense Intelligence Agency estimated the output of a particular defense plant or counted the production of missiles, submarines, tanks, manpower, or whatever, using all available sources, from satellite photographs to spies. The CIA then worked with American military contractors to cost this output in U.S. dollars, yielding an amount that it would cost the United States to duplicate every aspect of the Soviet military establishment while paying all personnel U.S. wage rates and making all purchases at U.S. prices.

This methodology had many flaws. The figure was distorted by the fact that the Soviet defense industries enjoyed subsidized buildings, electricity, and infrastructure. The real costs were almost impossible to ascertain.[45] One bizarre consequence of this dollar costing was that every time there was a cost-of-living increase in the United States, we had to increase our estimate of Soviet military expenditures.

To assess the impact of these military expenditures on the entire Soviet economy, the CIA applied ruble/dollar ratios and calculated the output in rubles.[46] For these ruble outlay figures, ruble prices were applied "to the estimated production of military equipment, ruble pay rates to estimates of military personnel and civilian employees of the Ministry of Defense, and ruble cost factors to estimates of operating and maintenance activity and defense-related construction."[47]

Within the CIA there was general dissatisfaction with the conceptual underpinnings of this methodology. According to a longtime and highly respected intelligence community economist, "In the Soviet Union, many more projects were commenced than finished. There were multiple research and development projects. Some were accelerated, some stood still for a long time, so altogether there was a confusing picture."[48]

A State Department economist described research on Soviet defense expenditures as "an exercise in meta-Intelligence. Analysts engage in the exegesis of obscure texts, guess at unexplained residues, hunt after analogues,

44. Ibid., 242.

45. Ibid.

46. Martin Walker, *The Cold War: A History* (New York: Henry Holt, 1993), 215; John Ranelagh, *The Agency: The Rise and Decline of the CIA* (New York: Simon & Schuster, 1986), 620; John Prados, *The Soviet Estimate: U.S. Intelligence Analysis and Soviet Strategic Forces* (Princeton: Princeton University Press, 1986), 246.

47. Noren, "The Controversy," 242.

48. Interview with Hans Heymann, October 11, 1990.

and indulge in assumptions."[49] "But," said one of the CIA analysts, "it was better than anything else."[50]

Those who thought that the CIA's figures were consistently low, such as William Lee, Eugene Rostow, and Steven Rosefielde, felt that "political pressures on the CIA to keep their estimates low are very strong."[51] On the other side, some thought that the agency analysts were convinced "that it was better to err on the side of overestimation."[52]

When James Schlesinger became secretary of defense, he started questioning "how . . . a country that is visibly deploying such weapons [can] do it with spending only 6–8 percent of its GNP on defense." Schlesinger had an "intuitive resistance to this notion and began to search for a way to abandon the old method of estimating."[53] Most of the critics of the building-block methodology thought it underestimated Soviet military expenditures. Since 1970 the Defense Intelligence Agency (DIA) had taken a share (roughly a third) of the state budget to be military and had come up with consistently higher figures than the CIA's.[54] The DIA's numbers became something of a cause célèbre among defense conservatives. When Lt. Gen. Daniel Graham became head of the DIA in 1974, he, too, challenged the building-block methodology.

Early in 1975, CIA and DIA analysts went "into the field" and obtained Soviet assessments of their own defense costs. Schlesinger certified the authority of this covertly obtained information.[55] At first the CIA questioned the reliability of these assessments. According to DCI Colby, "We scrubbed it as to whether it was real or not. Then it was accepted, although some in the analytical bureaucracy were slow to accept it."[56] The intelligence community also got Soviet budgetary data from a defector who had worked in a Soviet ministry and was assigned to perform an assessment of the Soviet defense budget. He had been sent into the "military-industrial complex" and

49. "The CIA's Goof in Assessing the Soviets," *Business Week*, February 28, 1977, 96–105.
50. Telephone interview with Hans Heymann, September 8, 1995.
51. Steven Rosefielde, "The Validity of the CIA's Ruble and Dollar Estimates of Soviet Defense Spending," testimony prepared for the Subcommittee on Oversight of the House Permanent Select Committee on Intelligence, 96th Cong., 2d sess., September 3, 1980, 50; idem, *False Science: Underestimating the Soviet Arms Buildup* (New Brunswick, N.J.: Transaction Books, 1982), 39; both cited in Noren, "The Controversy," 254.
52. Franklyn Holzman, "Are the Soviets Really Outspending the U.S. on Defense?" *International Security* 4, no. 4 (1980): 86–104, cited in Noren, "The Controversy," 255.
53. Interview with Hans Heymann, October 11, 1990.
54. Kennedy, "Sunshine and Shadow," 16.
55. "The CIA's Goof," 96–98.
56. Interview with William Colby, August 9, 1989.

granted a look at what was claimed to be the defense budget for two years.[57] The CIA also obtained a copy of the Soviet Politburo's Statistical Handbook, which gave the "real" figures of Soviet military spending.[58] The defector "was a so-so source; the more we delved, the less sure we were."[59]

By mid-1975, it was generally recognized that the CIA's January estimate that the Soviets were spending 20 percent more than the United States was an underestimate.[60] DCI Colby appointed a joint CIA-DIA study group, for the first time giving a non-CIA team of analysts weight equal to the agency's own. It was a major bureaucratic victory for the DIA, cemented when the CIA analysts accepted that their estimates of Soviet spending had been about half of what the Soviets had actually spent.[61]

Based on its conclusion "that the ruble prices it had been using to value military procurement and weapons maintenance were far too low,"[62] the CIA's February 1976 report SR 76-10053 stated that the Soviets were spending 40 percent more on defense than the United States and that this consumed 10–15 percent of their GNP rather than the 6–8 percent projected in previous NIEs.[63] In its official releases the CIA acknowledged that the new figures in no way indicated a revision of the previous estimated size of the Soviet military effort, but only of its cost.[64] In fact, the new data were interpreted to mean that the Soviet military sector of the economy was only half as efficient as had been thought.[65]

But this fact was lost in the public debate, which was vociferous. A pseudonymous author, a Soviet-area specialist working for the government, wrote that "the revised estimates were equated with a Soviet 'military buildup,' a description frequently preceded by the adjectives 'rapid,' 'massive,' 'unprecedented,' or 'relentless.' "[66] This was exemplified by Defense Secretary James Schlesinger, who wrote, just before he was fired by President Ford, in a letter to Senator John McClellan (D-Ark.), chairman of the Defense Subcommit-

57. Telephone interview with Hans Heymann, September 7, 1995.

58. Ranelagh, The Agency, 622.

59. Interview with Hans Heymann, October 11, 1990.

60. Prados, The Soviet Estimate, 247.

61. Ranelagh, The Agency, 622; Prados, The Soviet Estimate, 247; Cecil Brownlow, "CIA Threat-Juggling Confirmed," Aviation Week and Space Technology, May 3, 1976.

62. Noren, "The Controversy," 255–56.

63. Prados, The Soviet Estimate, 247.

64. Edward Aerie [pseud.], "Dollarizing the Russian Forces," The Nation, July 23, 1977, 78–81.

65. Prados, The Soviet Estimate, 248; Joint Economic Committee, Hearings: Allocation of Resources in the Soviet Union and China, 1975, 94th Cong., 2d sess., January 1976, 163.

66. Aerie, "Dollarizing the Russian Forces," 78.

tee of the Senate Appropriations Committee, "By most of the available measures, American power is declining and Soviet power is rising. No one can say precisely where the peril points lie as this process unfolds. But if real expenditures by the United States remain constant or continue to fall, while real Soviet outlays continue to rise, the peril points will occur in the relatively near future."[67] Shades of NSC 68 and the Gaither Report!

As the media picked up the news of the recalculation, the main thrust of the stories conveyed a sense of danger. In the first of three articles, Henry S. Bradsher, who later became a senior analyst at the CIA, wrote: "The new evaluation shows that the Kremlin's determination to drive toward greater military strength, its readiness to sacrifice for armed might, are much stronger than had been apparent." It was only in the twelfth paragraph that Bradsher admitted, "The new assessment of the economic effort which has made the military buildup possible does not change Pentagon estimates of Soviet armaments. The Soviet military machine is not suddenly being seen as twice as big as was previously believed."[68]

In the following day's story, the reader had to read through to the eighteenth paragraph to learn that "[t]he CIA reassessment indicates a much wider gap in dollars and therefore in economic effort, although it does not change the Pentagon estimates of actual troops, tanks, and missiles which the Soviet Union has."[69]

It took fifteen years for the true impact of these recalculations to be openly discussed by the economic community. In 1990 the House Permanent Select Committee on Intelligence asked the CIA to establish a panel of outside reviewers to evaluate CIA estimates of Soviet economic performance. Their findings were published in the summer of 1993. The authors, five academic economists, opined:

> We have found that the CIA's reporting of its findings on Soviet GNP and on general Soviet economic development has been satisfactory. With regard to CIA's findings on defense expenditures, however, we believe that the CIA presented their results in ways

67. James Schlesinger, letter to Senator John L. McClellan, chairman, Senate Appropriations Defense Subcommittee, October 23, 1975, 5, quoted in Les Aspin, "How to Look at the Soviet-American Balance," *Foreign Policy* 22 (spring 1976): 100.

68. Henry S. Bradsher, "CIA Uncovers Soviet Arms Shift," *Washington Star*, February 15, 1976.

69. Henry S. Bradsher, "Soviet Arms Spending Accelerating Yearly," *Washington Star*, February 16, 1976.

that contributed to misinterpretation and misrepresentation. For the most part, the effect of the form of presentation was to magnify the Soviet military threat to a level not warranted by the CIA's own findings.

. . . We believe it [the CIA] could have reduced the impact of its defense expenditure findings by directing less attention to them and by more diligently hammering away at the irrelevance of the spending figure for the assessment of the current military threat.[70]

Perhaps the most telling critique leveled by the report was of the CIA's basis for comparison:

> If the objective is to provide the best evidence regarding the military threat, however, the most appropriate subjects of comparison should have been NATO and the Warsaw Pact. The main reason is that, in our strategy for meeting the Soviet military threat, it was not U.S. military forces alone on which we counted but also the substantial forces of our NATO allies. A second reason is that in seeking to understand Soviet strategy, the U.S.S.R. should have been seen as facing not only U.S. military forces but those of Germany, Britain, and the other allies, including France in most circumstances. . . . We believe that by focusing on the U.S.S.R.-U.S. comparisons rather than on NATO, the great weight and authority of the CIA has served to bias the public debate on U.S. defense policy. Had greater attention been directed toward NATO–Warsaw Pact comparisons, the magnitude of the Soviet military threat would not have appeared as large as it appeared from the U.S.S.R.-U.S. comparisons alone.[71]

But large, indeed, is how the Soviet threat was seen by many in 1976, and the message seemed to be that the Russians were doing more on defense— and that so should the United States. Thus the stage was set when George Bush became the eleventh director of Central Intelligence early in 1976.

70. James R. Millar et al., "Survey Article: An Evaluation of the CIA's Analysis of Soviet Economic Performance, 1970–90," *Comparative Economic Studies* 35, no. 2 (1993): 47, 48.
71. Ibid., 49.

Bush as Director of Central Intelligence

Soon after George Bush was sworn in as the director of Central Intelligence, PFIAB renewed its request for a "Team B" approach. Within the agency Bush got mixed advice. Howard Stoertz, the NIO in charge of the NIE on Soviet strategic forces, advised against the experiment, as did many other analysts. According to one of them, "Most of us were opposed to it because we saw it as an ideological, political foray, not an intellectual exercise. We knew the people who were pleading for it."[72]

Others within the CIA were more sympathetic to such a study. Deputy Director E. Henry Knoche, a former college athlete who stands about six foot four, said in interview, "It wasn't a bad idea, because Henry Kissinger had begun tasking the intelligence community with highly technical questions. Kissinger was always interested in alternative views." Knoche "was confident that the agency's expertise would be vindicated. It was also a way of getting PFIAB off [the] backs [of the CIA]."[73] Eight months after this interview, Knoche expanded his answer in writing:

> Given the sensitivity of the subject and the high classification of the data involved, I didn't give enough weight to the possibility of leakage and it just did not occur to me that there would be those with a vested interest in public impugning of our national estimates. Certain hard-line elements, though, apparently saw a chance to do just that, and at the same time (1) build sentiment for increased U.S. defense spending and (2) further weaken an institution (the CIA) fresh out of the lurid investigation of '75 and '76—an institution perceived by some hard-liners as standing in the way of a true recognition of the evil empire.[74]

George Carver, Bush's deputy for national intelligence, had earlier told DCI Colby, when PFIAB first became concerned that a systemic underrating of the Soviets might have developed, "It was worth looking into."[75] Deputy Director for Intelligence Sayre Stevens recalled he had said, "Hell, let them do it. We have to be able to deal with contentions that we are wrong."[76]

72. Interview with Hans Heymann, October 11, 1990.
73. Interview with E. Henry Knoche, January 25, 1990.
74. E. Henry Knoche, letter to the author, September 27, 1990.
75. Interview with George A. Carver, January 17, 1990.
76. Interview with Sayre Stevens, February 21, 1990.

Bush discussed the request with William Hyland, the new deputy national security adviser, at a lunch also attended by Galvin and Foster. Hyland recommended that Bush proceed with the exercise, because he felt the CIA "had been getting too much flak for being too peacenik and detentish." Hyland felt that if two members of PFIAB wanted such a study, Bush, as the new CIA director, should pay attention to the request.[77] According to Hyland, "I encouraged him [Bush] to undertake the experiment, largely because I thought a new director ought to be receptive to new views."[78]

On May 12, Carver flew to Chicago to talk with Galvin about the proposed study.[79] Two weeks later Carver had drafted a letter for Galvin to send to Bush laying out the ground rules for the alternative assessment. Bush okayed it the same day, penning in, "[L]et her fly. OK, GB."[80] From the beginning it was understood that "[t]hose who are to be involved in preparing the competitive analysis conduct their work independently of the intelligence personnel and organizations involved in putting together the NIE itself." It was hoped that the results of the experiment would be "available at the same time that the new NIE on Soviet strategic forces is issued in the fall."[81]

A subsequent letter from Leo Cherne to Bush further elucidated the proposed process: Those working on the regular NIE 11-3/8-76 would be referred to as the A Team; the three issues to be included in the experiment would be selected by the DCI in consultation with the assistant to the president for national security affairs; on each of the three issues chosen for the experiment, the DCI, in consultation with the NIE Evaluation Committee, would select a B Team; each B Team would be given access to all of the information on its area of concern available to the U.S. government; the A and B Teams were to exchange drafts and comment on each other's drafts; and after the whole process was completed, the president's national security adviser was to "select a panel of senior consumers, civilian and military, to review the experiment and critique its results."[82]

By June 10, John Paisley, a retired deputy director of the CIA's Office of

77. Interview with William G. Hyland, September 26, 1989.

78. William G. Hyland, *Mortal Rivals: Superpower Relations from Nixon to Reagan* (New York: Random House, 1987), 85.

79. George A. Carver, memorandum for the record, June 30, 1976, obtained through FOIA.

80. George A. Carver, note for the director [of Central Intelligence], May 26, 1976, obtained through FOIA.

81. Henson DeBruler, briefing note for the DCI, June 2, 1976, obtained through FOIA.

82. Leo Cherne, letter to George Bush, June 8, 1976, obtained through FOIA.

Strategic Research, had agreed to manage the B Team process and to act as liaison between the A and B Teams. Paisley estimated the cost of Team B would be about $500,000.[83]

Now what was needed was to select the members of the three B Teams. This turned out not to be as easy as expected.

83. John Paisley, memorandum to Henson DeBruler, June 10, 1976, obtained through FOIA.

8

The Teams at Work

The Air Defense Panel

John Foster, the chief instigator of the PFIAB-mandated competitive threat assessment, was most interested in suggesting members of the three B Teams. He believed "it highly desirable to first select a team leader for each of the issues and then discuss with this individual the selection of additional team members." To chair the Soviet Air Defense Panel, Foster recommended Dan Fink, who was then a vice-president and general manager at General Electric and had been a deputy to Foster at the Department of Defense. If Fink was not available, Foster suggested James Drake of RDA (Research and Development Associates) as the team leader. As members he recommended Hank Hoffman of the Defense Intelligence Agency, Chris Nolan, Craig Hartzell, and Bruce Holloway, formerly commander of the Strategic Air Command.[1]

Although not on Foster's list, Charles Lerch of the Systems Planning Corporation (SPC) became the team leader, with Drake as his deputy.[2]

1. Lionel Olmer, memorandum for the record, June 30, 1976, obtained through FOIA.
2. "Soviet Low Altitude Air Defense: An Alternative View," Report of Team "B," Intelligence Community Experiment in Competitive Analysis, December 1976, obtained through FOIA.

Lerch had designed and supervised the building of the first big U.S. phased-array radar and had worked with Paul Nitze on the ABM Treaty.[3] Other members of this panel were mostly from SPC, the contractor engaged by the CIA to run this team. The reviewer was Daniel Fink.[4]

For both the Air Defense and Missile Accuracy Panels, as well as the Strategic Objectives Panel, the A-Team members were the intelligence analysts drafting the 1976 National Intelligence Estimate and included representatives from the CIA, Defense Intelligence Agency, National Security Agency, State Department, and Army, Navy, and Air Force Intelligence.

Soviet air defenses were a critical issue if U.S. B-52 bombers were to penetrate Soviet airspace in the event of war. The main controversy between the A Team and the B Team centered on the difference between the equipment of the Soviets, that is, their command and control capabilities and their detection and tracking capabilities, and, on the other hand, their tactics and operational practices.

According to Sayre Stevens, at the time the CIA deputy director of intelligence, the air defense controversy hinged on the question of netting Soviet air defense capabilities. Netting is a way of linking different parts of an organization or different weapons systems so that they operate more flexibly and efficiently. A current example is the Internet, which links different libraries and files around the world. In interview, Sayre remarked, "Team B said these things were netted together; the agency said they were not. The outcome was they were not netted but should be." Sayre continued, "The critics fell back on assertions of deceptions. It is hard to prove you haven't been deceived by the perfect deception scheme."[5]

The A Team made three separate judgments about Soviet low-altitude air defenses: present Soviet capabilities to stop or make inefficient a U.S. low-altitude attack consisting of B-52s and FB-111s armed with free-fall bombs and SRAMs (short-range attack missiles); future Soviet defense capabilities against the same current U.S. air-attack threat; and future Soviet defense capabilities against a future U.S. air attack force that might consist of some combination of B-52, B-1, and FB-111 bombers all armed with free-fall nuclear bombs and the SRAM and advanced cruise missiles, which could be launched from air, sea, or land launchers. Their judgment was that current Soviet air defenses were "unable to counter a large-scale low altitude bomber

3. Paul H. Nitze, *Tension Between Opposites: Reflections on the Practice and Theory of Politics* (New York: Charles Scribner's Sons, 1993), 12.
4. "Soviet Low Altitude Air Defense: An Alternative View," iv.
5. Interview with Sayre Stevens, February 21, 1990.

attack on the U.S.S.R." Furthermore, future Soviet air defenses were "not likely to be able to defend against the projected U.S. air threat . . . owing primarily to the probable Soviet inability to handle SRAM and cruise missiles."[6]

The B Team looked primarily at current Soviet defenses against current U.S. forces and concluded, "The performance of the Soviet system is formidable if it is operated to its full potential. It is marginal if operated only as observed in fragmentary data."[7] The B Team members examined Soviet air defense training manuals and said the Soviets ought to be able to do thus and so, to which Team A members responded, "But we can't confirm with firm intelligence data that they are actually doing that."[8] That is, Soviet training manuals, which were clandestinely obtained, were believed by Team B to describe operations U.S. intelligence couldn't observe.[9] In actuality, it is much more likely that Russian training manuals, just like American ones, described ideal systems that were rarely or never obtained in the course of day-to-day activities of the sort observable by intelligence agencies.

Given the November 1995 revelations of Soviet double agents planting false information to be fed to U.S. intelligence, there is the possibility, albeit small, that these manuals, too, were planted. A retired air force general who was a member of one of the other B Teams explained it this way: "Soviet air defense practices were then, had been, and remained mysterious. They do things we don't understand and fail to do things that seem utterly sensible to us. Lerch's team didn't shed much light on it."[10]

By and large, the meetings between the two teams were cordial. According to Dr. Peter Scop, one of the Team A participants, "Our meetings on air defense were very friendly. There were relatively few real differences. In some cases where the differences were important (in effect on air defense performance) it was usually because of the intelligence community's inability to confirm that Soviet air defenses were actually doing what Team B believed was entirely possible." Scop continued, "There were very few differences between what Team A and Team B thought were *possible* ways Soviet air defenses could operate. But since some of Team B's ideas could not be con-

6. "Soviet Low Altitude Air Defense: A Team Briefing to PFIAB," n.d., obtained through FOIA.

7. "Summary of B Team Findings—Low Altitude Air Defense," undated briefing paper, obtained through FOIA.

8. Peter Scop, Defense Intelligence Agency, written answers to submitted questions, June 26, 1990.

9. Interview with James Drake, May 10, 1990.

10. Interview with Gen. Jasper Welch, March 13, 1990.

firmed by firm intelligence data, these were not included in NIE 11-3/8"
(emphasis in original).[11]

"After all," said one of the B Team members, "everyone knew everyone,
it wasn't as though we were strangers." Yet, at the end, this same participant
felt there was dissatisfaction on everybody's part because the differences were
not resolved.[12]

Howard Stoertz, the national intelligence officer in charge of NIE 11-3/
8-75, said, "The main message I got was that there were lots of things the
Russians could change about their air defense system with organizational
changes to make improvements, so we ought to be careful and cautious about
ten-year forecasts. So forecasts that were not based on hard evidence were
deleted or softened."[13]

In a strange twist, a few years later, the Carter administration, which
ignored almost all of the Team B reports, used the B Team's contention that
the Soviets were developing very effective air defense radar in their arguments against developing the B-1. If the Soviet air defense system was so
good, the B-1 would soon be vulnerable and not worth the investment, they
argued.[14]

The Missile Accuracy Panel

For the team examining Soviet ICBM accuracy, Foster recommended Roland
Herbst of RDA as team leader and John Brett, retired air force general Bob
Duffy, John Kirk, Paul Levine, and Jim Merrick as members. Herbst, balding
and gray-haired, became the team leader, joined by Brett and Kirk as well as
Chuck Stowe, David Vaughn, and D. Welch, all of RDA, the company cho-
sen as the contractor.[15]

The accuracy of Soviet missiles was the subject of heated debate within
the U.S. defense community before the formation of Team B. For years, Dr.
Richard Latter had been pushing an alternative method for deriving the

11. Peter Scop, Defense Intelligence Agency, written answers to submitted questions, June
26, 1990.

12. Interview with James Drake, May 10, 1990.

13. Interview with Howard Stoertz, August 14, 1989.

14. Jim Klurfeld, "A New View on Nuclear War," Newsday, June 15, 1981, 6; telephone
interview with Lynn Davis, October 9, 1990.

15. "Soviet ICBM Accuracy: An Alternative View," Intelligence Community Experiment
in Competitive Analysis, Report of Team "B," December 1976, obtained through FOIA.

accuracy of Soviet missiles. His methodology was consistently judged invalid by the intelligence community. The 1975 NIE conclusion that Minuteman missiles would be safe until the mid-1980s was based on an estimate that the most accurate Soviet missiles—the SS-18s and -19s—had a CEP of about a quarter of a nautical mile.[16]

Quite small changes in estimates of CEP accuracy can produce quite dramatic changes in estimates of "kill" probabilities against silos. The lower the CEP, the higher the accuracy. Team B came up with much greater Soviet accuracies than did Team A. This implied a possible current threat to Minuteman, but Team B "used a methodology that had been considered and rejected in preparation not only of this year's 11-3/8 but of previous ones."[17] According to Herbst, "We didn't claim that we knew the CEP of the SS-18 and -19 at the present time. We said by the time the system is mature, the CEP will be X."[18]

Another disagreement between the two teams concerned an effect known as "fratricide"—the tendency of exploding warheads to destroy those following close behind. The air force, in defending the reputation of its own weapons systems, had long argued that this problem would hinder a disarming strike aimed at American missiles.[19] Now the questions were, Would the Soviets be able to have missiles arriving at different places without interfering with each other? Would they have satellites to observe what was going on? How would they plan quasi-simultaneous missions?

According to a Team B consultant at the Draper Laboratory, the major areas of disagreement concerned field performance: "How well did we think their instruments performed? Part is technology; part is usage and practice. If the Soviets decided to go mobile, would they have test flights from a proposed mobile missile site? The question was, What was accurate and under what firing velocity? How many could be set up to fire simultaneously?"[20] In all these matters, Team B credited the Soviets with much more technological sophistication than did Team A.

The A Team had two major objections to the B Team's approach.

16. Thomas Powers, "Choosing a Strategy for World War III," *Atlantic Monthly*, November 1982, 102. On CEP, see Chapter 5.
17. Richard Lehman, memorandum for the record, November 4, 1976, obtained through FOIA.
18. Interview with Roland Herbst, May 10, 1990.
19. Powers, "Choosing a Strategy," 102.
20. Telephone interview with Ken Fertig, a consultant to the Team B Missile Accuracy Panel, September 11, 1990.

First, applying any U.S. technological trend to the U.S.S.R. is immediately suspect for a variety of reasons and should only be used as a last resort where no data [exist]. For the B Team analogy to be valid, the Soviets would have to be on par with U.S. 1970 era technology not only in basic theory and laboratory instrument quality, but in mass production of precision instruments as well. In every area where data on inertial instruments [are] available, the Soviets lag the U.S. considerably, especially in mass production of precision equipment.

. . . [I]n the opinion of the A Team, the B Team approach of minimizing errors and mirror-imaging U.S. guidance instrument improvement trends leads to an artificially low estimate of Soviet ICBM accuracy.[21] (N.B. The writer of this memo obviously meant an artificially high estimate.)

Ironically, the Team B Strategic Objectives Panel scathingly accused the CIA of "mirror-imaging" U.S. doctrine and strategy. And this is precisely what the Team B Missile Accuracy Panel seemed to be doing. (I return to mirror-imaging in the next chapter.)

According to one of the Team B participants on the Missile Accuracy Panel, meetings with Team A were set up "to air our differences, to make sure both teams started from the same information. After all," he said, "it was not like a court of law, where you try to withhold information." But after a while "it got kind of acerbic and confrontational. It began passively, but eventually people got irritated with each other."[22]

The B Team chairman, Roland Herbst, didn't "believe the data available to either side were firm enough to make a solid judgment." He had hoped "to illustrate that decision makers ought to realize they had lots of uncertainty on their hands." According to Herbst, "nontrivial decisions get made without the decision maker being aware of the uncertainties."[23]

Now, in hindsight, we know that the Team B's analysis was even more inaccurate than Team A's. In 1985, the intelligence community lowered its estimate of the accuracy of the SS-19 by over 33 percent, so that it no longer was deemed a "hard-target" or "silo killer."[24] In other words, with a CEP of

21. "Summary of Intelligence Community ('A Team') Briefing to PFIAB on Soviet ICBM Accuracy," n.d., obtained through FOIA.

22. Telephone interview with Chuck Stowe, October 24, 1990.

23. Interview with Roland Herbst, May 10, 1990.

24. Michael R. Gordon, "CIA Downgrades Estimate of Soviet SS-19," *National Journal,*

four hundred meters, the SS-19 would not provide the Soviets with high confidence of destroying a U.S. missile silo even if two warheads from two different missiles were aimed at the same missile silo. A Pentagon official was quoted, "You could use three or four and still get low to moderate confidence."[25] Yet depicting the SS-19 as a silo killer encouraged the opening of the "window of vulnerability," the notion that U.S. land-based missiles were vulnerable to Soviet attack.

Strategic Objectives Panel

The only Team B panel that most people know about and the only one to receive widespread publicity was the Strategic Objectives Panel. It is also the panel that was substituted for one on Soviet antisubmarine warfare capabilities over the objections of several people. In June, National Security Council staffer Roger Molander met with Lionel Olmer, executive secretary of PFIAB, Henson DeBruler, and John Paisley, who had retired as deputy director of the CIA's Office of Strategic Research two years before and was the liaison between the CIA and the three B Teams, to firm up the topics for the experiment. "Molander had reservations about the usefulness of the topic of Soviet strategic objectives, but did not raise formal objection."[26] Richard Latter, a close adviser to the Missile Accuracy Panel, was opposed to a Strategic Objectives Panel because it would not be considering a technical subject and would be argumentative.[27]

Again, John Foster had his recommendations. For team leader he stated that Professor Richard Pipes of Harvard "had been highly recommended," but he was "not personally acquainted with Pipes. Sy [Seymour] Weiss would also be acceptable as team leader, as would Bill Van Cleave (preferred) or Gardner Tucker, Director of Research and Development for International Paper. Charles Herzfeld and Albert Wohlstetter should also be considered as members."[28] Again, Foster's recommendations were closely followed.

By the summer of 1976, Seymour Weiss had been ambassador to the Baha-

July 20, 1985, 1692–93; Jeffrey T. Richelson, "Old Surveillance, New Interpretation," *Bulletin of Atomic Scientists* 42, no. 2 (1986): 18–23.

25. Gordon, "CIA Downgrades Estimate," 1692–93.
26. CIA chronology of Team B events, n.d., obtained through FOIA.
27. Telephone interview with Richard Latter, February 28, 1990.
28. Lionel Olmer, memorandum for the record, June 30, 1976, obtained through FOIA.

mas for approximately two years. According to Weiss, he had been "exiled" there after Secretary of State Kissinger had "become fed up with" him and his views on detente.[29] Another reason for Kissinger's animosity, according to a National Security Council staffer at the time, was that Weiss called Kissinger by his first name "and Henry hated that!"[30] Weiss says he was offered several ambassadorial positions and chose the Bahamas "because of that country's proximity to Washington. There was a daily flight from the Bahamas to Washington which took a little over two hours. I believed, correctly as subsequent events proved, that I could continue to keep in touch with politico-military developments in Washington while serving as Ambassador to the Bahamas. It was after all, the politico-military matters that were of greatest interest to me and that I wished to influence."[31] According to Weiss, "PFIAB originally wanted me to chair Team B, but top State Department officials vetoed my nomination because it would be inappropriate to have a sitting ambassador take time from his normal duties for such a position."[32]

The man finally selected to serve as chairman of the Team B Strategic Objectives Panel was Richard Pipes, a Polish immigrant and professor of Russian history at Harvard University. Pipes had consistently labeled the Soviets an aggressive imperialistic power bent on world domination. He had been "discovered" by Richard Perle, who convinced his boss, Senator Henry Jackson, to hire Pipes as a consultant.[33] Pipes began to divide his time between Harvard University and the Washington office of the Stanford Research Institute (SRI). He was quite cognizant of the fact that he was not the first choice to head this Team B. According to Pipes, "Foy Kohler was the first choice to be chairman; Sy Weiss was second. And Weiss then proposed me."[34] Actually, William Van Cleave, a professor at the University of Southern California, and Gardiner Tucker had also been approached about becoming chairman, and "all indicated a willingness to participate in the study but could not commit the time to act as team leader."[35] Kohler, who

29. Seymour Weiss, "Competitive Intelligence Analysis: Team B," n.d.

30. Telephone interview with Jan Lodal, October 23, 1989.

31. Weiss, "Competitive Intelligence Analysis," 1.

32. Interview with Seymour Weiss, February 21, 1990.

33. Sidney Blumenthal, "Richard Perle's Nuclear Legacy: An Acolyte's Education and the Passing of the Torch," *Washington Post*, November 24, 1987, D-1.

34. Interview with Richard Pipes, August 15, 1990.

35. John Paisley, NIO coordinator, Competitive Analysis, memorandum to Daniel Sullivan, CIA, August 20, 1976, obtained through FOIA.

lived in Florida, apparently would not have been a good choice, since he did not attend a single meeting of the panel.[36]

Pipes is quite adamant that he named all the members of his panel: "It is possible that Paisley shopped around for potential members of Team B but I am confident that no formal invitation was extended to [anyone] since the final list was made up by me."[37] Pipes particularly denied that John Foster named anyone to his B Team.[38] Yet most of the names Pipes selected came from lists prepared by Foster and Paisley and included people Pipes did not know.[39]

Before Pipes was named, John Paisley, the former CIA official brought out of retirement to manage the whole Team A/Team B exercise, began calling people to invite them to join. Charles Herzfeld, who was on John Foster's list, said in interview that "someone from the agency called him long before the Team B panel was formed. There was talk that Sy Weiss would be chairman." Herzfeld said he would have to check with his bosses at the ITT Defense Space Group. "They said okay." A month later Herzfeld was called back by Paisley, and Herzfeld said he "would be glad to serve and never heard from [Paisley] again!"[40]

In a memo to his superior, Paisley reported, "I have not felt it appropriate for me to formally structure [Pipes's] team for him until he was fully cleared and briefed on the nature of the study and could participate in the decision, although I have spoken briefly to him about possible team members and have informally contacted a number of them to enquire about their willingness to participate in this exercise."[41]

Arnold Horelick of the RAND Corporation was also one of those contacted by Paisley before a chairman was selected. During the initial telephone conversation, Paisley mentioned Pipes and Weiss. Horelick didn't accept, because "it didn't sound to me like a new A–Z look by an impartial panel. It would not be blue ribbon. I might have participated if it were."[42] Others contacted by Paisley who indicated a willingness to serve were Alexander Flax, Foy Kohler, Paul Nitze, Eugene Rostow, Gardiner Tucker, Wil-

36. Interview with Richard Pipes, August 15, 1990.
37. Richard Pipes, letter to the author, October 17, 1990.
38. Interview with Richard Pipes, August 15, 1990.
39. Interview with Gen. John Vogt, October 11, 1990.
40. Interview with Charles Herzfeld, June 26, 1990.
41. John Paisley, memorandum for deputy director of Central Intelligence, August 11, 1976, obtained through FOIA.
42. Telephone interview with Arnold Horelick, June 12, 1990.

liam Van Cleave, Gen. John Vogt, Albert Wohlstetter, and Thomas Wolfe.[43] Most became members of Team B. By the end of August, the Security Office at the CIA was notified that fifteen "prominent Americans" had been "identified as candidates for membership in Team B." The five from this list who did not become team members were Herzfeld, Patrick J. Parker, Wohlstetter, Robert Fossum, and Alexander Flax.[44]

In interview Daniel Graham, in his spacious High Frontier office, claimed, "I was the first guy Pipes picked. He called me himself. I advised him not to put General Keegan [Gen. George Keegan, air force chief of intelligence] on the team. I suggested Johnny Vogt and Bill Van Cleave."[45] John Vogt, a Harvard-educated, retired four-star air force general who commanded the Seventh Air Force in Vietnam, and University of Southern California professor William Van Cleave, a short forty-year-old with strong square features who had been on the SALT delegation, were duly selected, as were Foy Kohler, a former assistant secretary and deputy undersecretary of state and ambassador to the Soviet Union, who was then teaching at the University of Miami's Graduate Center for Advanced Foreign Studies, and Seymour Weiss from Foster's list.

Pipes said in interview that he hadn't known Nitze before: "I went to his office in Arlington and introduced myself. I had seen him on TV and thought he was so good, and asked him to be on Team B, and he agreed to join." According to Pipes, "I picked Paul Wolfowitz [at the time working as special assistant for the Strategic Arms Limitation Talks to the director at the Arms Control and Disarmament Agency] because Richard Perle recommended him so highly."[46] Others selected were air force general Jasper Welch and Thomas Wolfe, a retired air force colonel working at the RAND Corporation.

Not only were most of the members suggested by people other than Pipes, but some additional people Pipes suggested were rejected by Paisley because the CIA simply did "not have time to complete the necessary security investigations in time for them to be of help."[47]

Pipes once wrote, "Team B was established and staffed by the Director of

43. John Paisley, memorandum for deputy director of Central Intelligence, August 11, 1976, obtained through FOIA.
44. Robert W. Gambino, director of security, memorandum to DCI, August 25, 1976, obtained through FOIA.
45. Interview with Daniel Graham, September 13, 1990.
46. Interview with Richard Pipes, August 15, 1990.
47. John Paisley, memorandum for deputy director of Central Intelligence, August 11, 1990, obtained through FOIA.

Central Intelligence."[48] However, based on advice from Deputy Assistant to the President for National Security William Hyland and his own tendency to "go along," CIA director George Bush did not exercise any control over the composition of any of the B Teams.[49] In a mid-July letter to the chairman of PFIAB, Leo Cherne, Bush wrote, "I am advised that the composition of the 'B' teams will conform closely to the Board members' suggestions."[50]

There was an almost incestuous closeness among most of the B Team members. In interview, General Welch said that he had known Tom Wolfe from his days at the RAND Corporation, that General Vogt's niece was a "dearly beloved teacher of [his] youngest son," and that he had met Nitze and Charlie Lerch in the 1960s when he was doing a damage-limiting study for Secretary of Defense Robert McNamara. Welch met Sy Weiss during his nuclear-targeting work, and knew Roland Herbst from Livermore in the early 1950s—"We designed bombs together." Furthermore, "Jim Drake and [Welch] had been in cruise missile work in the summer of 1967; [he] took Drake's job in the Office of the Secretary of Defense in 1971; John Foster was [his] first boss; Edward Teller was on [his] thesis committee at the University of California at Berkeley; [he] knew Paul Wolfowitz through Albert Wohlstetter and through work Wohlstetter did for the Defense Advanced Research Program Agency in the early 1970s."[51]

Apparently General Vogt also knew most of the Team B members. Paul Nitze had been his boss in 1961–65, when he was assistant secretary of defense for international security affairs and Vogt headed up the Defense Department's Policy Planning Staff, and he knew Generals Graham and Welch, as well as Sy Weiss.[52]

Two men not on the panel nevertheless played important behind-the-scenes roles: Albert Wohlstetter, whose influence was great, and John Lehman, deputy director of the Arms Control and Disarmament Agency. Paul Wolfowitz was Wohlstetter's former student, and the two remained in close contact, as did Wohlstetter and Weiss, and Vogt had worked with Wohlstetter in a New Alternatives Workshop.[53] According to Pipes, the panel used the Wohlstetter articles published in the previous year.[54] At their first meet-

48. Richard Pipes, "An Answer from 'Team B,'" *Washington Post*, January 9, 1977, C7.
49. Interviews with Robert Bowie, December 15, 1989, and William G. Hyland, September 26, 1989.
50. George Bush, letter to Leo Cherne, July 13, 1976, obtained through FOIA.
51. Interview with Gen. Jasper Welch, March 13, 1990.
52. Interview with Gen. John Vogt, October 11, 1990.
53. Interview with Ronald Stivers, October 24, 1989.
54. Interview with Richard Pipes, August 15, 1990.

ing, Team B discussed the possibility of sending their first draft to Wohlstet-ter, Edward Teller, and John Foster for critique.[55] Vogt and Weiss were both close friends of Lehman, and both joined Lehman's consulting firm within six months of his forming it.[56]

All these Team B members were white men who shared an almost apo-plectic animosity toward the Soviet Union. Nitze had staffed and partici-pated in writing the Gaither Report and NSC 68, each of which predicted impending Soviet superiority. Van Cleave was well known as a hard-line ideologue from his days on the SALT I negotiating team. According to a former student, "Van Cleave didn't tolerate anyone who questioned his posi-tion . . . and thought it was funny to make jokes about dropping bombs on people."[57] Vogt was called "the mad bomber" of Vietnam and Cambodia.[58]

Establishing the Ground Rules

The CIA went to great lengths to establish the ground rules for this experi-ment in competitive estimating. On May 12, 1976, George Carver, the dep-uty to the DCI for intelligence, flew to Chicago and spent two hours with Robert Galvin, chairman of the PFIAB NIE Evaluation Committee to work them out. In his memo to DCI Bush, Carver refers to it as "the PFIAB Treaty."[59] Carver drafted a letter to Bush to be signed either by Galvin or Leo Cherne, chairman of PFIAB.

The letter from Cherne to Bush was duly sent on June 8 and set out some rules: NIE 11-3/8-76 was to be prepared in the usual way by Team A. "Each B Team [would] be given access to all of the information on its area of con-cern available to the U.S. Government, i.e., it [would] have access to the same body of information and data on the issue which it [was] to address as [was] available to the A Team." Each B Team was to "adhere to the A Team's production schedule," so that all the drafts would be completed at the same time. The A and B Teams would then exchange drafts and meet "to discuss their respective findings and conclusions." Then both teams could revise

55. Donald J. Suda, memorandum for the record, August 19, 1976, obtained through FOIA.
56. Interview with Robert MacFarlane, October 18, 1989.
57. John S. Jensen, letter to the author, November 11, 1993.
58. Interview with Gen. John Vogt, October 11, 1990.
59. George A. Carver, note to the director [of Central Intelligence], May 26, 1976, ob-tained through FOIA.

their drafts and prepare comments on each other's revised drafts. The "entire package—basic Estimate draft, the three B Team drafts, and the comments of the A and B Teams—[would] then be studied . . . and discussed by the National Foreign Intelligence Board, chaired by the DCI." The B Team submissions would be forwarded to selected recipients together with the NIE. And after NIE 11-3/8-76, "along with the experimental volume, [was] forwarded, the Assistant to the President for National Security Affairs, in consultation with the DCI and the PFIAB, [would] select a panel of senior consumers, civilian and military, to review the experiment and critique its results."[60]

Three aspects of these ground rules later proved to be contentious. First, Pipes vehemently denied that any ground rules existed; in his own words: "No such 'ground rules' were spelled out."[61] However, at the first meeting of his team, Pipes distributed copies of Robert Galvin's letter to DCI Bush that "set forth the purpose of the experiment and the procedures to be followed," and noted that there was "no fixed definition of this Team's mandate from PFIAB, and perhaps that's just as well."[62] Van Cleave apparently thought the mandate came directly from the president: "We were charged by President Ford with reviewing intelligence estimates on Soviet strategic force programs and capabilities, looking backwards to see if they were wrong, what accounted for them being wrong, and then doing our own competitive estimate at this point in time."[63] Vogt claimed the task for Team B was defined as an "unbiased analytical study of estimating done by the CIA over the last decade. We were to look at the methods used and rationales given, and examine their authenticity."[64]

Second, right from the beginning, this Team B panel was determined to look at past NIEs, although the "treaty" made no mention of this. Welch stated, "We reviewed NIEs on Soviet strategic forces going back ten years to refresh our memories as to what they contained."[65] Indeed, the panel's report covered NIEs going all the way back to 1962. "I didn't foresee they would spend a lot of time going back over old estimates," said former NIO Howard Stoertz. "I didn't feel that the team drafting the chapter on Soviet strategic

---

60. Leo Cherne, letter to DCI Bush, June 8, 1976, obtained through FOIA.

61. Richard Pipes, letter to the author, October 5, 1990.

62. Donald J. Suda, memorandum for the record, August 19, 1976, obtained through FOIA.

63. Interview with William Van Cleave, March 9, 1990.

64. Interview with Gen. John Vogt, October 11, 1990.

65. Interview with Gen. Jasper Welch, March 13, 1990.

objectives bore any responsibility for estimates made under the old system, which had been abolished. But I misjudged the significance which would be attached to old answers."[66] When Pipes went to recruit Paul Nitze for the exercise, it was Nitze's impression, as recorded in his notes, that Team B was to discuss why past NIEs had been "consistently wrong."[67] Since Pipes had not been previously cleared, how could he have read the previous classified NIEs to ascertain whether they were right or wrong?

Third, Pipes and other members of Team B claimed they did not know about any plans for a "panel of senior consumers, civilian and military, to review the experiment and critique its results." In a response to several questions about the plans for such a team, Pipes wrote, "I am certain this is inaccurate."[68] When asked about such a senior review panel, Van Cleave replied, "It's news to me."[69] However, the note accompanying the Team B report states, "This document is one part of an experiment in competitive analysis undertaken by the DCI on behalf of the President's Foreign Intelligence Advisory Board."[70] In fact, not only were there three separate Team Bs, but there also was to be a subsequent review panel. John Foster went so far as to suggest members for this group: Sam Phillips and Richard Latter on accuracy; Gardiner Tucker, Foy Kohler, Albert Wohlstetter, and Paul Nitze for Soviet strategic objectives; Ben Ploymate and John Walsh for air defense; and Melvin Laird and Jim Schlesinger "as part of a senior review."[71]

Lionel Olmer, the executive secretary of PFIAB, corroborated that the Team A and Team B reports were to be presented to an outside impartial jury that would present a final report to PFIAB. In a December 1976 memo to PFIAB members, Olmer wrote:

> While reports of each team involved in the experiment have been completed, the next step in the experiment requires an evaluation by a senior review panel to be selected by the Assistant to the President for National Security Affairs, in consultation with the DCI and the PFIAB. Almost certainly, this step will not take place until after January 20, 1977 [i.e., after the inauguration of Jimmy Carter

66. Interview with Howard Stoertz, March 15, 1989.

67. Paul Nitze Papers, Team B File, Manuscript Division, Library of Congress.

68. Richard Pipes, letter to the author, October 5, 1990.

69. Interview with William Van Cleave, March 9, 1990.

70. "Intelligence Community Experiment in Competitive Analysis: Soviet Strategic Objectives: An Alternative View, Report of Team 'B,' December 1976," released by the CIA to the National Archives.

71. Lionel Olmer, memorandum for the record, June 30, 1976, obtained through FOIA.

as president]. Wherever it is possible to do so, the background to the experiment and its significance will be discussed with the appropriate Carter transition team members and designated incumbents in relevant national security affairs positions, to assure that this most important final step is not delayed.[72]

As Olmer explained, the idea for a review panel was an assurance of some level of objectivity: "Don't take the view of just these outsiders [the B Team]. Have outsiders under Henry Kissinger look at the implications. How does it smell? Does it pass the red-face test? If it turns up deficiencies may be present, would it represent an indictment of the process?" According to Olmer, "Pipes wouldn't have known about that because he was a factotum. He was to perform a somewhat ministerial function. He was not the chef de cabinet for the president. The PFIAB was."[73]

And finally, DCI Bush, in a letter to Gen. George Keegan, wrote, "My agreement with Leo Cherne and Brent Scowcroft is that a full joint review of the exercise will be conducted when this year's estimate is complete. Both the utility and validity of the results will then be addressed."[74]

Team B at Work

The first task was to obtain the necessary clearances for the team members. As is well known, there are different kinds of security clearances. According to a longtime CIA official, "The Team B members didn't go through a six-month process, any more than do congressmen. If there is no known derogatory information, they get cleared to be briefed."[75] In interview Pipes indicated his clearance was done in two weeks. "Paisley called me in my summer home in New Hampshire and said, 'You passed with flying colors,'" Pipes said with pride.[76]

One member about whom there *was* derogatory information was Van Cleave. Back in 1971, while he was a member of the SALT negotiating team,

72. Lionel Olmer, memorandum to PFIAB members, December 27, 1976, obtained through FOIA.
73. Interview with Lionel Olmer, November 8, 1990.
74. George Bush, letter to Gen. George Keegan, July 16, 1976, obtained through FOIA.
75. Interview with Edward Proctor, November 2, 1990.
76. Interview with Richard Pipes, August 15, 1990.

Van Cleave was suspected of having leaked the position of U.S. negotiators to William Beecher of the *New York Times*. President Nixon charged the newly constituted "plumbers" with ferreting out the source of the leak, and Van Cleave was subjected to a lie-detector test. Van Cleave made no secret of the fact that he was opposed to the U.S. negotiating approach and suspicious of Soviet motives and tactics.[77] He admitted having seen Beecher alone, a violation of Pentagon rules that required a press officer to be present when a reporter interviewed an official,[78] and told investigators that there was "some possibility that I might have said something that could be taken to be an indiscretion—but I didn't think so."[79] Although Van Cleave was cleared by the lie-detector test, he was dropped as a Pentagon consultant in November 1971, but he was rehired in the summer of 1973 when James Schlesinger became secretary of defense.[80]

During the Team B exercise, Van Cleave asked for access to two "special compartmented materials." Although Paisley told him "they were not relevant to his subject" and that "he had exposed the material" to Pipes and Wolfe, Van Cleave "insist[ed] that he need[ed] to study them personally himself." Paisley requested guidance on this matter, since he believed "Van Cleave [was] prepared to make an issue of the matter with members of PFIAB."[81] Paisley recommended that Van Cleave not be permitted to see these materials, and apparently he was not.

The first meeting of the Team B Strategic Objectives Panel took place on August 18. In mid-September they met with some consultants, including Gen. George Keegan, chief of Air Force Intelligence, who briefed them on lasers and other directed-energy weapons;[82] Gordon Negus of the Defense Intelligence Agency, who briefed them on Soviet command and control hardening as well as the thrust of the Soviet strategic effort; Andrew Marshall, director of net assessments in the Department of Defense, who discussed economic aspects of the Soviet strategic effort; Fritz Ermarth of the

77. David Wise, *The American Police State: The Government Against the People* (New York: Random House, 1976), 357.

78. Ibid., 359.

79. Ibid., 361.

80. Ibid., 365.

81. John Paisley, memorandum for Richard Lehman, deputy to the DCI for National Intelligence, September 21, 1976, obtained through FOIA.

82. Paul Nitze told his B Team mates that "he had heard Keegan on the subject and would not stay to hear him again." Donald J. Suda, "Summary of 4th Meeting of Team B on 15 September 1976," obtained through FOIA.

CIA, who told them about the NIE process; Sherman Kent, chairman of the Board of National Estimates from 1952 to 1967, who also briefed them on NIEs; and Richard Foster of SRI, who talked about Soviet strategic weapons and their role in Soviet strategic thinking.[83] Pipes was not present because of illness. All the A and B Teams met throughout September, and in mid-October the A and B Teams exchanged their first drafts. Within a few days, the first press report about this highly secret exercise appeared (see the next chapter).

Once the team was constituted, all the resources of the CIA were made available to it: satellite photographs, intercepts of Soviet signals, secret Soviet military documents, public documents, and reams of technical data.[84] By September 3, 1976, two weeks after the team was constituted, nearly forty documents were requested by John Paisley for Team B, including translations of such Russian publications as "Some Problems of Political Work Among Enemy Troops and Population in the Initial Period of War," "The Creation of a Marxist-Leninist Outlook Among the Students of Developing Countries Studying at Soviet Educational Institutions," and "Certain Problems in the Development of Soviet Military Art from 1953 to 1960."[85] Later that month sixty-seven additional documents were hand-carried to Pipes. These were mostly previous NIEs and drafts and minutes of intelligence community meetings and briefings.[86] According to NIO Howard Stoertz, at his first meeting with Pipes he tried "to assure this fellow no intelligence material would be held back."[87] And indeed, none was. In a break with its standards of secrecy, the CIA granted this group access to the most sensitive data on Soviet military strength, data that had been culled from satellite photos and reports of agents in the field, defectors, and current informants. As Robert Scheer points out, "Never before had outside critics of government policy been given such access to the data underlying that policy. Bush did not extend similar privileges to dovish critics of prevailing policy."[88]

83. Donald J. Suda, "Summary of 4th Meeting of Team B on 15 September 1976," obtained through FOIA.

84. Klurfeld, "A New View on Nuclear War," 6–15.

85. "Documents Compiled for John Paisley's Project," September 3, 1976, obtained through FOIA.

86. "Material Hand-Carried to Richard Pipes," undated CIA list indicating all materials were returned by September 29, 1976, obtained through FOIA.

87. Interview with Howard Stoertz, March 15, 1989.

88. Robert Scheer, *With Enough Shovels: Reagan, Bush, and Nuclear War* (New York: Vintage Books, 1983), 53.

The A and B strategic objectives teams met face-to-face at CIA headquarters at Langley on November 5. By all accounts this first meeting was a rout of the A Team analysts, who were outgunned by such stalwarts as Paul Nitze. One of the Team A participants remembers, "We were overmatched. People like Nitze ate us for lunch."[89] A CIA official stated, "It was like putting Walt Whitman High versus the Redskins. I watched poor GS-13s and -14s [middle-level analysts] subjected to ridicule by Pipes and Nitze. They were browbeating the poor analysts. Team B was not constructive."[90]

According to Pipes, this first confrontation between Teams A and B

> proved a "disaster" for Team A. This outcome was at least in some measure due to the Agency's unwise decision to field against senior outside experts a troop of young analysts, some of them barely out of graduate school, who, even if they had a better case to make, could not help feeling intimidated by senior government officials, general officers, and university professors. The champion for Team A had barely begun his criticism of Team B's effort, delivered in a condescending tone, when a member of Team B [Paul Nitze] fired a question that reduced him to a state of catatonic immobility: we stared in embarrassment as he sat for what seemed an interminable time with an open mouth, unable to utter a sound. Later Stoertz came to the rescue, but he did not save the Agency and his office from emerging badly mauled.[91]

Looking back, Stoertz stated, "If I had appreciated the adversarial nature, I could have wheeled up different guns. I thought it was not intended to be a zero-sum discussion."[92] It was clear that Team B was out to humiliate their prey, not merely to defeat their foes. After this confrontation, both teams reworked their drafts in preparation for presenting their work to PFIAB and the intelligence community. Three days after the initial confrontation, Jimmy Carter defeated Gerald Ford for the presidency of the United States.

89. Interview with Jay Kalner, July 20, 1989.
90. Interview with Sidney Graybeal, April 28, 1989.
91. Richard Pipes, "Team B: The Reality Behind the Myth," *Commentary*, October 1986, 25–40.
92. Interview with Howard Stoertz, March 15, 1989.

PFIAB and the Intelligence Community Receive the Team Reports

In early December, the chairmen of both teams presented their findings to PFIAB with DCI Bush present.[93] Stoertz remembers it as a "pretty formal meeting with the principals not engaging much."[94] Pipes immodestly wrote that PFIAB members were " 'thunderstruck' at hearing what many of its members regarded as the first realistic assessment of Soviet strategic intentions to come before it."[95]

On December 21, the six A and B Teams presented their findings to the National Foreign Intelligence Board in the main auditorium (called the Igloo) at CIA headquarters in Langley, Virginia. The room was packed, since there were lots of visitors from the intelligence community. Pipes remembers that the B Teams "sat on the right side and Bush sat with Team A on the left."[96] Again, the chairman of each team made its presentation. General Graham remembered that after Roland Herbst presented the Team B Missile Accuracy Panel's report, which declared Soviet missiles were very accurate, "General Keegan [soon to be retired air force chief of intelligence] got up and said they were not all that accurate."[97] Adm. Daniel Murphy, deputy director for the intelligence community, thought he was going to get a briefing on the alternate estimates. What he got instead was "a lecture by Pipes and then technical talks on particle beams, CEPs, and the Backfire bomber."[98] Herbst remembers that "Pipes and Stoertz had a long debate."[99] After the team presentations, Stoertz explained how and why the conclusions in the draft NIE differed from the estimates that had been volunteered by the Pipes panel. On each of the topics he discussed, Stoertz explained what the intelligence community's estimate was and the basis for it.[100]

After the presentations were finished, DCI Bush thanked everyone and invited them all to lunch. Years later, Pipes was still smarting over the seating arrangements at the lunch. He commented, "There were no assigned seats

93. Pipes, "Team B," 34.
94. Interview with Howard Stoertz, July 23, 1990.
95. Pipes, "Team B," 34.
96. Interview with Richard Pipes, August 15, 1990.
97. Interview with Daniel Graham, September 13, 1990.
98. Interview with Adm. Daniel Murphy, November 9, 1989.
99. Interview with Roland Herbst, May 10, 1990.
100. Telephone interview with Howard Stoertz, November 6, 1995.

except for the director's table, and there was not a single member from my Team B at that table."[101] The tables were arranged according to subject matter, and Bush sat at the air defense table. James Drake, a short, wiry, friendly man who sat at that table, recalled that Bush said he was pleased with the exercise and that it validated the system as it existed.[102] According to Roland Herbst, someone at Bush's table asked, "What happens next?" and Bush's reply was, "Nothing. I have to go along with my own guys."[103]

What Did DCI Bush Think of the Experiment?

Because DCI Bush later became president of the United States, there has been much speculation about what he thought of the B Team exercise. There are numerous indications that Bush was not enamored of it. According to former deputy national security adviser William Hyland, "Bush didn't buy on to Team B. There was no institutional way for Bush to say 'I believe in Team B and not Team A.' "[104] A longtime CIA analyst said that "early on, Bush thought Team B was the right thing to do for President Ford's attempt to play open, play fair, and restore confidence in the capability of the intelligence community to provide good estimates. As time went on, he changed his mind and thought he had made a mistake, that he should not have approved it and that it was not a useful exercise. It had become a political hobbyhorse for some."[105] This view was echoed by PFIAB chairman Cherne with his usual loquacity: "I must believe he viewed the process with reserve and at a maximum with some degree of apprehension and reserve and concern, if not dislike."[106]

When Bush appeared on *Face the Nation* following articles in the press about the exercise, the DCI said, "I am here to defend the integrity of the intelligence process. . . . The CIA has great integrity. It would never take directions from a policy-maker, me or anybody else, in order to come up with conclusions to force a President-elect's hand or a President's hand, or to comply with a President's directive."[107]

101. Interview with Richard Pipes, August 15, 1990.
102. Interview with James Drake, May 10, 1990.
103. Interview with Roland Herbst, May 10, 1990.
104. Interview with William G. Hyland, September 26, 1989.
105. Interview with Hans Heymann, October 11, 1990.
106. Interview with Leo Cherne, August 2, 1990.
107. *Face the Nation*, transcript, January 2, 1977, 2.

A talking paper prepared for Bush's meeting with the National Security Council on January 13, 1977, states, "It appears in retrospect that in view of the highly charged and controversial nature of interpretations of Soviet objectives, it would have been desirable to include a broader range of viewpoints on the B team."[108]

Further evidence of Bush's feelings about the exercise appears in a memo he wrote to PFIAB chairman Cherne on his last day as DCI.

> The B Team's charge that "soft" factors affecting Soviet motivation do not receive "thorough" analytical attention is simply not true. . . . The recommendation that adversarial procedures similar to the B Team experiment be continued, perhaps every other year, is one I oppose. It is not that the experiment was a total failure; to the contrary, the B Team on low altitude air defense made a particular contribution. Rather, it is that, when one sets out to establish an adversarial B Team, one sets in motion a process that lends itself to manipulation for purposes other than estimative accuracy. I am already getting recommendations that should the process ever be repeated, a C team of a persuasion opposed to the B Team should be established to review the estimate at the same time. I would prefer to convene panels of experts with a mix of views.[109]

A different view was expressed by David Binder of the *New York Times*, who interviewed DCI Bush: "For Bush, Team B was a ghastly outcome. Bush is not disloyal downward; these were his own people. He was in an absolute tizzy to have been shown that there were flaws in the most priceless product of the agency, its *Hauptaufgabe*. I confronted a man who was miserable about the outcome and about being confronted with a journalist from the *New York Times*. Bush was an embarrassed, unhappy man, who seemed to have accepted Team B's grimmer, more horrific scenario."[110]

Pipes has always claimed that Bush agreed with Team B: "I do recall attending a dinner sometime in 1977 at which Bush spoke to a large audience and fully identified with the Team B point of view."[111]

The truth is that Bush was probably of at least two minds about the exer-

108. Talking paper for the DCI, NSC meeting, January 13, 1977, obtained through FOIA.

109. George Bush, memorandum for chairman, President's Foreign Intelligence Advisory Board, January 19, 1977, 2 and 7–8, obtained through FOIA.

110. Interview with David Binder, October 8, 1990.

111. Richard Pipes, letter to the author, October 17, 1990.

cise. Bush exhibited great loyalty to his CIA analysts and always treated them with respect and courtesy. Longtime CIA officials who had seen various DCIs come and go remarked on that. One said that "at his first official appearance Bush was greeted with icy politeness. Within ten days, he had everyone eating out of his hand."[112] Another declared that Bush "was extremely good in talking to analysts and listening to them. He had great rapport with people. He asked good questions." This former CIA official continued, "If Bush were to get up in the auditorium and say to his people, 'We have a problem,' everyone would have said, 'How can we solve it together?' If Turner [Adm. Stansfield Turner, DCI under President Carter] were to get up in the auditorium and say, 'We have a problem,' the reaction would have been, 'You've got a problem.' "[113]

Bush certainly abhorred the leaks and correctly suspected they came from Team B members. In his memorandum distributing the final NIE to the intelligence community, Bush wrote, "[I]nspired by these selective leaks, allegations have appeared in the press that the judgments appearing in this official *Estimate* were shaped by pressure from the 'Team B.' There is no truth to such allegations." Yet, at some level, Bush probably bought at least some of the more pessimistic and gloomy forecasts of Team B. His ambivalence is exhibited in the same memo: "The views of these experts [Team B] did have some effect." But then, defending his agency, he continues, "But to the extent that this *Estimate* presents a starker appreciation of Soviet strategic capabilities and objectives, it is but the latest in a series of estimates that have done so as evidence has accumulated on the continuing persistence and vigor of Soviet programs in the strategic offensive and defensive fields."[114]

What did the Team B Strategic Objectives Panel say? How did it differ from NIE 11-3/8-76? Was NIE 11-3/8-76 toughened up in response to Team B's criticisms? Who leaked the Team B report? What was the aftermath of this experiment in competitive threat assessments? These are the questions I take up in the next chapter.

112. Interview with Hans Heymann, October 11, 1990.
113. Interview with Sidney Graybeal, November 11, 1990.
114. George Bush, memorandum for recipients of National Intelligence Estimate 11-3/8-76, "Soviet Forces for Intercontinental Conflict Through the Mid-1980s," January 7, 1977, obtained through FOIA.

9

Team B Panel Report on Strategic Objectives

The Gist of the Report

The fifty-five-page final report of the Team B Strategic Objectives Panel, written in the four months between August and December 1976, consists of three parts and an annex. Pipes has said in interview that he wrote most of the first section, which addresses and critiques the methodology of past NIEs.[1] It accuses the CIA of consistently underestimating the "intensity, scope, and implicit threat" posed by the Soviet Union, because "the hard evidence on which the NIEs are based relates primarily to the adversary's capabilities rather than his intentions, his weapons rather than his ideas, motives and aspirations."[2]

However, the capability-versus-intention argument is complicated. National Intelligence Estimates (NIEs) are prepared for various policymakers, including Defense Department officials. Former chief of the Strategic Air Command Gen. John T. Chain Jr. put it well: "As a military officer my job

---

1. Interview with Richard Pipes, August 15, 1990.
2. "Intelligence Community Experiment in Competitive Analysis: Soviet Strategic Objectives: An Alternative View, Report of Team 'B,' December 1976," 1 and 9, released by the CIA to the National Archives; hereafter referred to as Team B report.

is to worry about capability, not intentions."[3] Defense officials would not be happy with an NIE that focused on intentions, for as they know so well, intentions, ideas, motives, and aspirations are subject to unpredictable and rapid change. In addition, capabilities also can be ambiguous because weapons can be used in more than one way.

Team B decried the NIEs' "judgments of Soviet past and present behavior" and stated, "The evidence suggests that the Soviet leaders are first and foremost offensively rather than defensively minded."[4] But the Team B analysts slanted their evidence. In asserting that "Russian, and especially Soviet political and military theories are distinctly *offensive* in character," Team B claimed "their ideal is the 'science of conquest' (*nauka pobezhdat*) formulated by the 18th century Russian commander, Field Marshall A. V. Suvorov in a treatise of the same name, which has been a standard text of Imperial as well as Soviet military science."[5] However, Raymond Garthoff, the highly respected senior fellow at the Brookings Institution, maintains that the correct translation of *nauka pobezhdat* is "the science of winning" or the "science of victory."[6] All military strategists strive to achieve a winning strategy. Our own military writings are devoted to winning victories, but this is not commonly viewed as a policy of conquest.

The report accused the NIEs of indulging in "mirror-imaging," attributing to Soviet decision makers forms of behavior that might be expected from their U.S. counterparts under analogous circumstances. "This conceptual flaw is perhaps the single gravest cause of the misunderstanding of Soviet strategic objectives found in past and current NIEs."[7] Although the B Team report decried mirror-imaging, it engaged in the practice itself. In discussing the Soviet Backfire bomber, the report stated, "We consider our FB-111 a strategic bomber and plan its use against Soviet targets even though its unrefueled radius falls short of even the lowest estimates of Backfire performance. Our strategic air command plans multiple refueling of the aircraft which gives it, on a typical mission a range (with 2 refuelings) of about 6400 nautical miles."[8]

3. Tom Kenworthy, "Eyeball-to-Eyeball at SAC Headquarters," *Washington Post*, February 14, 1990, 8.

4. Team B report, 2.

5. Ibid., 14.

6. Interview with Raymond Garthoff, February 10, 1989; Anne Hessing Cahn, "Team B: The Trillion-Dollar Experiment," *Bulletin of Atomic Scientists* 49, no. 3 (1993): 22–27.

7. Team B report, 1.

8. Ibid., 28.

Team B went on to claim that for the Soviet bomber "there is no question therefore that the *aircraft has the inherent capability for strategic missions, should the Soviets chose to use it this way*" (emphasis in original).[9] In later years, the Defense Intelligence Agency lowered its estimate of the range of the Backfire by about 20 percent when fully loaded. This meant that the Backfire could not have carried out round-trip missions against the United States without midair refueling. These later intelligence reports indicated that the Backfire lacked a probe for aerial refueling, and we now know that the Soviets never developed a large tanker capability, both of which would have been necessary in order to use the bomber for missions against the United States.[10] The Team B panel report guessed that the Backfire would probably "be produced in substantial numbers, with perhaps 500 aircraft off the line by early 1984."[11] In fact, the Soviets had less than half that many, 235, in 1984.

Pipes has been called the intellectual godfather of the thesis that the Soviets rejected nuclear parity and were bent on fighting a nuclear war.[12] Paul Wolfowitz and some other Team B members believed that if the Soviets ever achieved superiority, they would use it in a conventional sense, such as in Angola or Afghanistan, not that they would start a nuclear war.[13] However, the report admonished the intelligence community for failing

> to acknowledge that the Soviets believe that the best way to paralyze U.S. strategic capabilities is by assuring that the outcome of any nuclear exchange will be as favorable to the Soviet Union as possible; and, finally they ignore the possibility that the Russians seriously believe that if, for whatever reason, deterrence were to fail, they could resort to the use of nuclear weapons to fight and win a war. *The NIEs tendency to view deterrence as an alternative to a warfighting capability rather than as complementary to it,* is in the opinion of Team 'B', a grave and dangerous flaw in their evaluations of Soviet strategic objectives." (Emphasis in original)[14]

9. Ibid.
10. Michael R. Gordon, "Pentagon Reassesses Soviet Bomber," *New York Times*, October 1, 1985, 8; Jeffrey T. Richelson, "Old Surveillance, New Interpretation," *Bulletin of Atomic Scientists* 42, no. 2 (1986): 18–23.
11. Team B report, 28–29.
12. Robert Scheer, *With Enough Shovels: Reagan, Bush, and Nuclear War* (New York: Vintage Books, 1983), 55.
13. Interview with Paul Wolfowitz, July 23, 1990.
14. Team B report, 2.

Both mirror-imaging and the report's descriptions of Soviet behavior share the common flaw of assuming that an opponent can't and won't do something new and different in the future.

The report also viewed Soviet strategic thinking as monolithic. However, information was available indicating that between mid-1973 and late 1974 a debate occurred in the Soviet press about the nature of nuclear war and the significance of strategic military power. One group, mostly political commentators associated with the USA Institute in Moscow, stressed the futility of the strategic arms competition, the economic benefits of arms control, the declining political value of military power, and the emptiness of any concept of "victory" in nuclear war. The second group, mainly military writers affiliated with the Main Political Directorate of the Armed Forces, stressed the need for vigilance despite detente, the continuing political utility of military power, and the belief that "victory" in nuclear war remained possible. Most observers concluded that this debate about the nature of nuclear war would continue.[15]

The second part of the Team B report, "A Critique of NIE Interpretations of Certain Soviet Strategic Developments," was, according to Pipes, the most highly classified.[16] This section, consisting of eighteen pages, or about one-third of the entire study, looked briefly at ten specific aspects of Soviet strategic force developments, including economic restraints, Soviet antisatellite capabilities, and Soviet antisubmarine warfare capabilities. For each, Team B gave a brief estimating history and their own conclusions. Team B attempted to discredit Team A by showing that the old estimates were never right. It was this part of the Team B report that Stoertz reviewed when the teams made their presentations to the National Foreign Intelligence Board at Langley (discussed in the last chapter).

Wherever Team B looked at "hard" data, it saw the worst possible case. Antiballistic missiles (ABM) and directed-energy weapons research and development were examined together. Team B asserted, "Mobile ABM system components combined with the deployed SAM [surface-to-air missile] system could produce a significant ABM capability." But that never occurred. Team B assumed that Murphy's Law was not operative in the Soviet Union in these forefront technological areas: "Understanding that there are differ-

15. "The 'Great Debate': Soviet Views on Nuclear Strategy and Arms Control," CIA Intelligence Report, August 1975, 1, obtained through FOIA.

16. Interview with Richard Pipes, August 15, 1990.

ing evaluations of the potentialities of laser and CPB [charged-particle beam] for ABM, *it is still clear that the Soviets have mounted ABM efforts in both areas of a magnitude that it is difficult to overestimate*" (emphasis in original).[17]

Overestimating is precisely what the United States did! A facility at the Soviet Union's nuclear test range in Semipalatinsk was touted by Gen. George Keegan as a site for tests of Soviet nuclear-powered beam weapons. Instead, it was used to test nuclear-powered rocket engines and was totally unrelated to so-called nuclear directed-energy weapons. According to Gregory Canavan, a physicist at the Los Alamos National Laboratory who toured the supposed Russian directed-energy facilities, "We had overestimated both their capability and their [technical] understanding. They were five years behind where I expected them to be."[18]

This mistaken interpretation of Soviet capabilities in strategic defense weapons helped build support for a costly but ultimately unsuccessful attempt by the United States to develop our own arsenal of nuclear directed-energy weapons. According to John Pike of the Federation of American Scientists, "It laid the foundation for all of SDIO's [Strategic Defense Initiative Office's] directed energy programs."[19]

When Team B couldn't find a deployed Soviet nonacoustic antisubmarine system, the report mused that "the absence of a deployed system by this time is difficult to understand. The implication could be that the Soviets have, in fact, deployed some operational nonacoustic systems and will deploy more in the next few years."[20] But our submarine force never was vulnerable. For Team B, it wasn't a question of the Russians coming. They were already here!

Another brickbat hurled by Team B was that the CIA consistently underestimated Soviet military expenditures. With the advantage of hindsight, we now know that Soviet military spending increases began to slow down precisely as Team B was writing about "an intense military buildup in nuclear as well as conventional forces of all sorts, not moderated either by the West's self-imposed restraints or by SALT."[21] In 1983, Deputy Director of the CIA Robert Gates testified, "The rate of growth of overall defense costs is lower because procurement of military hardware—the largest category of defense

17. Team B report, 34.
18. Vincent Kiernan, "Russians: Site Tested Rockets, Not Beam Weapon," *Space News,* October 12–18, 1992, 1.
19. Ibid.
20. Team B report, 32.
21. Ibid., 5.

spending—was almost flat in 1976–1981. . . . Practically all major categories of Soviet weapons were affected—missiles, aircraft, and ships."[22] In January 1984, a separate NATO study agreed with and substantiated Gates's findings.[23] Three years later, the CIA and the Defense Intelligence Agency agreed that "the slowdown in procurement growth began in the year 1975. That is, 1975 over 1974, was the first year of slow procurement growth."[24] So even as Team B was writing its report, the CIA and the rest of the intelligence community were overestimating, not underestimating, Soviet military expenditures.

While Team B panelists waxed eloquent about "conceptual failures," they themselves were unable to grasp how the future may differ radically from the past. In 1976, with rising mortality rates for the entire Soviet population, declining life expectancy, declining numbers of new entrants into the labor force, and declining agricultural output, Team B wrote confidently, "Within what is, after all, a large and expanding GNP . . . *Soviet strategic forces have yet to reflect any constraining effect of civil economy competition, and are unlikely to do so in the foreseeable future*" (emphasis in original).[25] Fourteen years later, the Soviet Union no longer existed.

The third section, "Soviet Strategic Objectives," emphasized again an ultimate Soviet goal of world domination and saw Soviet military programs as striving for strategic superiority. The report stated, "The main thrust of Soviet doctrine has been that in the event of a failure of deterrence, war-winning and national survival prospects can be improved by having in readiness balanced forces superior to those of the adversary, together with an effective civil defense system."[26]

Repeating the earlier doomsday threat assessments, Team B panelists wrote:

22. "Allocation of Resources in the Soviet Union and China—1983," Hearings before the Subcommittee on International Trade, Finance, and Security Economics of the Joint Economic Committee, 98th Cong., 1st sess., pt. 9, June 28 and September 20, 1983, 230; Rhodri Jeffreys-Jones, *The CIA and American Democracy* (New Haven, Conn.: Yale University Press, 1989), 243; Bob Woodward and Patrick E. Tyler, "Officials Hope Gates Will Bring Calm to CIA," *Washington Post*, April 10, 1986, 12.

23. Jeffreys-Jones, *The CIA and American Democracy*, 242.

24. "Allocation of Resources in the Soviet Union and China—1985," Hearings before the Subcommittee on Economic Resources, Competitiveness, and Security Economics of the Joint Economic Committee, 99th Cong., 2d sess., pt. 11, March 19, 1986, 101.

25. Team B report, 23.

26. Ibid., 45.

An intensified military effort has been under way designed to provide the Soviet Union with *nuclear as well as conventional superiority*
both in strategic forces for intercontinental conflict and theater or regional
forces. While hoping to crush the 'capitalist' realm by other than
military means, *the Soviet Union is nevertheless preparing for a Third*
World War as if it were unavoidable. . . .

Soviet leaders believe that their ultimate objectives are closer to
realization today than they have ever been before. *Within the ten year*
period of the National Estimate the Soviets may well expect to achieve a
degree of military superiority which would permit a dramatically more
aggressive pursuit of their hegemonial objectives, including direct military challenges to Western vital interests, in the belief that such
superior military force can pressure the West to acquiesce or, if not,
can be used to win a military contest at any level. (Emphasis in
original)[27]

What was beginning to be known at that time was that the Soviet armed
forces had a high alcoholism rate, inadequate food, and poor morale. Now,
of course, we know that within the ten-year period, the Soviet Union began
to implode.

The annex examines NIEs on Soviet strategic forces from 1962 to 1975
and, not surprisingly, finds them wanting. The mind-set of Team B led them,
for example, to state that "since there were more pessimistic interpretations
occasionally contained in footnotes—it can be argued that they [the NIEs]
were more optimistic than warranted by available contemporary evidence."[28]
It could be argued just as well (or more accurately) that the pessimistic footnotes were wrong!

The Pipes panel recommendations, signed by Richard Pipes, William Van
Cleave, and Daniel Graham as team members and Paul Nitze, Seymour
Weiss, and Paul Wolfowitz as advisers, were submitted directly to PFIAB and
were concerned with methodology and procedures. Foy Kohler, John Vogt,
Jasper Welch, and Tom Wolfe did not sign the recommendation memo.

To avoid "mirror-imaging," Team B recommended that NIEs should "inte-
grate observed and projected Soviet weapons' programs and force deployments derived from the 'hard' physical data with more thorough analysis of

27. Ibid., 45–46, 47.
28. Ibid., 51.

historical, political, institutional, and other 'soft' factors shaping Soviet motives and intentions."[29]

But such "soft" factors as Soviet military doctrine had been included in every NIE, years before Team B. A special National Estimate for 1973 stated, "Since the early 1960s, the Soviet military has articulated a view of strategic requirements that links deterrence with the ability actually to wage strategic war to the point of some form of victory."[30] NIE 11-8-73 discussed Soviet objectives as "probably includ[ing] an opportunistic desire to press ahead and achieve a margin of superiority if they can."[31] Nevertheless, Stoertz, writing eleven years after the Team B experiment, acknowledges that "more emphasis is now placed on Soviet military doctrine and on the operational practices of Soviet strategic forces and for this, the B Teams deserve some of the credit."[32]

In reading NIE 11-3/8-76 it is hard to find any evidence that Soviet objectives and military doctrine were judged in U.S. rather than in Soviet terms. For example, the NIE stated, "The Soviets' belief in the eventual supremacy of their system is strong. They see their forces for intercontinental conflict as contributing to their ultimate goal of achieving a dominant position over the West, particularly the United States, in terms of political, economic, social, and military strength."[33]

Even before the B Team experiment, a previous NIE had stated, "Deeply held ideological and doctrinal convictions impel the Soviet leaders to pose as an ultimate goal the attainment of a dominant position over the West, particularly the U.S., in terms of political, economic, social, and military strength. We do not doubt that if they thought they could achieve it, the Soviets would try to attain the capability to launch a nuclear attack so effective that the U.S. could not cause devastating damage to the U.S.S.R. in retaliation."[34]

29. "Memorandum for Chairman, President's Foreign Intelligence Advisory Board, 'Recommendations of Team B—Soviet Strategic Objectives,'" n.d., 1, obtained through FOIA; hereafter referred to as Team B Recommendations.

30. "Soviet Strategic Arms Programs and Detente: What Are They Up To?" Special National Estimate, 11-4-73, September 10, 1973, 7, Record Group 263, Folder 57, National Archives.

31. "Soviet Forces for Intercontinental Attack," National Intelligence Estimate 11-8-73, January 25, 1974, Record Group 263, Folder 58, National Archives.

32. Howard Stoertz, letter to the editor, Commentary, March 1987, 18.

33. "Soviet Forces for Intercontinental Conflict Through the Mid-1980s," National Intelligence Estimate, December 21, 1976, 3, obtained through FOIA.

34. "Soviet Forces for Intercontinental Conflict Through the Mid-1980s," National Intelligence Estimate 11-3/8-75, November 17, 1975, 5, Record Group 263, Folder 60, National Archives.

The Pipes panel recommended that net assessments, that is, judgments of the balance of U.S. and Soviet military capabilities, should be avoided but, when used, "should be done explicitly, analytically, and thoroughly, not implicitly or perfunctorily."[35] However, any estimate of the technical capability of a weapon system requires some kind of an interaction analysis, that is, some appraisal of how well it performs against the force it was designed to fight. That in essence is a net assessment. But the detailed analyses that would look at operational factors, leadership, training, morale, and so forth are explicitly not incorporated in NIEs. Ever since 1973 an Office of Net Assessment has existed in the Defense Department to perform this very function.

According to Team B, weapons systems and force developments should "be examined in a more integrated manner to yield 'combined evaluations' more indicative of Soviet total military capabilities."[36] But the NIEs were arranged according to the way the United States planned its forces—strategic offensive, strategic defensive, and general-purpose forces—because that is the way the consumers, that is, the policymakers, wanted them to be presented.[37]

Another recommendation was to minimize policy pressures on the intelligence estimating process. But the very people who supervised the NIE process, the DCI, the NIOs, and the CIA analysts, did not represent any department involved in the policy-making process. Moving the chief estimative officer and a staff to the executive office of the president, as Team B recommended, would have politicized the process and maximized policy pressures on the NIEs.

Team B also recommended enlisting "the part-time services of a panel of prominent outside specialists for the purpose of reviewing estimates so as to identify judgments that are based on questionable assumptions concerning Soviet strategic doctrine and behavior."[38] (Could they have been thinking of themselves?) The last recommendation was to convene a Team B "adversarial" panel of outsiders every second year.[39] However DCI Bush opposed continuing adversarial procedures "similar to Team B" and concluded that

35. Team B Recommendations, 2.

36. Ibid.

37. George Bush, memorandum to chairman, President's Foreign Intelligence Advisory Board, January 19, 1977, 4, obtained through FOIA.

38. Team B Recommendations, 4.

39. Richard Pipes, William Van Cleave, Daniel Graham, Paul Nitze, Seymour Weiss, and Paul Wolfowitz, "Recommendations of Team 'B'—Soviet Strategic Objectives," memorandum for chairman of PFIAB, n.d., obtained through FOIA.

he "would prefer to convene panels of experts with a mix of views."[40] Outside consultants with diverse opinions are now more widely used during the preparation of estimates, but according to Stoertz, "Their role is that of advisers, rather than competitors, and they are selected to represent a broader range of viewpoints than the B teams of 1976."[41]

Overall, the Team B report contains more pontification and polemics than hard analyses. Team B failed to come to grips with the key question faced by Soviet military planners, that is, how to turn an appetite for superior military power into the real thing, given constraints and limits such as economic considerations, bureaucratic pressures, and concerns about U.S. countermoves. Colby was prescient in his skepticism about a Team B exercise: "It is hard for me to envisage how an ad hoc 'independent' group of government and non-government analysts could prepare a more thorough, comprehensive assessment of Soviet strategic capabilities—even in two specific areas—than the Intelligence Community can prepare."[42] And his skepticism was certainly borne out.

Differences Between Team B and NIE 11-3/8-76

The major difference between the Pipes Team B report and NIE 11-3/8-76, approved by the National Foreign Intelligence Board in December 1976, hinged on the question whether the Soviets could reasonably expect to achieve clear strategic superiority during the next ten years. Team A wrote that while "the Soviets may be optimistic about their long-term prospects in this competition [with the United States] . . . they cannot be certain about future U.S. behavior or about their own future strategic capabilities relative to those of the U.S."[43]

This statement, as well as much of the rest of the NIE, is heavily footnoted. The director of the State Department's Bureau of Intelligence and Research opined that Soviet leaders "do not entertain, as a practical objective in the foreseeable future, the achievement of what could reasonably be

40. George Bush, memorandum for chairman, President's Foreign Intelligence Advisory Board, January 19, 1977, 8, obtained through FOIA.

41. Stoertz, letter to the editor, 18.

42. William Colby, letter to President Gerald Ford, November 21, 1975, 4, obtained through FOIA.

43. "Soviet Forces for Intercontinental Conflict Through the Mid-1980s," National Intelligence Estimate, December 21, 1976, 3, obtained through FOIA.

characterized as a 'war-winning' or 'war-survival' posture." Army, Navy, and Air Force Intelligence as well as the Defense Intelligence Agency and the Energy Research and Development Administration believed "that the Soviets do, in fact, see as attainable their objective of achieving the capability to wage an intercontinental nuclear war, should such a war occur, and survive it with resources sufficient to dominate the postwar period."[44] The NIE concludes that the Soviets could not overcome deficiencies in their present low-altitude air defenses until after 1980. Team B felt that the United States could be adversely surprised by discounted or undetected capabilities. The NIE's estimates of Soviet ICBM accuracies implied no severe threat to Minuteman until about 1980. Team B implied that such a threat could materialize much sooner.[45] Now we know that both Team A and Team B overestimated many characteristics of Soviet strategic forces, with the more pessimistic Team B report further off the mark.

A careful reading of both documents leads me to conclude that the difference was more a question of tone than of substance. The Team B report expressed extreme alarm, while the NIE expressed concern. No one could read NIE 11-3/8-76 without worrying about the Soviet buildup. The NIE stated, "[T]he Soviets are striving to achieve war-fighting and war-survival capabilities which would leave the U.S.S.R. in a better position than the U.S. if war occurred."[46] The real question is, Did Team B influence the tone of the NIE?

Pipes claimed the final NIE was "a very different report from the initial draft." He felt it was "much closer to our [Team B's] point of view."[47] Writing about the December 2 meeting when the six A and B Teams presented their findings to PFIAB, Pipes stated, "I listened with mounting disbelief as Team A advanced an estimate that in all essential points agreed with Team B's position." In that article, written when George Bush was vice-president and the heir apparent, Pipes continued, "I strongly suspect that George Bush intervened to have Team A substantially revise its draft to allow for Team B's criticism."[48] Given what is known about Bush's directorship of CIA, and

44. Ibid., 4.

45. These differences are summarized in a January 1977 congressional briefing document prepared for the DCI, "DCI Congressional Briefing, Experiment in Competitive Analysis," obtained through FOIA.

46. "Soviet Forces for Intercontinental Conflict Through the Mid-1980s," National Intelligence Estimate, December 21, 1976, 3, obtained through FOIA.

47. Interview with Richard Pipes, August 15, 1990.

48. Richard Pipes, "Team B: The Reality Behind the Myth," *Commentary*, October 1986, 34.

the fact that I have examined nearly three hundred documents, classified and unclassified, and have not seen a single piece of paper documenting any such intervention, I doubt very much that any such intervention by DCI Bush took place.

How much was the NIE changed to respond to Team B's criticisms? Stoertz, the retired CIA official who was the NIO for strategic programs from 1973 to 1980 and the leader of Team A, has said that throughout the process of producing NIEs, changes are constantly being made, as new information comes in, as technologies improve, and as the document wends its way through the bureaucracy, with the aim of reaching consensus wherever possible and clarifying important differences where not. Team A was never a unified group, nor was it intended to be. Air force intelligence chief General Keegan was a vigorous, and sometimes virulent, source of alternative views in the intelligence community for many years. His representative on the chapter team (the group responsible for producing a specific chapter) always reflected his views and fought hard to have those views appear in the NIE.[49] Depending on specific circumstances, NIE 11-3/8 sometimes changed more, sometimes less, during its long gestation. The specific effect of Team B or any other political protuberance on a given year's NIE would be very subtle. To some extent every analyst is influenced by what goes on around him or her in the broader political arena. That is a pervasive phenomenon and was not peculiar to this NIE.

Stoertz does admit that some statements about Soviet intentions were changed in the direction of Team B. Mostly this consisted of deleting statements not based on hard evidence. Stoertz told his analysts to "make sure to include a brief description of the evidence behind your major points. Document your findings very carefully. Don't offer undocumented opinions." When asked, "Didn't you say that every year?" he answered, "Yes, but perhaps not so strongly."[50] According to Stoertz, no changes were made as a result of the Pipes panel's comments on antisubmarine warfare, the Backfire bomber, civil defense, and so forth.[51]

The real question is, How did NIE 11-3/8-76 differ from previous NIEs, and to what extent was any "hardening" due to Soviet actions rather than the hot breath of Team B? Since 1973, each successive NIE showed increasing concern about the scope, vigor, and persistence of Soviet strategic pro-

49. Telephone interview with Howard Stoertz, March 17, 1989; interview with Howard Stoertz, July 23, 1990.
50. Telephone interview with Howard Stoertz, November 14, 1995.
51. Interview with Howard Stoertz, July 23, 1990.

grams. In a Special Intelligence Estimate dated September 10, 1973, the intelligence community warned of "the vigorous pursuit of weapons development programs that portend substantial improvements in Soviet strategic capability."[52] Four months later, in NIE 11-3/8-1973, we read, "The Soviets are now well into a broad range of programs to augment, modernize and improve their forces for intercontinental attack. This new round of programs . . . follows hard on a large-scale sustained deployment effort which left the U.S.S.R. considerably ahead of the U.S. in numbers of ICBM launchers and in process of taking the lead in SLBM [sea-launched ballistic missile] launchers. . . . [A]t least in the field of ICBM development, they represent a breadth and concurrency of effort which is virtually unprecedented."[53] Hardly a complacent assessment!

By November 1975 the NIE warned, "The capability of the Soviet ICBM force to destroy U.S. Minuteman silos is growing. It will probably pose a major threat in the early 1980s. A more rapid increase in this threat is possible but unlikely." The same NIE stated, "We do not doubt that if they thought they could achieve it, the Soviets would try to attain the capability to launch a nuclear attack so effective that the U.S. could not cause devastating damage to the U.S.S.R. in retaliation."[54]

If the Team B exercise had any positive influence on that year's NIE, perhaps it contributed to the more complete documentation of conclusions and more precision in terminology, especially about Soviet doctrine. It also seemed to spell out for the policymaker more clearly the evidence behind the phrase "we believe." In reading over all these NIEs, I was struck by how often the terms "probably," "conceivably," "possibly," "likely," and "almost certainly" appeared. Sherman Kent, the California-bred Yale-trained historian turned intelligence officer who for fifteen years headed the CIA office that produced National Intelligence Estimates, tried to quantify some of these phrases: " 'Almost certain' should denote a 99–87% area of possibility, 'probable,' 87–63%, 'chances about even,' 40–60%, 'probably not,' 40–20% and 'almost certainly not' 12–2%."[55]

52. "Soviet Strategic Arms Programs and Detente: What Are They Up To?" Special Intelligence Estimate 11-4-1973, September 10, 1973, 1, Record Group 263, Folder 57, National Archives.

53. "Soviet Forces for Intercontinental Attack," National Intelligence Estimate 11-8-73, January 25, 1974, 7, Record Group 263, Folder 58, National Archives.

54. "Soviet Forces for Intercontinental Conflict Through the Mid-1980s," National Intelligence Estimate 11-3/8-75, November 17, 1975, 2 and 5, Record Group 263, Folder 60, National Archives.

55. Sherman Kent, "Words of Estimative Probability," in *Sherman Kent and the Board of*

Even before the Pipes panel report was officially presented to PFIAB, the chairman was anxious to publicize its findings. Pipes opened a December 7 meeting of his panel by discussing the possibility of declassifying the Team B report. Since the declassification option was rejected by a CIA official, Pipes said "he would urge PFIAB to make the Team B report available to as large an audience as possible. If his appeal to PFIAB were rejected . . . he mentioned . . . the publication of articles on the general subject of the Team B report without reference to classified information. . . . Pipes also raised the possibility of using the Freedom of Information Act to get the report into the public domain."[56] But as Pipes knew well, the story had already appeared in the press six weeks before, right after the initial exchange of papers between the A and B Teams.

The Leak

On October 20, 1976, William Beecher broke the story about Team B in a front-page story in the *Boston Globe*. Beecher had most of the facts correct: He named Pipes as chairman and Nitze, Graham, Vogt, and Van Cleave as members, omitting Kohler, Weiss, Welch, Wolfe, and Wolfowitz. The article stated that the group was charged with coming up with a parallel NIE executive summary for 1976 by November 7 and recommending ways to "minimize institutional bias in the existing analytical process."

The concluding paragraph of Beecher's story stated that "the Pipes group is believed to be considering moving the staff involved in drawing up the NIE out of CIA headquarters and mak[ing] it directly responsible to the President, rather than the director of Central Intelligence."[57] At that time, all of the recommendations were in draft form. Only one member of Team B, Gen. Daniel Graham, had made that particular recommendation. It seems obvious that he, directly or indirectly, communicated with Beecher.[58]

Most probably there were several leakers. According to the *New York*

National Estimates: Collected Essays, ed. Donald P. Steury (Washington, D.C.: Center for the Study of Intelligence, Central Intelligence Agency, 1994), 133.

56. Donald J. Suda, memorandum for the record, December 7, 1976, obtained through FOIA.

57. William Beecher, "Special Unit Analyzing U.S. Spy Data," *Boston Globe*, October 20, 1976, 1.

58. "Team B Recommendations," Papers of Paul Nitze, Manuscript Division, Library of Congress; interview with Daniel Graham, October 30, 1990.

Times reporter who was scooped on this story, "People on Team B were talking to Gen. George Keegan, who was due to retire in a few months. Keegan, who had an ax to grind, was hanging out with retired army general Danny Graham, the former director of the Defense Intelligence Agency."[59] General Vogt said in interview, "The Team B report was gaining a great deal of credibility in the Defense Intelligence Agency, Air Force Intelligence, etc. I worked with them daily. They thought, great—here's an opportunity to even up some scores with the CIA. Sock it to them!"[60]

As the Pipes B Team was being formed in the late summer, Deputy Director for Intelligence Henry Knoche wrote a farsighted memo to DCI Bush: "Dick Lehmann [national intelligence officer for warning] and Paisley [John Paisley, the CIA liaison with Team B] were not exactly overwhelmed with the idea advanced by Professor Pipes that Danny Graham become a member of the Estimates Evaluation Committee, nor am I. My own concerns go largely to the fact that Danny has not been the most discreet ex-intelligence official around town." However Knoche felt that "it would create very controversial—and perhaps public criticism—if we were to prevent his membership," and so he "reluctantly" agreed "that he should be among those selected." DCI Bush appended a handwritten note: "I do not feel Graham has to be on the panel. I do not think we should be committed to him but I do not object! Use own judgment."[61]

But strangely, Beecher's story was not picked up by other media. However, this first public mention of the existence of Team B caused an incensed CIA director Bush to "storm into" the office of PFIAB chairman Leo Cherne, in the Old Executive Office Building. According to Cherne, it was the first time that he had a personal visit from the DCI. Bush was irate over the leak and suspected it came from PFIAB. Cherne, for his part, felt that "members of PFIAB were sufficiently smart to recognize that any publicity would invalidate what had been a serious effort. I would not be as sure about the members of Team B. Their egos might have felt a sense of loss if the public did not become aware of what they had been doing."[62]

When a one-paragraph story about Team B appeared in *U.S. News and World Report* on November 15, Bush sent it to Cherne with a short letter: "The attached is the kind of publicity that I am sure you would agree is very

59. Interview with David Binder, October 8, 1990.
60. Interview with Gen. John Vogt, October 11, 1990.
61. E. Henry Knoche, note to director [of Central Intelligence], August 30, 1976, obtained through FOIA.
62. Interview with Leo Cherne, May 23, 1990.

damaging. I really don't think there is much we can do about it at this point, but I worry about it."[63] But despite Bush's worry, the story seemed to go largely unnoticed.

As soon as the story appeared in the *Boston Globe*, David Binder, the *New York Times* correspondent covering the intelligence community, called the CIA and was promised that if he didn't write about the Team B exercise until it was completed, he would be given the full story.[64] Binder lost no time in talking to some of his sources. During November, he spoke with Team B members Danny Graham, William Van Cleave, Seymour Weiss, and Tom Wolfe, as well as William Miller and Spencer Davies of the Senate Select Committee on Intelligence, David Aaron of the transition team, about-to-retire General Keegan, Deputy Assistant to the President for National Security Affairs William Hyland, former DCI Colby, and, most important, CIA director Bush.[65]

On November 19, DCI Bush and his deputy, E. Henry Knoche, flew to Plains to brief President-elect Jimmy Carter. During the six-hour meeting Carter apparently turned aside Bush's hint that up to this point CIA directors had not changed with an incoming administration.[66] Immediately thereafter, George Bush, the great foe of leaks, agreed to meet with David Binder of the *New York Times*. The same CIA director who wrote to President Ford in August 1976, "I want to get the CIA off the front pages and at some point out of the papers altogether"[67]—by granting Binder an on-the-record interview—assured that Team B would, indeed, become front-page news. Binder's interview with DCI Bush occurred on November 26 at 2:30 P.M. in Bush's office at CIA headquarters in Langley, and lasted about forty minutes.[68] On the same day, Binder also met with Richard Lehman, director of the Office of Strategic Research at the CIA, to learn about the "nuts and bolts of Team B."[69]

On December 21, the day that all the Teams A and B squared off before

---

63. "Washington Whispers," *U.S. News and World Report*, November 15, 1976, 5, and George Bush, letter to Leo Cherne, November 8, 1976, Leo Cherne Papers, Box 1, Folder: Bush, George, Gerald R. Ford Library, Ann Arbor, Mich.

64. Interview with David Binder, October 8, 1990.

65. Telephone interview with David Binder, October 10, 1990.

66. Bob Woodward and Walter Pincus, "At CIA, a Rebuilder 'Goes with the Flow,'" *Washington Post*, August 10, 1988, 1; Jimmy Carter, handwritten comments on a letter sent to him by the author, December 20, 1990.

67. Pincus and Woodward, "At CIA, a Rebuilder."

68. Daily logs of DCI George Bush, obtained through FOIA. Also interview with David Binder, October 8, 1990.

69. Interview with David Binder, October 8, 1990.

the National Foreign Intelligence Board, Binder interviewed Richard Pipes, who had been his tutor at Harvard, although the two hadn't seen each other in twenty-five years.[70] That meeting took place before Pipes's return to Boston, at the American Airline Admiral's Club at National Airport, and lasted about half an hour.[71] According to Binder, when he met him, "Pipes was jubilant. They had triumphed, they had poked holes at the agency's analyses."[72]

Binder's article was the lead story on the front page of the *New York Times* on Sunday, December 26, "prime time" in the newspaper business. For Binder, the stocky, gravelly-voiced reporter, this was a "big deal." "I hadn't done that for a while," he said.[73] Binder's article quoted "high-ranking officials of the Central Intelligence Agency" saying the NIE "was more somber than any in more than a decade." According to a top-level military intelligence officer, "It was more than somber—it was very grim. It flatly states the judgment that the Soviet Union is seeking superiority over United States forces." Binder quoted DCI Bush as saying, "There are some worrisome signs and the viewpoints, interpretations and comments on these will be adequately reflected in the estimate."[74] The day of Binder's story, Bush appeared on *Meet the Press,* and three separate congressional committees vowed to hold hearings on the whole exercise.

A week later, Murrey Marder's front-page story about Team B appeared in the *Washington Post*. It didn't add much new except that Team B panelists gave a laudatory and self-serving account of their work ("we just licked them on a great number of points"), which exacerbated the overtly political nature of the whole exercise.[75]

The leak was an attempt, first, to produce an "October surprise" and influence the November presidential election. When that failed to materialize, the leakers hoped to influence President-elect Jimmy Carter, an inexperienced Georgia governor. The new administration, however, was not particularly impressed by the Team B report. Indeed, one of Carter's first acts was to abolish PFIAB.

70. Ibid.
71. Interview with Richard Pipes, August 15, 1990.
72. Interview with David Binder, October 8, 1990.
73. Ibid.
74. David Binder, "New CIA Estimate Finds Soviet Seeks Superiority in Arms," *New York Times*, December 26, 1976, 1.
75. Murrey Marder, "Carter to Inherit Intense Dispute on Soviet Intentions," *Washington Post*, January 2, 1977, 1.

Congress Steps In

When the new Congress convened in January 1977, it entered the "Battle of the Estimates." The Senate Intelligence Subcommittee on Collection, Production, and Quality of Intelligence, headed by Senator Adlai E. Stevenson (D-Ill.) announced it would look into the question whether the official estimates were slanted by the Team B experiment. Another inquiry was begun by Senator William Proxmire (D-Wis.) of the Senate Defense Appropriations Subcommittee. The Senate Foreign Relations Committee, in an initiative begun before the Team B dispute, was planning hearings on the U.S.-Soviet strategic balance.[76] Thirteen liberal House members wrote a letter to President-elect Jimmy Carter on January 7, 1977, expressing their concern "with the recent politicization of the analysis process which produces the National Intelligence Estimate." They noted that "[t]he participants on the outside panel unfortunately included several persons who had already developed conclusions on the matter and who are actively engaged in lobbying efforts to shape policy to meet their conclusions."[77]

The Senate Select Committee staff began meeting with Team B participants and CIA officials in mid-February 1977. The initial discussion with Charles Lerch, chairman of the B Team Air Defense Panel, was apparently entirely substantive and friendly.[78] However, the meeting between committee staffers Harold Ford and Ted Ralston and panel chairman Richard Pipes was not as clear-cut.

As Pipes tells it, "When Ford came to see me, he didn't tell me he was working for the Senate Select Committee. I thought he was working for the agency."[79] Ford is sure he told Pipes he was from the committee. He says he and Ralston "were there about an hour. It was all very pleasant. Pipes and I knew each other. I was coordinator for academic relations in the agency. I would gather together some experts, and we met in Boston, or New York or Washington. Pipes came to a couple of those. They were all unclassified. I

76. Murrey Marder, "Congress Enters the Debate on Soviet-U.S. Power," *Washington Post*, January 6, 1977, A4.

77. Congressmen Ronald Dellums, Berkly Bedell, John Burton, William Clay, John Conyers, Don Edwards, Jim Johnson, Michael Harrington, Robert Kastenmeier, Robert Leggett, Parren Mitchell, Richard Ottinger, and Henry Reuss, letter to Governor Jimmy Carter, January 7, 1977, obtained through FOIA.

78. Howard Stoertz, memorandum for chief, Congressional Support Staff, DDI, CIA, February 22, 1977, obtained through FOIA.

79. Interview with Richard Pipes, August 15, 1990.

explained to Pipes I had been out of the agency for over a year."[80] Pipes claimed "the questions were pro forma so [Ford] could say he interviewed me."[81]

By late April CIA officials were responding to a draft Senate Select Committee report on the Team A/Team B experiment.[82] The CIA, not surprisingly, objected to language such as "NIEs inadequately serve the needs of the President and senior policy-makers, . . . fail to set strategic force developments in a broader context, . . . contain subsumed net assessments, . . . reflect a preoccupation with Soviet strategic weapons."[83] A short time later, the new DCI, Adm. Stansfield Turner, enclosed fourteen pages of detailed comments on the draft in a letter to Senator Stevenson.[84]

Angelo Codevilla, Senator Malcolm Wallop's staffer on the Senate Select Committee, alerted Daniel Graham and William Van Cleave about the draft Senate committee report. Codevilla told them the report vilified Team B and was an ad hominem attack on the motivations and qualifications of Team B members. Graham said in interview, "Pipes was accused of having written the whole report before we ever gathered together. I thought Pipes and I ought to take a look at it. Pipes, because he was being vilified; I, because I knew a lot about it. I would not have recommended that Paul Nitze come along, because Nitze and I never got along much."[85] On his next trip to Washington, Van Cleave went to see Senator Wallop and Codevilla to discuss the draft committee report.[86]

In July Pipes wrote to Senator Stevenson: "[E]arlier this year I spent an hour or so discussing the work of 'Team B' with Mr. Hal Ford who is on your staff, but I have not been given an opportunity to see the draft of the study, nor, to the best of my knowledge, has it been seen [by] any other member of 'Team B.'" Pipes requested that he and "perhaps a couple other members of what had been 'Team B'. . . be given the opportunity to read and comment on it."[87] Paul Nitze called Senator Stevenson with a similar request, and

80. Interview with Harold Ford, October 11, 1990.

81. Interview with Richard Pipes, August 15, 1990.

82. Howard Stoertz, memorandum to deputy to the DCI for intelligence, April 28, 1977, obtained through FOIA.

83. Sidney Graybeal, director, Office of Strategic Research, CIA, memorandum to NIO for Special Programs, May 6, 1977, obtained through FOIA.

84. Stansfield Turner, letter to Senator Adlai E. Stevenson, May 11, 1977; William Miller, letter to Howard Stoertz, May 24, 1977; both obtained through FOIA.

85. Interview with Daniel Graham, September 13, 1990.

86. Interview with William Van Cleave, March 9, 1990.

87. Richard Pipes, letter to Senator Adlai Stevenson, July 9, 1977, provided by Gen. Daniel Graham.

soon the committee voted to give Pipes, Nitze, and Graham access to the draft report, although the CIA (with good reason) worried about "unauthorized disclosures."[88]

The draft Senate report was about thirty pages long. Pipes, Graham, and Nitze were aghast at what they read. According to Pipes, the report was scurrilous and "accused [Team B] of coming up with preconceived notions, working with PFIAB, and [implied] that the purpose was to force Carter to increase DOD expenditures."[89] (To me, all three charges ring true.) Pipes left his comments on the draft with Ford and wrote to Senator Inouye that he was "deeply disturbed by the tone of the Report and by the aspersions it casts on the integrity of Team B and the motives of its members."[90]

After seeing the draft report, Nitze wrote Bill Miller, the chief of staff of the Senate committee, "a long memorandum with fifty-odd instances where he was wrong."[91]

The committee staff was told to revise the report. Abe Shulsky, Senator Moynihan's staffer on the committee, flew to Chicago to interview Robert Galvin, chairman of the NIE Evaluation Committee of PFIAB. Galvin confirmed that Team B had not abided by the ground rules that he had helped to set up. Shulsky's criticism of the Senate draft lessened after that.[92] While the draft report was being revised, Pipes and Ford exchanged several "Dear Hal, Dear Dick" letters clarifying such things as dates of the B Team meetings. The revised committee report finally appeared in February 1978. According to Ford, "It was not terribly shortened or terribly different."[93] Graham insisted "he didn't get to look at the revised report before it came out, but it was a lot better."[94]

According to the published report, "The B Team made some valid criticisms of the NIE's, especially concerning certain technical intelligence questions, and some useful recommendations concerning the estimative process, but those contributions were less valuable than they might have been be-

88. Senator Adlai Stevenson, letter to Richard Pipes, July 14, 1977; Senator Daniel Inouye, letter to Richard Pipes, July 25, 1977; both kindly made available by Gen. Daniel Graham. Senator Daniel Inouye, letter to Stansfield Turner, July 20, 1977; Stansfield Turner, letter to Senator Daniel Inouye, August 1, 1977; both obtained through FOIA.

89. Interview with Richard Pipes, August 15, 1990.

90. Richard Pipes, letter to Senator Daniel Inouye, August 7, 1977, provided by Gen. Daniel Graham.

91. Interview with Paul Nitze, March 7, 1990.

92. Interview with Abe Shulsky, August 18, 1989; interview with Harold Ford, October 11, 1990.

93. Interview with Harold Ford, October 11, 1990.

94. Interview with Daniel Graham, September 13, 1990.

cause (1) the exercise had been so structured by the PFIAB and the Director of Central Intelligence that the B Team on Soviet objectives reflected the views of only one segment of the spectrum of opinion; and (2) that Team spent much of its effort on criticizing much earlier NIE's rather than, as had been earlier agreed upon by the PFIAB and the DCI, producing alternative estimates from certain of those of the 1976 NIE."[95]

The report stated that Binder's conclusion "that the B Team challenge turned the NIE 'around 180 degrees' is incorrect." The committee endorsed the use of competitive and alternative analyses but said, "Panels representing only one perspective, whether 'hard' or 'soft,' are not desirable." The NIE was faulted for not addressing "the question of how Soviet strategic weapons development fits into important larger concerns (the entire panoply) of Soviet domestic, military, diplomatic, economic, and cultural efforts. As a consequence, the NIE's discussion of Soviet objectives was too brief to be useful."[96]

Committee members Gary Hart, Daniel Patrick Moynihan, and Malcolm Wallop issued separate views. Predictably, liberal Senator Hart pointed out that "the pro–B Team leak and public attack on the conclusions of the NIE represent but one element in a series of leaks and other statements which have been aimed at fostering a 'worst case' view for the public of the Soviet threat. In turn, this view of the Soviet threat is used to justify new weapons systems."[97]

The more conservative Senator Moynihan endorsed the idea of "calling in outside experts from time to time [as] a healthy corrective against the tendency of any organization to become set in its own way of thinking. The particular panel of experts chosen, however, will always be subject to charges of being 'unrepresentative' or 'biased' by those who do not like its findings, including those in the intelligence community who are, after all, the ones being criticized." Moynihan continued, "The objective standard will be to look at how well one institutional arrangement, or one line of argument, has predicted and explained recent events." He concluded that "[t]he National Intelligence Estimates of the past dozen years have, by and large, failed this test. . . . The B Team report . . . was a credible attempt to place recent developments in a context which makes them more understandable, and

95. Senate Select Committee on Intelligence, Subcommittee on Collection, Production, and Quality, *The National Intelligence Estimates A-B Team Episode Concerning Soviet Strategic Capability and Objectives*, February 16, 1978, 2.
96. Ibid., 3, 5, and 4.
97. Ibid., 8.

which offers the possibility of greater predictive success."[98] We now know that these sentiments did not square with the facts.

Senator Wallop (R-Wyo.) found the committee report "fundamentally flawed" because it made "no attempt to judge which group's estimates concerning the U.S.S.R. [were] correct." However, the Senate committee members were not intelligence estimators and had no mandate or expertise to make that judgment. Wallop sided with Team B in asserting that the Soviet Union rejected the notion of "Mutual Assured Destruction" and was going for "decisive superiority—the capability to fight and win a nuclear war."[99]

Coming more than a year after the experiment was finished, the release of the Senate report did not generate much news coverage. After all, it was yesterday's mashed potatoes! But Team B did not fade from public attention. The panel members were well placed to keep the report's conclusions before the public for the next four years. Through op-ed pieces, radio and television interviews, and the large outreach program of the Committee on the Present Danger, the mantra of the United States falling behind the Soviet Union in military might was repeated over and over again. The fact that the report remained classified for eighteen years made it difficult to refute.

98. Ibid., 10–11.
99. Ibid., 13.

Epilogue

The events in this book took place at the beginning of a great debate in the United States about U.S.-Soviet relations, detente, and national defense. For a quarter century the United States had worried that the Soviet Union was on the road to military superiority. This concern was a major point of Barry Goldwater's presidential campaign in 1964. In the mid-seventies it began to gain force again. This was a time of national shock stemming from America's departure from Vietnam, and heightened Soviet-bloc assertiveness in the Third World. Conservatives became distressed over President Nixon's policy of detente with the USSR and the signing of the Strategic Arms Limitation Talks (SALT) Treaty. They felt that Nixon and Kissinger had understated the Soviet Union's intentions and capabilities and had oversold detente, promising more than was delivered. They feared that detente would deter or weaken support for new U.S. weapons programs. Flagrant Soviet human rights abuses, interventions in the Third World and the expulsion of Aleksandr Solzhenitsyn were also significant factors in creating disillusionment with detente.

Another reason for the demise of detente and the rise of a more militant policy vis-à-vis the Soviet Union was that a weak President Ford, running for reelection and challenged by the Right, showed no leadership and capitulated to the hawks. He abolished the word "detente" from his political vocabulary and ceased trying to get a SALT II agreement negotiated before the 1976 presidential election.

In addition, the CIA was reeling from the onslaughts of DCI Schlesinger on the operational personnel and from the revelations about the "family jewels" to congressional committees. The old consensus about the value and importance of an intelligence organization evaporated, and the agency became vulnerable to a right-wing attack on its intelligence estimates. The rapid turnover in DCIs during that period accentuated the agency's vulnerability.

The CIA's weakness was compounded by the choice of George Bush as the new DCI. Bush, the former chairman of the Republican National Committee, naturally turned to the White House for guidance when faced with the PFIAB request to permit an alternative assessment by outsiders. Whereas DCI Colby, the career CIA man, fought successfully to protect his agency, Bush, the political man with ambitions of his own, capitulated without a struggle. Furthermore, by agreeing to an official interview with David Binder of the *New York Times*, Bush guaranteed that news about the B Teams would become a major media story.

The intelligence community itself was fragmented over the question of the Soviet threat. NIE 11-3/8-76 is riddled with footnotes, denoting dissent from the main text. Widely differing opinions were registered over directed-energy weapons, Soviet military objectives and doctrines, the Backfire bomber, radars and antiballistic missiles, surface-to-air missiles, civil defense, particle-beam-weapons research, Soviet attitudes toward SALT and the ABM Treaties, defense expenditures, and the ICBM force. There was hardly a paragraph in the estimate with which the entire intelligence community concurred.

The primary target of the conservatives always was to destroy detente. Along the way, various subgoals emerged. First was to belittle, besmirch, and tarnish Henry Kissinger, seen as the primary architect of detente. Second was to force the intelligence community to present a more frightening and pessimistic view of Soviet capabilities and intentions, hence the Team B exercise. Next came the bruising battle to oppose the appointment of Paul Warnke as the director of the Arms Control and Disarmament Agency. During those hearings, Nitze, who seemed to take dovishness in others as a personal affront, said he thought he was a better American than Warnke. The closeness of that vote (fifty-eight in favor, forty opposed) signaled the rise of a new militant coalition bent on destroying detente. Later fights revolved around President Jimmy Carter and his attempt to have SALT II ratified. Then in 1980 the battleground shifted to the presidential election, and with Ronald Reagan's election, detente ended and the conservatives finally won.

Team B's Influence

At first it appeared that the Team B story would have a very short hold on the public's attention. The outgoing Ford administration seemed to go out of its way to distance itself from the Team B report. In a farewell interview with Hugh Sidey of *Time* magazine, President Ford was asked, "What are the

Soviet objectives in a nuclear arms race?" He answered, "The Soviet buildup is not a sudden surge. It has been a long-range problem. I don't necessarily think that buildup is for adventures around the world. It is my feeling that they are doing it because they feel it is necessary for their own security."[1] On the same day, Secretary of State Henry Kissinger, at a National Press Club farewell, dismissed Team B as nothing more than an effort to "sabotage SALT II."[2] In his last State of the Union Address, President Ford confidently reaffirmed, "We are maintaining stability in the strategic nuclear balance and pushing back the specter of nuclear war."[3]

The immediate reaction of the incoming Carter administration to Team B was likewise negative. To some on the transition team it looked like blackmail calculated to head off any moves toward more accommodation with the Soviet Union. Carter's DCI, Stansfield Turner, said in interview that the exercise "was not a big thing. I had a lot of other things on my platter."[4] Robert Bowie, Turner's deputy for national intelligence, agreed, and was of the opinion that Team B did not have much impact on the Carter administration. "This was a fight for the soul of the Republican party, for getting control of foreign policy within one branch of the party."[5]

Soon, however, it became clear that the B Teams' viewpoints were gaining currency. When President Carter named Zbigniew Brzezinski as his national security adviser, it was foreordained that detente with the Soviet Union was in for rough times. First came the March 1977 ill-fated arms control proposal, which departed from the Vladivostok Agreement and was leaked to the press before it was presented to the Soviets. By April, Carter was pressing the NATO allies to rearm, demanding a firm commitment from all NATO members to start increasing their defense budgets by 3 percent per year. In the summer of 1977 Carter's Presidential Review Memorandum-10 called for an "ability to prevail" if war should come, wording that smacked of the Team B view. The administration also decided to respond to the deployment of Soviet SS-20 intermediate-range missiles in Eastern Europe by matching them with cruise and Pershing missiles in Western Europe. Before leaving office, Carter sent 35,000 additional troops to Europe, boosting the U.S. contingent

1. "Parting Words from President Ford," interview by Hugh Sidey, *Time*, January 10, 1977, 15.
2. Richard Pipes, "Team B: The Reality Behind the Myth," *Commentary*, October 1986, 25–40.
3. Quoted in Raymond Garthoff, *Detente and Confrontation: American-Soviet Relations from Nixon to Reagan* (Washington, D.C.: Brookings Institution, 1985), 551.
4. Interview with Stansfield Turner, April 7, 1989.
5. Interview with Robert Bowie, December 15, 1989.

to more than 300,000. Stealth technology, microcircuitry, smart bombs, satellite communications, and laser-targeting systems were all initiated in the Carter administration.[6]

The Committee on the Present Danger

Ultimately, however, the major impact of Pipes's Team B was that it provided intellectual fodder for the reconstituted Committee on the Present Danger (CPD), which held its first press conference at the National Press Club in Washington, D.C., with more than a hundred media representatives present, two days after the 1976 presidential election. On that occasion, the committee released its first policy statement, "Common Sense and the Common Danger," which stated that "the principal threat to our nation, to world peace and to the cause of human freedom is the Soviet drive for dominance based upon an unparalleled military buildup. The Soviet Union has not altered its long-held goal of a world dominated from a single center— Moscow."[7]

It is not surprising that these words sound familiar, because Team B members Richard Pipes, Foy Kohler, Paul Nitze, and William Van Cleave became founding board members of the CPD. They, and other CPD members, were disappointed when not a word of the event appeared on television or radio that evening. Nor did a line appear in the *New York Times, Washington Post,* or *Washington Star.* Nitze complained that when the committee was mentioned elsewhere, its members were referred to as "cold warriors," "hawkish," or as representatives of "the military-industrial complex."[8]

In the spring of 1977, the CPD issued a policy statement, "What Is the Soviet Union Up To?" written by Richard Pipes. This time, the response was very different both in extent and tone. AP and UPI filed substantial stories, which were widely reprinted. Many of the major newspapers published favorable companion editorials. Additionally, ABC-TV and CBS-TV carried special interviews with Eugene Rostow and Paul Nitze. More important, now the Committee was described as "a public interest group," "an organization

6. Martin Walker, "Playing the Carter Card," *Washington Post,* June 19, 1994, C2.
7. Charles Tyroler, ed., *Alerting America: The Papers of the Committee on the Present Danger* (Washington, D.C.: Pergamon-Brassey's, 1984), 3.
8. Paul H. Nitze, with Ann M. Smith and Steven L. Rearden, *From Hiroshima to Glasnost: At the Center of Decision, a Memoir* (New York: Grove Weidenfeld, 1989), 359.

comprised of many leading Americans from all segments of the political spectrum," and a "nonpartisan committee."[9]

Over the next three years, the CPD relentlessly repeated and disseminated the views of Team B. The CPD and most of the drafters of the Team B report went on to oppose ratification of SALT II and advocate greatly expanded U.S. military programs. By 1980, Team B members Daniel Graham, Richard Pipes, William Van Cleave, John Vogt, and Seymour Weiss had become key foreign policy advisers to presidential candidate Ronald Reagan. They and the Team B report bolstered Bush's and Reagan's assertions in the 1980 campaign that the Soviets had betrayed the hopes of detente and were bent on attaining nuclear superiority. It was the leaked Team B study that led to the charge during the campaign that the United States had allowed the Soviets to gain nuclear superiority and the call for it to "rearm."[10] With the election of Ronald Reagan, the B Team essentially became the A Team.

Given this track record, it is not surprising that conservatives view the initial exercise with great fondness, despite the fact that all three Team B panels greatly overestimated the prowess of the Soviet Union, both in the short and particularly in the long term. Whenever they are unhappy with existing policies or advisers, sooner or later the call goes out to form another Team B.

Team B Lives On

Kenneth Adelman, who became director of the Arms Control and Disarmament Agency during the Reagan years, wanted Congress to "promote independent rival centers of intelligence collection" and perpetuated the myth that "the now famous Team B . . . reached conclusions on the Soviet threat which have fared far better than those of Team (CI)A's."[11]

Senator Jesse Helms (R-N.C.) has been an ardent defender of Team B. In 1986 he submitted an amendment to the CIA Authorization Bill mandating competitive estimates for thirty-two topics ranging from "the role of Soviet Bloc intelligence services in the international drug trade" to "the possibility

9. Ibid.
10. Robert Scheer, *With Enough Shovels: Reagan, Bush, and Nuclear War* (New York: Vintage Books, 1983), 54.
11. Kenneth L. Adelman, "Intelligence: The Wrong Debate?" *Wall Street Journal*, April 8, 1980, 24.

of Soviet Bloc sabotage being among the human errors causing the Space Shuttle Challenger and other recent U.S. strategic space mission explosions."[12]

On the House side, the Permanent Select Committee on Intelligence in 1990 urged "that the DCI consider forming an independent panel composed of outside authorities—including economists and experts on the Soviet Union—to evaluate the data base and methodologies which historically have been used in formulating estimates of the Soviet economy and defense spending. This panel should consider arguments advanced by both supporters and critics of the system, with the goal of identifying improvements to statistical and qualitative analyses by U.S. intelligence in these areas." However, the paragraph immediately preceding this exhortation states, "[I]t is debatable what impact more accurate intelligence analyses would have had on U.S. policy."[13]

In 1990 Frank Gaffney, a deputy assistant secretary of defense in the Reagan administration, asserted that Team B's analysis "was validated" and wrote, "Now is the time for a new Team B and a clear-eyed assessment of the *abiding* Soviet (and other) challenges that dictate a continued, robust U.S. defense posture" (emphasis added).[14]

As the Soviet Union was disintegrating, Defense Secretary Richard Cheney and DCI William Webster disagreed about the extent to which the Soviet Union remained a military threat. The International Security Council took out an ad in the *New York Times* urging that a new B Team be formed. The ad claimed that the original Team B "not only corrected over a decade's mis-estimation of the size, scope and purpose of Brezhnev's buildup of strategic forces, but also raised the standard of intelligence analysis for a decade."[15]

William Safire is another admirer of Team B and calls for a new Team B every few years. Invited by DCI William Webster to an "on-the-record" luncheon to discuss the latest revisions in estimates of Soviet GNP in 1988, Safire wrote, "Well, isn't it time to set up a Team B, I asked, pocketing an agency ashtray, to present a different view of reality?"[16] A few years later, he

12. Jesse Helms, in *Congressional Record*, September 24, 1986, S 13567.

13. *Intelligence Authorization Act for Fiscal Year 1991*, 101st Cong., 2d sess., September 19, 1990, 10.

14. Frank Gaffney, "Second Opinion on Defense," *Washington Times*, May 8, 1990, F2.

15. International Security Council, "Bring on the B-Team," *New York Times*, July 18, 1990, A21.

16. William Safire, "Through Different Eyes," *New York Times*, April 21, 1988, 31.

suggested that a "prestigious Team B" be formed "to suggest an alternative Russia policy to Mr. Clinton."[17]

The belief that outside experts will improve the quality of intelligence estimates continues unabated. Following the November 1994 election, the Heritage Foundation sponsored a study that urged the United States to launch a crash program to develop global defenses against ballistic missiles. The foundation called the report's authors "Team B" and compared their recommendations to the "self-constrained and go-slow programs of 'Team A' [the Clinton administration]."[18]

Why these recurrent calls for Team Bs? Because the original Team B, with the help of the CPD, is correctly perceived to have played a major role in turning public opinion in the United States against the policy of detente with the Soviet Union. By virtue of the billboard effect of publicizing their views that the Soviet Union was stronger than the United States and getting stronger all the time, that it meant to achieve world domination, that it was the fount and origin of all radical movements around the world, that detente and arms control negotiations were a snare and a delusion, Team B and the CPD prevented the intelligence community and the public from correctly interpreting the many signs of the coming demise of the Soviet Union. That is the real legacy of Team B.

The Legacy of Inflated Threat Assessments

The indicators of deep problems in the Soviet Union were numerous and obvious. Beginning in the mid-1960s American Sovietologists became aware of severe problems in the Soviet economy. As early as 1966 a study prepared for the congressional Joint Economic Committee reported that "both official Soviet data and Western estimates show a marked decline in the rate of growth of industrial production in the U.S.S.R."[19] In 1968 Egon Neuberger predicted that "[t]he centrally planned economy eventually would meet its

---

17. William Safire, "Needed: A 'Team B,' " *New York Times*, March 10, 1994, 25.

18. "Defending America: A Near and Long-Term Plan to Deploy Missile Defenses" (Heritage Foundation, Washington, D.C., 1995), 1.

19. "New Directions in the Soviet Economy," studies prepared for the Joint Economic Committee, 89th Cong., 2d sess., 1966, 275.

demise, because of its demonstrably growing ineffectiveness as a system for managing a modernizing economy in a rapidly changing world."[20]

Murray Feshbach at the Foreign Demographic Analysis Division of the Bureau of the Census, in his yearly submissions to the Joint Economic Committee and elsewhere, pointed to the adverse demographic trends that began in the late 1960s.[21] The decline in the rate of growth of oil production was known, as were the fuel shortages. In 1974 Marianna Slocum wrote that "shortfalls of fuel energy and raw materials are escalating, . . . and the Soviet Union is faced with an energy crisis."[22] This article was widely circulated; all members of the President's Foreign Intelligence Advisory Panel received copies.

It was also public knowledge that Soviet agriculture was a catastrophe, with annual shortfalls of millions of tons of grain. By the 1970s, according to Gertrude E. Schroeder, Sovietological discussion focused "on the clearly worsening plight of the Soviet economy and the dilemmas it posed for the political leadership. By then the growth retardation was old news, as were the ever-higher costs by which even reduced growth was being achieved." The analysts within and outside the government "accurately portrayed the Soviet economy as one with secularly deteriorating performance and under increasing strain, especially after 1970. The large and growing technological and qualitative lags behind the West were also identified."[23]

Through testimony before the Joint Economic Committee, at academic conferences and symposia, in periodicals, books, and speeches, Sovietologists described the worsening economic situation in the Soviet Union. But they weren't the only ones drawing attention to the economic weakness within the Soviet Union. Senator Henry Jackson (D-Wash.), the conservative foe of detente and advocate of increased U.S. military spending, addressing a

20. Egon Neuberger, "The Legacies of Central Planning," RM 5530-PR, Rand, June 1968, quoted in Gertrude E. Schroeder, "Reflections on Economic Sovietology," *Post-Soviet Affairs* 11 (July–September 1995): 197–234.

21. Murray Feshbach, "Employment," in Joint Economic Committee, *Annual Economic Indicators for the USSR*, February 1964, 43–65; "Employment," in Joint Economic Committee, *Current Economic Indicators for the USSR*, July 1965, 63–90; "Manpower in the USSR: A Survey of Recent Trends and Prospects," in Joint Economic Committee, *New Directions in the Soviet Economy*, July 1966, 703–88; "Population," in Joint Economic Committee, *Economic Performance and the Military Burden in the Soviet Union*, September 1970, 60–70; "Labor Constraints in the USSR," in Joint Economic Committee, *Soviet Economic Prospects for the Seventies*, July 1973, 485–563.

22. Marianna Slocum, "Soviet Energy: An Internal Assessment," *Technology Review* 77, no. 1 (1974): 17–33.

23. Schroeder, "Reflections on Economic Sovietology," 219 and 226.

dinner at the University of Florida in Gainesville in November 1973, said, "The growth of the Soviet economy—the means by which the Soviet Union has so long been hoping to 'overtake and surpass' the U.S.—has begun to falter badly. . . . The inflexible Soviet economy has found it increasingly difficult to assimilate modern technology. Even massive infusion of their own capital no longer promises to sustain economic growth."[24]

Former secretary of defense Melvin Laird, surely no dovish liberal, wrote in 1974:

> By any assessment the Soviet economy is in trouble. The growth rate of Soviet productivity has been declining. Her technological industries, so vital in today's world, have shown a marked incapacity to come up with economical, efficient and innovative products. The loss of the "moon race," which was felt very acutely by the Soviets, is but one indicator of this. The wheat deal . . . was forged to save the Soviets from the results of a disastrous agricultural program. The availability of consumer goods in the Soviet Union is still among the lowest of the developing nations.[25]

What about Soviet dissidents inside the Soviet Union? What were they saying about conditions in their homeland, and were these views available in the United States? The most prominent dissident, Andrei Sakharov, in Memorandum No. 2, addressed to Brezhnev, Kosygin, and Podgorny in 1970, wrote:

> The more novel and revolutionary the aspect of the economy, the wider becomes the rift between the USA and ourselves. We are ahead . . . in the production of coal but behind them in the production of oil, gas, and electric power, ten times behind in chemistry and immeasurably behind in computer technology. The latter is especially essential, for the introduction of electronic computers into the national economy is of decisive importance which could radically change the face of the system of production and culture in general. . . . The total capacity of our computers is hundreds of times less than in the USA, and as for the use of electronic computers in

---

24. Henry M. Jackson speech, University of Florida Blue Key Dinner, November 16, 1973, Box 10, Folder 92, Henry M. Jackson Papers, University of Washington Libraries.

25. Melvin Laird, "Let's Not Fool Ourselves About U.S.-Soviet Detente," *Reader's Digest* 104, no. 622 (1974): 57–60.

the national economy, here the rift is so enormous that it is impossible to measure. We are simply living in a different era.

Sakharov pointed out that despite the fact that the USSR was the first to launch a sputnik and the first to send a man into space, the United States won the race to the moon, and according to Sakharov, "This is one of the outward signs of an essential and ever-growing gap." As a result, the Soviet Union could "gradually revert to the status of a second-rate provincial power." This memo was publicly disclosed in 1973.[26]

So in the mid-1970s, at the time of Team B, it was clear that the Soviet economy was running out of steam and was being dragged into stagnation and decline. Everyone who visited the Soviet Union came back with reports of empty grocery-store shelves, busses and trucks constantly breaking down, and nonfunctioning elevators, so that the most desirable apartments or offices were not in the penthouse but on the ground floor. Despite declining growth rates, shortages of goods and services, and recurrent poor harvests, Team B looked only at the military sector and noted that military power, military research and development, and military foreign trade were increasing. And even here, we now know that this sector, too, began to falter at that time. As Soviet defectors were telling us in anguished terms that the system was collapsing, Team B looked at the quantity but not the quality of missiles, tanks, and planes, at the quantity of Soviet men under arms, but not their morale, leadership, alcoholism, or training.

By 1976, lots of information was also available about the political and social factors within the Soviet Union. Prominent dissident Andrei Amalrik wrote:

> There is another powerful factor which works against the chance of any kind of peaceful reconstruction and which is equally negative for all levels of society: this is the extreme isolation in which the regime has placed both society and itself. This isolation has not only separated the regime from society, and all sectors of society from each other, but also put the country in extreme isolation from the rest of the world. This isolation has created for all—from the bureaucratic elite to the lowest social levels—an almost surrealistic picture of the world and of their place in it. Yet the longer this state

26. Quoted in I. F. Stone, "The Sakharov Campaign," *New York Review of Books*, October 18, 1973, 3–6.

of affairs helps to perpetuate the status quo, the more rapid and decisive will be its collapse when confrontation with reality becomes inevitable.

Amalrik predicted the collapse of the regime would occur between 1980 and 1985.[27]

In February 1976, Secretary of State Henry Kissinger cabled all European diplomatic posts: "There are serious underlying pressures and tensions in the Soviet system itself. The base from which imperialism asserts itself has serious problems in the economic and social sectors. There are also internal nationalist groups which are growing. Non-Russian nationalist groups in Russia are growing at a disproportionally faster rate, which will add to these tensions in the base whence springs Soviet imperialism."[28]

All of these political and economic indicators and conditions, were, of course, well known to analysts in the intelligence community, but what we now take to be some pretty obvious conclusions to be drawn from these data were not taken seriously then. This was partly because the Soviet military sector was just beginning to slow down in 1975 and, more important, because the consequences of underestimating the Soviets were so much more dire than the consequences of overestimation.

No one can state that the official intelligence community analyses were without defect or totally accurate. The "group-think" that exists to some extent in all bureaucracies certainly made it very difficult for anyone in 1976 to contemplate the collapse of the Soviet Union. It is a fact that analysts and other experts who have been deeply engrossed in a certain field of study for a long time are hard-pressed to conceive of discontinuities. They tend to imagine the future as a bounded version of the present, about which they know so much. That is why alternative estimates have a place.

If the Pipes Team B had undertaken an honest effort to conduct an impartial assessment of the threat posed by the Soviet Union, it would have deserved respect. If that Team B had looked at the same evidence as Team A and then specified on what points their interpretations of the evidence differed from those of Team A, it would have deserved praise. If a "C" team of experts with a more liberal approach had been granted the same access as

27. Andrei Amalrik, *Will the Soviet Union Survive Until 1984?* (New York: Harper & Row, 1970), 33.

28. Henry Kissinger, "U.S. Policy Toward USSR and Eastern Europe," cable to all European Diplomatic Posts, February 1976, Gerald R. Ford Library, Ann Arbor, Mich., obtained under mandatory review.

Team B, then the experiment might have deserved repetition. But Team B failed these tests.

It is true, of course, that the Soviet Union was repressive and expansion-ist. But Team B insisted that there was a continuous Soviet increase, when, in fact, in 1975 the growth of Soviet military spending declined sharply, from 4–5 to 2 percent, and procurement of weapons was flat. Conservatives used the allegations of a continuous, dangerous Soviet buildup to justify a real American and NATO buildup in the late 1970s and early 1980s.

Conservatives have made much of the purported impact of the Reagan military buildup in making Soviet leaders realize that they could not win an arms race with the United States. A more likely explanation is that the Soviets accepted the ABM Treaty, the SALT I Interim Agreement, SALT II, the INF Treaty, and START I and II because their leaders saw that neither side could win a lasting victory in a nuclear arms race and that neither country could survive a nuclear war.

More important, we, the American people, paid dearly for our military buildup. In the 1980s we spent over a trillion and a half dollars on defense. In the 1980s we turned ourselves into a debtor nation to pay for those arms. In the 1980s we allowed our education system to cease functioning for mil-lions of students, our health-care system to neglect millions of citizens, our cities, roads, and bridges to deteriorate, our drinking water to become unsafe, our family life to become dependent on two wage earners—all this to counter the threat of a nation that was itself collapsing.

Appendix:
CIA Directors and Their Tenures

Sidney W. Souers	January 1946–June 1946
Hoyt S. Vandenberg	June 1946–May 1947
Roscoe H. Hillenkoetter	May 1947–October 1950
Walter Bedell Smith	October 1950–February 1953
Allen W. Dulles	February 1953–November 1961
John A. McCone	November 1961–April 1965
William F. Raborn Jr.	April 1965–June 1966
Richard Helms	June 1966–February 1973
James R. Schlesinger	February 1973–July 1973
William E. Colby	September 1973–January 1976
George Bush	January 1976–January 1977
Stansfield Turner	March 1977–January 1981
William J. Casey	January 1981–January 1987
William H. Webster	May 1987–August 1991
Robert M. Gates	November 1991–January 1993
R. James Woolsey	February 1993–January 1995
John M. Deutch	May 1995–December 1996

Glossary

ABM: Antiballistic missile.

ABM Treaty: Antiballistic missile treaty signed in 1972, limited each side to two defensive sites.

ACDA: Arms Control and Disarmament Agency.

AFL-CIO: American Federation of Labor–Congress of Industrial Organizations.

ASM: Air-to-surface missile.

ASW: Antisubmarine warfare.

AWACS: Airborne Warning and Control System, a flying command post with the capability to detect hostile radar systems and aircraft and to direct friendly forces.

Backfire bomber: A Soviet supersonic bomber of the 1970s, whose range and mission became a controversial issue.

BNE: Board of National Estimates.

CEP: Circular error probability, a measure of missile accuracy that refers to the radius of the circle around the target within which 50 percent of the warheads aimed at that target will fall.

CIA: Central Intelligence Agency, established in 1947.

Coalition for a Democratic Majority: A conservative committee formed in 1972 to back the presidential quest of Senator Henry Jackson.

counterforce targeting: Directing military strategies, attacks, or weapons against an opponent's military forces, command posts, and other war-fighting targets.

CPD: Committee on the Present Danger, originally formed in 1950, reconstituted in 1976 to oppose the policy of detente with the Soviet Union.

cruise missile: A pilotless, jet-propelled guided missile.

CSCE: Conference on Security and Cooperation in Europe, a thirty-five-nation conference held in 1975 that produced agreements on human rights, economics, and confidence-building measures such as notification of major military maneuvers.

DCI: Director of Central Intelligence.

DDCI: Deputy director of Central Intelligence, second person in line of command at the CIA.

DDI: Directorate for Intelligence, created in 1952, responsible for production of intelligence and for collection of overt information.

DDP: Directorate for Plans, created in 1952, also known as the "Clandestine Service"; responsible for clandestine collection, counterintelligence, and covert operations; renamed the Directorate for Operations in 1973.

DDR&E: Directorate of Defense Research and Engineering.

Defense Science Board: A Department of Defense advisory board.

DIA: Defense Intelligence Agency, created by Secretary of Defense Robert McNamara in 1961, responsible for production of military intelligence.

equivalent megatonnage: A technical term used to compare different forces by estimating the total area on which they could inflict structural damage.

"family jewels": The name given to an internal CIA document detailing many of the serious charges brought against the agency in the 1970s.

Gaither Report: A threat assessment written in 1957 that warned of a "missile gap" and said 1959 was year of "maximum danger"; remained classified until 1973.

hard targets: Targets, such as land-based missiles, that are protected against the blast, heat, and radiation effects of nuclear weapons.

Hudson Institute: A conservative think tank.

ICBM: Intercontinental ballistic missile.

INR: Bureau of Intelligence and Research, the State Department's intelligence analysis unit.

intelligence community: Consists of all the intelligence services in the U.S. government, including Army, Navy, and Air Force Intelligence, the Defense Intelligence Agency, the National Security Agency, the Bureau of Intelligence and Research in the State Department, and the counterintelligence unit of the FBI.

IOC: initial operational capability, when the first unit becomes operational in field forces.

Jackson-Vanik amendment: Blocked all trade advantages for the Soviet Union until emigration from that country was liberalized; remained in effect for twenty years.

linkage: The attempt to reward appropriate Soviet behavior in international matters with most-favored-nation (MFN) trade status, technology transfers, and generous access to credits from the Export-Import Bank.

MAD: Mutual Assured Destruction, the official targeting policy of the United States during the Cold War.

MFN: Most-favored nation, provides for nondiscriminatory trade, rather than favored treatment; nations not granted MFN are subject to tariffs designed to inhibit trade.

Minuteman missile: The mainstay of the American missile force in the 1960s.

MIRV: Multiple independently targetable reentry vehicle; two or more warheads are carried by a single missile and deliverable to separate targets.

MRV: Multiple targetable reentry vehicle; two or more warheads are carried by a single missile but released almost simultaneously so they fall on or near the same target.

MX missile: A highly accurate ten-warhead U.S. intercontinental ballistic missile.

NATO: North Atlantic Treaty Organization.

Neocons: Neoconservatives, former liberals concerned that America's post-Vietnam anti-interventionist mood combined with an eagerness to curry favor with Moscow would make the United States a less staunch defender of Israel.

net assessment: A comparison of the relative military postures of two opponents.

NFIB: National Foreign Intelligence Board, successor to the U.S. Intelligence Board; a senior interagency body responsible for coordinating intelligence activities among the intelligence agencies.

NIE: National Intelligence Estimate, a predictive judgment of the capabilities, vulnerabilities, and actions of foreign nations; includes both current *knowledge* and *predictions* of what will happen within a given future period, usually five or sometimes ten years; represents the composite view of the intelligence community.

NIOs: National Intelligence Officers, a senior group of analysts, organized in 1973 to replace ONE; responsible for the management of intelligence collection and production.

NSC: National Security Council, established in 1947, the senior decision-making body in the executive branch; consists of the president, the vice president, the secretaries of state and defense, the chairman of the Joint Chiefs of Staff, and the national security adviser.

NSC 68: A comprehensive U.S. national security review written in 1950 just after the Soviets exploded their first nuclear bomb; it designated 1954 as the "year of maximum danger."

ONE: Office of National Estimates, established in 1950 to produce National Intelligence Estimates; abolished in 1973.

OSS: Office of Strategic Services, precursor to CIA, established during the Second World War and abolished after the war.

PNET: Peaceful Nuclear Explosion Treaty, limited nuclear explosions used for peaceful purposes to 150 kilotons; signed by President Ford and General Secretary Brezhnev in May 1976.

PFIAB (pronounced "piffy-ab"): President's Foreign Intelligence Advisory Board, the official watchdog over the intelligence community.

RAND Corporation: A think tank formed by the Air Force after the Second World War.

Rockefeller Commission: Officially, the Commission on CIA Activities Within the U.S., created by President Ford in 1975, after revelations of illegal CIA activities.

RV: Reentry vehicle, the part of a ballistic missile containing a nuclear warhead and designed to reenter the earth's atmosphere in the final portion of the missile's trajectory.

Safeguard: The U.S. antiballistic missile system briefly deployed in Grand Forks, North Dakota, in the 1970s.

SALT I: Strategic Arms Limitation Talks; signed in 1973, it limited the number of offensive intercontinental ballistic missiles to 1,410 land-based missiles and 950 submarine-launched missiles on the Soviet side, and 1,000 land-based missiles and 710 submarine-launched weapons on the U.S. side.

SAM: Surface-to-air missile.

Sentinel: The original name given to a proposed antiballistic system in 1967 to defend fifteen U.S. cities; changed to the Safeguard system by the Nixon administration in 1969.

SLBM: Submarine-launched ballistic missile.

SRAM: Short-range attack missile, a nuclear air-to-surface missile designed to attack ground targets and suppress enemy air defenses.

SS-9: A Soviet intercontinental ballistic missile of the 1970s.

SS-19: A Soviet intercontinental ballistic missile originally thought to be accurate enough to be a silo or "hard-target" killer; estimates of its accuracy were lowered in 1985 by over one-third.

SS-20: A mobile triple-warhead Soviet intermediate-range missile deployed in Eastern Europe in the 1970s.

SSBN: Strategic nuclear ballistic missile submarine.

telemetry: Electronic signals transmitted from a missile during a flight test that provide information about the missile's performance.

throw weight: The lift capacity of a missile, which determines what weight and number of warheads it can carry.

USIB: U.S. Intelligence Board, an interdepartmental body established in 1958, chaired by the director of Central Intelligence; members are representatives from the Defense Intelligence Agency, Army, Navy, and Air Force intelligence branches, the State Department, the FBI, the Department of Energy, and the National Security Agency; superseded by the National Foreign Intelligence Board (see NFIB).

Verification Panel: An interagency high-level group formed in July 1969 to ascertain whether Soviet compliance with various arms control proposals could be verified by U.S. intelligence.

Vladivostock Agreement: A joint statement outlining a framework for SALT II, signed by President Ford and General Secretary Brezhnev in November 1974.

Warsaw Treaty Organization, or Warsaw Pact: An Eastern European security alliance formed in 1955; its members included the USSR, Bulgaria, Czechoslovakia, East Germany, Hungary, Poland, and Romania.

Watergate: Originally referred to the June 1972 break-in at the Democratic Party's national headquarters in the Watergate complex of apartments and office buildings in Washington, D.C.; former and present CIA employees were arrested; ensuing revelations of wiretapping, burglary, violations of campaign-financing laws, and the attempted use of government agencies to harm political opponents resulted in the resignation of President Richard Nixon in 1974.

Bibliography

Books and Chapters

Amalrik, Andrei. *Will the Soviet Union Survive Until 1984?* New York: Harper & Row, 1970.

Ashton, S. R. *In Search of Detente: The Politics of East-West Relations Since 1945.* New York: St. Martin's Press, 1989.

Barnet, Richard J. *The Giants: Russia and America.* New York: Simon & Schuster, 1977.

Berkowitz, Bruce D. *American Security: Dilemmas for a Modern Democracy.* New Haven: Yale University Press, 1986.

Berkowitz, Bruce D., and Allan E. Goodman. *Strategic Intelligence for American National Security.* Princeton: Princeton University Press, 1989.

Bialer, Seweryn. *The Soviet Paradox: External Expansion, Internal Decline.* New York: Knopf, 1986.

Bock, Joseph G. *The White House Staff and the National Security Assistant: Friendship and Friction at the Water's Edge.* New York: Greenwood Press, 1987.

Brands, H. W. *The Devil We Knew: Americans and the Cold War.* New York: Oxford University Press, 1993.

Breckinridge, Scott D. *The CIA and the U.S. Intelligence System.* Boulder, Colo.: Westview Press, 1986.

Bush, George, with Victor Gold. *Looking Forward.* Garden City, N.Y.: Doubleday, 1987.

Caldwell, Dan. *American-Soviet Relations from 1947 to the Nixon-Kissinger Grand Design.* Westport, Conn.: Greenwood Press, 1981.

Codevilla, Angelo. "Comparative Historical Experience of Doctrine and Organization." In *Intelligence Requirements for the 1980s: Analysis and Estimates,* edited by Roy Godson. New Brunswick, N.J.: Transaction Books, 1980.

Colby, William, and Peter Forbath. *Honorable Men: My Life in the CIA.* New York: Simon & Schuster, 1978.

Cox, Arthur Macy. *Russian Roulette: The Superpower Game.* New York: Times Books, 1982.

Dionne, E. J., Jr. *Why Americans Hate Politics.* New York: Simon & Schuster, 1991.

Dobrynin, Anatoly. *In Confidence: Moscow's Ambassador to America's Six Cold War Presidents (1962–1986).* New York: Times Books, 1995.

Fain, Tyrus G. *The Intelligence Community: History, Organization, and Issues.* New York: R. R. Bowker, 1977.

Fitzgerald, A. Ernest. *The Pentagonists: An Insider's View of Waste, Mismanagement, and Fraud in Defense Spending.* Boston: Houghton Mifflin, 1989.

Ford, Gerald. *A Time to Heal: The Autobiography of Gerald R. Ford.* New York: Harper & Row, 1979.

Foreign Relations of the United States, 1950. Washington, D.C.: GPO, 1950.

Freedman, Lawrence. *U.S. Intelligence and the Soviet Strategic Threat*. 2d ed. Princeton: Princeton University Press, 1986.

Gaddis, John Lewis. *The United States and the End of the Cold War*. New York: Oxford University Press, 1992.

Garthoff, Raymond. *Detente and Confrontation: American-Soviet Relations from Nixon to Reagan*. Washington, D.C.: Brookings Institution, 1985.

Gelman, Harry. *The Brezhnev Politburo and the Decline of Detente*. Ithaca, N.Y.: Cornell University Press, 1984.

Godson, Roy, ed. *Intelligence Requirements for the 1980s: Analysis and Estimates*. New Brunswick, N.J.: Transaction Books, 1980.

Halliday, Fred. *The Making of the Second Cold War*. London: Verso, 1983.

Hersh, Seymour M. *The Price of Power: Kissinger in the Nixon White House*. New York: Summit Books, 1983.

Hershberg, James. *James B. Conant: Harvard to Hiroshima and the Making of the Nuclear Age*. New York: Knopf, 1993.

Hyland, William G. *Mortal Rivals: Superpower Relations from Nixon to Reagan*. New York: Random House, 1987.

Isaacson, Walter. *Kissinger: A Biography*. New York: Simon & Schuster, 1992.

Jeffreys-Jones, Rhodri. *The CIA and American Democracy*. New Haven, Conn.: Yale University Press, 1989.

Johnson, Loch K. *America's Secret Power*. New York: Oxford University Press, 1989.

Kalb, Marvin, and Bernard Kalb. *Kissinger*. Boston: Little, Brown, 1974.

Kaldor, Mary. *The Disintegrating West*. London: Allen Lane, Penguin Books, 1978.

Kampelman, Max M. *Entering New Worlds: The Memoirs of a Private Man in Public Life*. New York: Harper Collins, 1991.

Kent, Sherman. "Words of Estimative Probability." In *Sherman Kent and the Board of National Estimates: Collected Essays*, edited by Donald P. Steury. Washington, D.C.: Center for the Study of Intelligence, Central Intelligence Agency, 1994.

Kissinger, Henry. *The White House Years*. Boston: Little, Brown, 1979.

———. *Years of Upheaval*. Boston: Little, Brown, 1982.

Krepon, Michael. *Strategic Stalemate: Nuclear Weapons and Arms Control in American Politics*. New York: St. Martin's Press, 1984.

LaFeber, Walter. *The American Age: United States Foreign Policy at Home and Abroad Since 1750*. New York: W. W. Norton, 1989.

Locher, Frances C., ed. *Contemporary Author*. Vols. 97–100. Detroit: Gale Research, 1981.

McCormick, Thomas J. *America's Half-Century: United States Foreign Policy in the Cold War*. Baltimore: Johns Hopkins University Press, 1989.

Menges, Constantine C. *The Twilight Struggle: The Soviet Union v. the United States Today*. Washington, D.C.: AEI Press, 1990.

Nitze, Paul H. *Tension Between Opposites: Reflections on the Practice and Theory of Politics*. New York: Charles Scribner's Sons, 1993.

Nitze, Paul H., with Ann M. Smith and Steven L. Rearden. *From Hiroshima to Glasnost: At the Center of Decision, a Memoir*. New York: Grove Weidenfeld, 1989.

Nixon, Richard M. *The Real War*. New York: Warner Books/Random House, 1980.

Nolan, Janne. *Guardians of the Arsenal: The Politics of Nuclear Strategy*. New York: Basic Books, 1989.

Ognibene, Peter J. *Scoop: The Life and Politics of Henry M. Jackson*. New York: Stein & Day, 1975.

Powers, Thomas. *The Man Who Kept the Secrets: Richard Helms and the CIA*. New York: Pocket Books, 1979.

Prados, John. *The Soviet Estimate: U.S. Intelligence Analysis and Soviet Strategic Forces*. Princeton: Princeton University Press, 1986.

Ranelagh, John. *The Agency: The Rise and Decline of the CIA*. New York: Simon & Schuster, 1986.

Richelson, Jeffrey. *The U.S. Intelligence Agency*. Cambridge, Mass.: Ballinger, 1985.

Rosefielde, Steven. *False Science: Underestimating the Soviet Arms Buildup*. New Brunswick, N.J.: Transaction Books, 1982.

Sanders, Jerry W. *Peddlers of Crises*. Boston: South End Press, 1983.

Scheer, Robert. *With Enough Shovels: Reagan, Bush, and Nuclear War*. New York: Vintage Books, 1983.

Stern, Paula. *Water's Edge: Domestic Politics and the Making of American Foreign Policy*. Westport, Conn.: Greenwood Press, 1979.

Stubbing, Richard A. *The Defense Game*. New York: Harper & Row, 1986.

Talbott, Strobe. *The Master of the Game: Paul Nitze and the Nuclear Peace*. New York: Knopf, 1988.

Tyroler, Charles, ed. *Alerting America: The Papers of the Committee on the Present Danger*. Washington, D.C.: Pergamon-Brassey's, 1984.

Walker, Martin. *The Cold War: A History*. New York: Henry Holt, 1993.

Wise, David. *The American Police State: The Government Against the People*. New York: Random House, 1976.

Journal and Magazine Articles

Aerie, Edward [pseud.]. "Dollarizing the Russian Forces." *The Nation*, July 23, 1977.

Alsop, Joseph. "The Challenge America Must Meet." *Reader's Digest* 107, no. 640 (1975).

"Arming to Disarm in the Age of Detente." *Time*, February 11, 1974.

Aspin, Les. "Debate over U.S. Strategic Forecasts: A Mixed Record." *Strategic Review* 8 (summer 1980).

———. "How to Look at the Soviet-American Balance." *Foreign Policy* 22 (spring 1976).

Berkowitz, Bruce D. "Intelligence in the Organization Context: Coordination and Error in National Estimates." *Orbis* 29, no. 3 (1985).

Brownlow, Cecil. "CIA Threat-Juggling Confirmed." *Aviation Week and Space Technology*, May 3, 1976.

Burnham, James. "Too Much Intelligence." *National Review*, July 4, 1975.

Cahn, Anne Hessing. "Team B: The Trillion-Dollar Experiment." *Bulletin of Atomic Scientists* 49, no. 3 (1993).

Callen, Earl, and Edward A. Stern. "Abuses of Scientific Exchanges." *Bulletin of Atomic Scientists* 31, no. 2 (1975).

Chace, James. "The Kissinger Years: A Gravely Flawed Foreign Policy." *New Republic*, November 9, 1974.

"The CIA's Goof in Assessing the Soviets." *Business Week*, February 28, 1977.

Clark, Joseph. "Notes on Detente." *Dissent* 21 (summer 1974).

Diamond, Edwin. "Time Warner Marches On." *New York*, May 21, 1990.

Draper, Theodore. "Detente" and "Appeasement and Detente." *Commentary*, June 1974.

———. "The Enemy Within." *Progressive*, February 1975.

"Evgeny Levich—An Appeal." *Bulletin of Atomic Scientists* 29, no. 10 (1973).

Flanagan, Stephen. "Managing the Intelligence Community." *International Security* 10, no. 1 (1985).

Flieger, Howard. "Loose-Fitting Cap." *U.S. News and World Report*, December 23, 1974.

Ford, Gerald. "Parting Words from President Ford." Interview by Hugh Sidey. *Time*, January 10, 1977.

Gates, Robert. "The CIA and American Foreign Policy." *Foreign Affairs* 66, no. 2 (1987–88).

Gordon, Michael R. "CIA Downgrades Estimate of Soviet SS-19." *National Journal*, July 20, 1985.

Herling, John. "George Meany and the AFL-CIO." *New Republic*, October 4, 1975.

Holst, Johan Jorgen. "What Is Really Going On?" *Foreign Policy* 19 (summer 1975).

Holzman, Franklyn. "Are the Soviets Really Outspending the U.S. on Defense?" *International Security* 4, no. 4 (1980).

———. "Politics and Guesswork." *International Security* 14, no. 2 (1989).

Jacobsen, Sally. "On the Freedom of Emigration." *Bulletin of Atomic Scientists* 30, no. 2 (1974).

Karnow, Stanley. "Jackson's Bid: Walking the Long Road to the White House." *New Republic*, May 25, 1974.

Kiernan, Vincent. "Russians: Site Tested Rockets, Not Beam Weapon." *Space News*, October 12–18, 1992.

"Kissinger on Balance." *New Republic*, March 30, 1974.

Kornbluh, Peter, and James G. Blight. "Dialogue with Castro: A Hidden History." *New York Review of Books*, October 6, 1994.

Laird, Melvin R. "Is This Detente?" *Reader's Digest* 107, no. 639 (1975).

———. "Let's Not Fool Ourselves About U.S.-Soviet Detente." *Reader's Digest* 104, no. 622 (1974).

———. "Let's Stop Undermining the CIA." *Reader's Digest* 108, no. 649 (1976).

Long, F. A. "Should We Buy the Vladivostok Agreement?" *Bulletin of Atomic Scientists* 31, no. 2 (1975).

Lourie, Richard. "Soviet Dissidents and Balance of Power." *Dissent* 21 (winter 1974).

Millar, James R., et al. "Survey Article: An Evaluation of the CIA's Analysis of Soviet Economic Performance, 1970–90." *Comparative Economic Studies* 35, no. 2 (1993).

Morris, Roger. "Solzhenitsyn with a Grain of SALT." *New Republic*, August 16 and 23, 1975.

Nacht, Michael L. "The Delicate Balance of Error." *Foreign Policy* 19 (summer 1975).

Nitze, Paul H. "Assuring Strategic Stability in an Era of Detente." *Foreign Affairs* 54, no. 2 (1976).

Noren, James H. "The Controversy over Western Measures of Soviet Defense Expenditures." *Post-Soviet Affairs* 11 (July–September 1995).

"No Time to Say Hello, Goodby." *New Republic*, July 26, 1975.

Osborne, John. "Arming Up." *New Republic*, December 14, 1974.

Pipes, Richard. "Team B: The Reality Behind the Myth." *Commentary*, October 1986.

Podhoretz, Norman. "Making the World Safe for Communism." *Commentary*, April 1976.

Powers, Thomas. "Choosing a Strategy for World War III." *Atlantic Monthly*, November 1982.

Richelson, Jeffrey T. "Old Surveillance, New Interpretation." *Bulletin of Atomic Scientists* 42, no. 2 (1986).

Robinson, Clarence A. "Cabinet Shifts May Speed SALT." *Aviation Week and Space Technology*, November 10, 1975.

Schlesinger, James R. "The Continuing Challenge to America." *Reader's Digest* 108, no. 648 (1976).

Schroeder, Gertrude E. "Reflections on Economic Sovietology." *Post-Soviet Affairs* 11 (July–September 1995).

Slocum, Marianna. "Soviet Energy: An Internal Assessment." *Technology Review* 77, no. 1 (1974).

Solzhenitsyn, Aleksandr. "No More Concessions!" *Reader's Digest* 107, no. 642 (1975).

Stoertz, Howard. Letter to the editor. *Commentary*, March 1987.

Stone, I. F. "The Sakharov Campaign." *New York Review of Books*, October 18, 1973.

Szulc, Tad. "Pentagon Cool." *Washingtonian Magazine* 10, no. 1 (1974).

Teller, Edward. "Arms Deal: A Defense." *U.S. News and World Report*, December 30, 1974.

Treverton, Gregory F. "Estimating Beyond the Cold War." *Defense Intelligence Journal* 3, no. 2 (1994).

"Washington Whispers." *U.S. News and World Report*, November 15, 1976.

Wheelon, Albert. "History of PFIAB." *Periscope* 10, no. 3 (1985).

Wohlstetter, Albert. "Is There a Strategic Arms Race?" *Foreign Policy* 15 (summer 1974).

———. "Legends of the Strategic Arms Race, Part I: The Driving Engine." *Strategic Review* 2 (fall 1974).

———. "Optimal Ways to Confuse Ourselves." *Foreign Policy* 20 (fall 1975).

———. "Rivals but No 'Race.' " *Foreign Policy* 16 (fall 1974).

———. "The Uncontrolled Upward Spiral." *Strategic Review* 3 (winter 1975).

Newspaper Articles

Achenbach, Joel. "So It Was a Fair Race . . . and We Won." *Washington Post*, July 1, 1994.

Adelman, Kenneth L. "Intelligence: The Wrong Debate?" *Wall Street Journal*, April 8, 1980.

Akmentine, Osvalds. "A 'Miserable' Treaty." Letter. *New York Times*, July 25, 1975.

Alsop, Joseph. "The CIA Analysts: Changes at the Top." *Washington Post*, February 23, 1973.

Bartlett, Kay. "Letting Light into the Lobby Club." *Milwaukee Journal*, July 7, 1974.

Beecher, William. "Special Unit Analyzing U.S. Spy Data." *Boston Globe,* October 20, 1976.

Binder, David. "New CIA Estimate Finds Soviet Seeks Superiority in Arms." *New York Times,* December 26, 1976.

Blumenthal, Sidney. "Richard Perle's Nuclear Legacy: An Acolyte's Education and the Passing of the Torch." *Washington Post,* November 24, 1987.

Bradsher, Henry S. "CIA Uncovers Soviet Arms Shift." *Washington Star,* February 15, 1976.

————. "Quality Intelligence Analysis: The Key Factor That Ford Ignored." *Washington Star,* February 19, 1976.

————. "Soviet Arms Spending Accelerating Yearly." *Washington Star,* February 16, 1976.

Brinkley, Douglas. "The Unexpected President." *Washington Post Book World,* February 6, 1994.

Charlton, Linda. "Drive for Stronger U.S. Defense." *International Herald Tribune,* April 5, 1977.

"The CIA's Goof in Assessing the Soviets." *Business Week,* February 28, 1977.

Daly, Christopher B. "Ex-Director Faults CIA of Carter Era." *Washington Post,* December 3, 1994.

Delaney, William. "Trying to Awaken Us to Russia's 'Present Danger.' " *Washington Star,* April 4, 1977.

"European Security and Real Detente." *New York Times,* July 21, 1975.

"Ex-Im Bank Lets Soviets Borrow $180 Million at 6%." *Wall Street Journal,* May 22, 1974.

Finney, John W. "SS-9 Helps Administration Score Points in Missile Debate." *New York Times,* March 24, 1969.

Gaffney, Frank. "Second Opinion on Defense." *Washington Times,* May 8, 1990.

Goodman, Melvin A. "We Need Two C.I.A.'s." *New York Times,* July 21, 1994.

Gordon, Michael R. "Pentagon Reassesses Soviet Bomber." *New York Times,* October 1, 1985.

Gwertzman, Bernard. "Democrats Score Nixon on Detente." *New York Times,* August 1, 1974.

————. "Solzhenitsyn Says 'Ford Joins in Eastern Europe's Betrayal.' " *New York Times,* July 22, 1975.

Herbers, John. "Ford, Brezhnev Agree to Curb Offensive Nuclear Weapons; Final Pact Would Run to 1985." *New York Times,* November 25, 1974.

"Himalayan Confrontation?" Editorial. *New York Times,* August 1, 1971, Week in Review.

Horrock, Nicholas. "1973 Arms Cover-up Is Laid to Kissinger." *New York Times,* December 18, 1975.

International Security Council. "Bring on the B-Team." *New York Times,* July 18, 1990.

Jackson, Henry. "First, Human Detente." *New York Times,* September 9, 1973.

Jehl, Douglas. "Clinton Frees Russia from Curbs on Trade." *New York Times,* September 21, 1994.

Kenworthy, Tom. "Eyeball-to-Eyeball at SAC Headquarters." *Washington Post,* February 14, 1990.

Klose, Kevin. "Bearing Witness in a New Europe." *Washington Post,* November 25, 1990.

Klurfeld, Jim. "A New View on Nuclear War." *Newsday,* June 15, 1981.

Kraft, Joseph. "The Limits of Detente." *Washington Post,* August 7, 1975.

Krauthammer, Charles. "Goodbye, Monroe Doctrine." *Washington Post,* August 2, 1994.

Lippman, Thomas W. "McNamara Writes Vietnam Mea Culpa." *Washington Post,* April 9, 1995.

Lippman, Thomas W., and Bradley Graham. "Helms Offers Bill to Force U.S. out of ABM Treaty." *Washington Post,* February 8, 1996.

Marder, Murrey. "Carter to Inherit Intense Dispute on Soviet Intentions." *Washington Post,* January 2, 1977.

———. "Congress Enters the Debate on Soviet-U.S. Power." *Washington Post,* January 6, 1977.

Oberdorfer, Don. "Report Saw Soviet Buildup for War." *Washington Post,* October 12, 1992.

"On the Money." *Pine Bluff Commercial,* September 15, 1975.

Pincus, Walter. "Ex-CIA Chief Backs Smaller Spy Agency." *Washington Post,* December 10, 1994.

Pincus, Walter, and R. Jeffrey Smith. "Costs Linked to CIA Data Under Study." *Washington Post,* November 2, 1995.

Pipes, Richard. "An Answer from 'Team B.'" *Washington Post,* January 9, 1977.

Reston, James. "Soviets Invoke Helsinki." *New York Times,* August 13, 1975.

Rostow, Eugene V. "Defining Detente in Terms of the United Nations Charter." *New York Times,* April 27, 1974.

"Rules for Coexistence." *New York Times,* May 30, 1972.

Safire, William. "Needed: A 'Team B.'" *New York Times,* March 10, 1994.

———. "Through Different Eyes." *New York Times,* April 21, 1988.

Schlesinger, Arthur M. "The Price of Detente." *Wall Street Journal,* September 27, 1973.

Schweber, S. S. "The Hawk from Harvard." *Washington Post Book World,* February 6, 1994.

"Spurring the Arms Race." *New York Times,* December 4, 1974.

"State Dept. Summary of Remarks by Sonnenfeldt." *New York Times,* April 6, 1976.

"Symbolic Journey . . ." *New York Times,* July 27, 1975.

"Transcript of the President's News Conference on Foreign and Domestic Affairs." *New York Times,* April 19, 1969.

"U.S. Negotiator on Arms Quits, Citing the Effects of Watergate." *New York Times,* June 15, 1974.

"Vladivostok Arms Pact." *New York Times,* November 29, 1974.

Walker, Martin. "Playing the Carter Card." *Washington Post,* June 19, 1994.

Weiner, Tim. "CIA's Chief Says Russians Duped the U.S." *New York Times,* December 9, 1995.

———. "Military Accused of Lies over Arms." *New York Times,* June 28, 1993.

Whalen, Richard J. "The Ford Shakeup: Politics vs. Policy." *Washington Post,* November 9, 1975.

Wilson, George C. "U.S. Said to Lead Soviets in Arms." *Washington Post,* August 17, 1975.

Wohlstetter, Albert. "Clocking the Strategic Arms Race." *Wall Street Journal,* September 24, 1974.

Woodward, Bob, and Walter Pincus. "At CIA, a Rebuilder 'Goes with the Flow.' " *Washington Post*, August 10, 1988.

Woodward, Bob, and Patrick E. Tyler. "Officials Hope Gates Will Bring Calm to CIA." *Washington Post*, April 10, 1986.

Congressional Hearings and Reports

"Allocation of Resources in the Soviet Union and China—1983." Hearings before the Subcommittee on International Trade, Finance, and Security Economics of the Joint Economic Committee. 98th Cong., 1st sess., pt. 9, June 28 and September 20, 1983.

"Allocation of Resources in the Soviet Union and China—1985." Hearings before the Subcommittee on Economic Resources, Competitiveness, and Security Economics of the Joint Economic Committee. 99th Cong., 2d sess., pt. 11, March 19, 1986.

Cherne, Leo. Statement before House Select Committee on Intelligence, December 12, 1975.

Chwat, John Steven. "The President's Foreign Intelligence Advisory Board: An Historical and Contemporary Analysis (1955–1975)." Library of Congress, Congressional Research Service, Manuscript Division, November 13, 1975.

"Deterrence and Survival in the Nuclear Age: Report to the President of the Security Resources Panel of the Science Advisory Committee." November 7, 1957. Printed for the use of the Joint Committee on Defense Production, 94th Cong., 2d sess., 1975.

Feshbach, Murray. "Employment." In Joint Economic Committee, *Annual Economic Indicators for the USSR*, February 1964.

———. "Employment." In Joint Economic Committee, *Current Economic Indicators for the USSR*, July 1965.

———. "Labor Constraints in the USSR." In Joint Economic Committee, *Soviet Economic Prospects for the Seventies*, July 1973.

———. "Manpower in the USSR: A Survey of Recent Trends and Prospects." In Joint Economic Committee, *New Directions in the Soviet Economy*, July 1966.

———. "Population." In Joint Economic Committee, *Economic Performance and the Military Burden in the Soviet Union*, September 1970.

Helms, Jesse. In *Congressional Record*, September 24, 1986.

Intelligence Authorization Act for Fiscal Year 1991. 101st Cong., 2d sess., September 19, 1990.

Kohler, Foy. "Soviet 'Peaceful Coexistence' Is Not Western 'Detente.' " Testimony before Subcommittee for Europe, House Committee on Foreign Affairs, May 15, 1974.

"New Directions in the Soviet Economy." Studies prepared for the Joint Economic Committee, 89th Cong., 2d sess., 1966.

Rosefielde, Steven. "The Validity of the CIA's Ruble and Dollar Estimates of Soviet Defense Spending." Testimony prepared for the Subcommittee on Oversight of the House Permanent Select Committee on Intelligence. 96th Cong., 2d sess., September 3, 1980.

Sakharov, Andrei. "An Open Letter to the Congress of the United States from Andrei Sakharov." September 14, 1973. Reprinted in Senate Committee on Finance, *The Trade Reform Act of 1973, Hearings,* 93d Cong., 2d sess., 1974.

Wohlstetter, Albert. Testimony before the Senate Armed Services Committee on ABM. 91st Cong., 1st sess., April 23, 1969. *Congressional Record,* 115, pt. 8:10956.

"United States/Soviet Military Balance: A Frame of Reference for Congress." Library of Congress, Congressional Research Service, 94th Cong., 2d sess., January 1976.

U.S. Congress. Joint Economic Committee. *Hearings: Allocation of Resources in the Soviet Union and China, 1975.* 94th Cong., 2d sess., June 18 and July 21, 1975.

U.S. Senate Armed Services Committee. *Nomination of George Bush to Become Director of Central Intelligence.* 94th Cong., 1st sess., January 6, 1976. S. Rept. 94-21.

U.S. Senate Select Committee on Intelligence. Subcommittee on Collection, Production, and Quality. *The National Intelligence Estimates A-B Team Episode Concerning Soviet Strategic Capability and Objectives.* February 16, 1978.

U.S. Senate Select Committee to Study Governmental Operations with Respect to Intelligence Activities. Final report, bk. 1, "Foreign and Military Intelligence." 94th Cong., 2d sess., 1976.

U.S. Senate Select Committee to Study Governmental Operations with Respect to Intelligence Activities. Final report, bk. 4. 94th Cong., 2d sess., April 23, 1976.

Congressional Record. July 19, 1994.

Unpublished Reports and Papers

Bush, George. Letter to Leo Cherne. December 31, 1975.

Cahn, Anne Hessing. "Eggheads and Warheads: Scientists and the ABM." Ph.D. diss., Center for International Studies, Massachusetts Institute of Technology, Cambridge, Mass., 1971.

Cunningham, Kevin Roy. "Scientific Advisers and American Defense Policy: The Case of the Defense Science Board." Ph.D. diss., University of Michigan, 1991.

"Defending America: A Near and Long-Term Plan to Deploy Missile Defenses." Heritage Foundation, Washington, D.C., 1995.

Face the Nation. Transcript. January 2, 1977.

Ford, Harold P. "Estimative Intelligence: The Purposes and Problems of National Intelligence Estimating." Defense Intelligence College, Washington, D.C., 1989.

————. "The U.S. Government's Experience with Intelligence Analysis: Pluses and Minuses." August 1994.

Humphrey, Hubert H. Letter to Leo Cherne. February 10, 1976.

Inouye, Daniel, Senator. Letter to Richard Pipes. July 25, 1977.

Kennedy, David M. "Sunshine and Shadow: The CIA and the Soviet Economy." Case study, Intelligence and Policy Program, Kennedy School of Government, Harvard University, 1991.

Luce, Clare Boothe. Letter to Leo Cherne. December 29, 1975.

Lundberg, Kirsten. "CIA and the Fall of the Soviet Empire: The Politics of 'Getting It Right.' " C16-94-1251.0, case study of the Kennedy School of Government, Harvard University, 1994.

———. "The SS-9 Controversy: Intelligence as Political Football." Case study of the Kennedy School of Government, Harvard University, 1989.

Neuberger, Egon. "The Legacies of Central Planning." RM 5530-PR, Rand, June 1968.

Olmer, Lionel. "Watchdogging Intelligence." In "Seminar on Command, Control, Communications, and Intelligence." Center for Information Policy Research, Harvard University, 1980.

Pipes, Richard. Letter to Senator Adlai Stevenson. July 9, 1977.

Price, Victoria S. "The DCI's Role in Producing Strategic Intelligence Estimates." Naval War College Center for Advanced Research, January 1980.

Rumsfeld, Donald H. Letter to Leo Cherne. January 5, 1976.

Schlesinger, James. Letter to Senator John L McClellan, chairman, Senate Appropriations Defense Subcommittee. October 23, 1975.

Shultz, George P. Letter to Leo Cherne. December 22, 1975.

Stevenson, Adlai, Senator. Letter to Richard Pipes. July 14, 1977.

Teller, Edward. "The Advantages of Vladivostok." Paper submitted to U.S. News and World Report, December 16, 1974.

Weiss, Seymour. "Competitive Intelligence Analysis: Team B." n.d.

Freedom of Information Documents

Air Force:

Keegan, George. Letter to William Colby, November 21, 1975.

Central Intelligence Agency:

Acting Chief, Office of Strategic Research (OSR). Memorandum to chief, Congressional Support Staff Center for Policy Support. March 14, 1977.

Attachment to Henson DeBruler briefing memorandum for the director of Central Intelligence. June 2, 1976.

Bush, George. Daily logs of Director of Central Intelligence George Bush.

———. Letter to Gen. George Keegan. July 16, 1976.

———. Letter to Leo Cherne. July 13, 1976.

———. Memorandum for chairman, President's Foreign Intelligence Advisory Board. January 19, 1977.

———. Memorandum for recipients of National Intelligence Estimate 11-3/8-76, "Soviet Forces for Intercontinental Conflict Through the Mid-1980s." January 7, 1977.

Carver, George A. Memorandum for Mr. Knoche, Admiral Murphy, and Mr. Proctor. May 5, 1976.

———. Memorandum for the record. June 30, 1976.

———. Memorandum to director of Central Intelligence. April 24, 1976.

———. Note for the director [of Central Intelligence]. May 26, 1976.

CIA chronology of Team B events. n.d.

Colby, William. Letter to George Anderson, comments on George Anderson's August 8, 1975, letter to President Ford. December 2, 1975.

————. Letter to John E. Rielly. July 25, 1974.

————. Letter to President Gerald Ford. May 18, 1974.

————. Letter to President Gerald Ford. November 21, 1975.

"DCI Congressional Briefing, Experiment in Competitive Analysis." January 1977.

DeBruler, Henson. Briefing note for the director of Central Intelligence. June 2, 1976.

————. Memorandum for the record. August 8, 1975.

————. Memorandum for the record. September 15, 1975.

————. Memorandum for the record. December 8, 1975.

————. Memorandum for the record. April 28, 1976.

"Documents Compiled for John Paisley's Project." September 3, 1976.

Galvin, Robert. Letter to George A. Carver. December 11, 1975.

Gambino, Robert W., director of security. Memorandum to director of Central Intelligence. August 25, 1976.

Graham, Daniel. Memorandum to Director of Central Intelligence William Colby. July 1, 1974.

Graybeal, Sidney, director, Office of Strategic Research, CIA. Memorandum to NIO for Special Programs. May 6, 1977.

"The 'Great Debate': Soviet Views on Nuclear Strategy and Arms Control." CIA Intelligence Report, August 1975.

Hewitt, Robert L., Dr. John Ashton, Dr. John H. Milligan. "The Track Record in Strategic Estimating: An Evaluation of the Strategic National Intelligence Estimates, 1966–1975." February 6, 1976.

Knoche, E. Henry. Note to director [of Central Intelligence]. August 30, 1976.

Lehman, Richard. Memorandum for the record. November 4, 1976.

"Material Hand-Carried to Richard Pipes." Undated CIA list indicating all materials were returned by September 29, 1976.

Memorandum for the record. December 11, 1975.

Memorandum for the record. December 17, 1975.

Memorandum for the record. March 10, 1976.

"More on the Military Estimates." *Studies in Intelligence* 19, no. 2 (1975).

Paisley, John. Memorandum for deputy director of Central Intelligence. August 11, 1976.

————. Memorandum for Richard Lehman, deputy to the director of Central Intelligence for National Intelligence. September 21, 1976.

————. Memorandum to Daniel Sullivan. August 20, 1976.

————. Memorandum to Henson DeBruler. June 10, 1976.

"Soviet Forces for Intercontinental Conflict Through the Mid-1980s." National Intelligence Estimate. December 21, 1976.

"Soviet Low Altitude Air Defense: A Team Briefing to PFIAB." n.d.

Stoertz, Howard. Memorandum for chief, Congressional Support Staff, DDI, CIA. February 22, 1977.

————. Memorandum for Robert Galvin. December 23, 1975.

————. Memorandum to deputy to the director of Central Intelligence for Intelligence. April 28, 1977.

————. "Observations on the Content and Accuracy of Recent National Intelligence Estimates on Soviet Strategic Forces (NIE 11-3/8)." Memorandum. July 25, 1978.

Suda, Donald J. Memorandum for the record. August 19, 1976.
———. Memorandum for the record. December 7, 1976.
———. "Summary of 4th Meeting of Team B on 15 September 1976."
"Summary of B Team Findings—Low Altitude Air Defense." Undated briefing paper.
"Summary of Intelligence Community ('A Team') Briefing to PFIAB on Soviet ICBM
        Accuracy." n.d.
Talking paper for the director of Central Intelligence, NSC meeting, January 13, 1977.
Turner, Stansfield. Letter to Senator Adlai E. Stevenson. May 11, 1977.
———. Letter to Senator Daniel Inouye. August 1, 1977.
"Wohlstetter, Soviet Strategic Forces, and National Intelligence Estimates." *Studies in
        Intelligence* 19, no. 1 (1975).

Department of State:

"Politburo Approval of Summit: Warmer Than July." Cable. November 1974.
Sonnenfeldt, Helmut. Memorandum for Secretary of State Kissinger. July 22, 1975.
"The Soviets Look at the Vladivostok Summit." Cable. November 1974.

National Security Council:

Kissinger, Henry. Memorandum to Director of Central Intelligence William Colby. Sep-
        tember 8, 1975.

The White House:

Cherne, Leo. Letter to George Bush. June 8, 1976.
Memorandum of conversation. March 26, 1974.
Memorandum of conversation. March 27, 1974.
Olmer, Lionel. Memorandum for the record. June 30, 1976.
———. Memorandum to PFIAB members. December 27, 1976.

Other FOIA Sources:

Dellums, Ronald, Berkly Bedell, John Burton, William Clay, John Conyers, Don Edwards,
        Jim Johnson, Michael Harrington, Robert Kastenmeier, Robert Leggett, Parren
        Mitchell, Richard Ottinger, and Henry Reuss, congressmen. Letter to Governor
        Jimmy Carter. January 7, 1977.
Inouye, Daniel, Senator. Letter to Stansfield Turner. July 20, 1977.
"Intelligence Community Experiment in Competitive Analysis: Soviet Strategic Objec-
        tives: An Alternative View, Report of Team 'B,' December 1976."
"Memorandum for Chairman, President's Foreign Intelligence Advisory Board, 'Recom-
        mendations of Team B—Soviet Strategic Objectives.' " n.d.
Miller, William. Letter to Howard Stoertz. May 24, 1977.
Pipes, Richard, William Van Cleave, Daniel Graham, Paul Nitze, Seymour Weiss, and
        Paul Wolfowitz. "Recommendations of Team 'B'—Soviet Strategic Objectives."
        Memorandum for chairman of PFIAB. n.d.

"Soviet ICBM Accuracy: An Alternative View." Intelligence Community Experiment in
    Competitive Analysis, Report of Team "B." December 1976.
"Soviet Low Altitude Air Defense: An Alternative View." Report of Team "B." Intelli-
    gence Community Experiment in Competitive Analysis. December 1976.

Archives

Clare Boothe Luce Papers, Manuscript Division, Library of Congress.
George Kistiakowsky Papers, Harvard University Archives.
The George Meany Memorial Archives, Silver Spring, Maryland.
Gerald R. Ford Library, Ann Arbor, Michigan.
Henry M. Jackson Papers, University of Washington Libraries.
National Archives, Washington, D.C.
Paul Nitze Papers, Manuscript Division, Library of Congress.
Richard Nixon Presidential Papers, National Archives, Washington, D.C.

Polls

Gallup Organization, May 1973.
Gallup Organization, April 1974.
Louis Harris and Associates, December 1974.
Roper Organization, July 1974.
Gallup Organization and Louis Harris and Associates, December 1974.

Interviews

Unless otherwise noted, all interviews were conducted in person.
William Bader, telephone, October 23, 1990.
William Beecher, September 29, 1989.
Bruce Berkowitz, February 7, 1989.
David Binder, October 8, 1990; telephone, October 10, 1990.
Robert Bowie, December 15, 1989.
David Branwein, telephone, January 16, 1990.
Jimmy Carter, handwritten comments on a letter sent to him by the author, December
    20, 1990.
George A. Carver, January 17, 1990.
Leo Cherne, telephone, May 23, 1990; August 2, 1990.
Ray Cline, October 3, 1989.
William Colby, August 9, 1989; August 18, 1989; September 17, 1990.
Lynn Davis, telephone, October 9, 1990.
James Digby, September 8, 1990; letter to the author, September 20, 1990.
James Drake, May 10, 1990.

Sidney D. Drell, letter to the author, October 5, 1990.
Ken Fertig, telephone, September 11, 1990.
Noel Firth, January 11, 1990.
Charles Floweree, April 17, 1990.
Harold Ford, August 5, 1989; October 11, 1990; October 29, 1990.
John Foster, May 9, 1990; telephone, September 1, 1990.
Richard Foster, January 16, 1990.
Joseph Fromm, telephone, September 27, 1990, and October 17, 1993.
Alton Frye, November 1, 1990.
Robert Galvin, September 24, 1990.
Raymond Garthoff, February 10, 1989.
James Goodby, February 9, 1990.
Sanford Gottlieb, telephone, July 14, 1994.
Daniel Graham, September 13 and October 30, 1990.
Sidney Graybeal, April 28, 1989; November 11, 1990.
William Harris, telephone, June 1, 1990.
Roland Herbst, May 10, 1990.
Charles Herzfeld, June 26, 1990.
Hans Heymann, October 11, 1990; telephone, September 7 and 8, 1995.
Richard Holbrooke, telephone, July 9, 1993.
Arnold Horelick, telephone, June 12, 1990.
John Huizenga, November 27, 1990.
William G. Hyland, September 26, 1989.
Adm. Bobby Inman, May 4, 1989.
John S. Jensen, letter to the author, November 11, 1993.
Gerald Johnson, May 17, 1990.
T. K. Jones, May 4, 1990.
Jay Kalner, July 20, 1989.
Richard Kaufman, February 14, 1989.
E. Henry Knoche, January 25, 1990; letter to the author, September 27, 1990.
William Krimer, telephone, December 4, 1990.
Richard Latter, telephone, February 28, 1990, and August 12, 1993.
Richard Lehman, telephone, April 4, 1990.
Jan Lodal, telephone, October 23, 1989.
Mark Lowenthal, February 8, 1989.
Gordon MacDonald, April 20, 1989.
Robert MacFarlane, October 18, 1989.
Stephen Miller, July 25, 1989.
William Miller, July 25, 1989; telephone, March 6, 1990.
Roger Molander, October 5, 1989.
Adm. Daniel Murphy, November 9, 1989.
Michael Nacht, March 11, 1989.
Paul Nitze, March 7, 1990.
Lionel Olmer, November 8, 1990.
Richard Pipes, August 15, 1990; letters to the author, October 5 and 17, 1990.
Anthony Pocarro, telephone, April 22, 1991.

John Prados, telephone, March 8, 1989.

Edward Proctor, January 3, 1990; November 2, 1990.

Ted Ralston, telephone, May 23, 1990.

Peter Scop, written answers to submitted questions, June 26, 1990.

William and Harriet Scott, January 31, 1990.

Abe Shulsky, August 18, 1989.

Walter Slocombe, October 4, 1989; telephone, October 23, 1990.

Helmut Sonnenfeldt, March 9, 1990.

John Steinbruner, November 21, 1988; November 29, 1990.

Sayre Stevens, February 21, 1990.

Ronald Stivers, October 24, 1989.

Howard Stoertz, March 15, 1989; August 14 and 15, 1989; July 23, 1990; telephone, March 17, 1989, and November 6 and 14, 1995.

Chuck Stowe, telephone, October 24, 1990.

Stansfield Turner, April 7, 1989.

William Van Cleave, March 9, 1990.

Gen. John Vogt, October 11, 1990.

Seymour Weiss, February 21, 1990.

Gen. Jasper Welch, March 13, 1990.

Sam Wells, November 16, 1989.

Fred Wikner, October 30, 1990.

Paul Wolfowitz, July 23, 1990.

Index

Aaron, David, 178
ABM treaties, 7, 18–19, 20, 50, 51, 63, 64, 102, 112, 186
ABMs (Anti-Ballistic Missiles), 7, 15, 50, 94, 95, 96, 129, 166–67
ACDA (Arms Control and Disarmament Agency), 19–20
Adelman, Kenneth, 189
Afghanistan, 69, 165
AFL-CIO, 32, 36–38, 55
Agnew, Spiro, 79, 98
"Agreed Statements" (SALT and ABM treaties), 64
Agreement on the Prevention of Nuclear War, 49, 51
Agreement on the Prevention of War, 31
Air Defense Panel, 141–44
Air Force Intelligence, 15, 91, 173
Air Force Systems Command, 94
Allen, Richard, 27, 30
Allende, Salvador, 54, 75, 79
Allison, Royal B., 20
Alsop, Joseph, 65, 83
Amalrik, Andrei, 69, 194–95
American Psychiatric Association, 35
American Security Council, 29
Americans for Democratic Action, 45
Ames, Aldrich, 1
Amitay, Morris, 44
Anderson, George W., Jr., 101, 113
  background of, 104
  on composition of PFIAB, 103
  on creation of parallel NIE, 112
  criticisms of NIE, 115–16, 130
  objections to NIE 11-8-73, 110
  on suppression of intelligence by Kissinger, 22
Angola, 47, 53, 54, 55–57, 68, 165
Anti-Ballistic Missiles. See ABMs
antisubmarine warfare. See ASW
"Arms Competition and Strategic Doctrine" (conference), 11–14

arms control. See ABM treaties; *entries beginning with* SALT; Soviet Union: compliance with arms control
Arms Control and Disarmament Agency (ACDA), 19–20
arms race
  American public opinion about, 68
  consequences of, 1–2
  conservatives' view of, 53, 196
  decade-of-neglect argument and, 67–68
  Ford on, 46
  Jackson on, 18, 61
  parity in, 62, 67
  SANE and, 35
  Soviet versus U.S. superiority debate, 64–69
  Wohlstetter on, 11–13, 64–65, 109
Army Intelligence, 15, 173
Ashton, John, 128
assassination schemes, 75, 79–81, 102
ASW (antisubmarine warfare), 116, 126–27, 147
Atlantic Charter, 58

B-1 bombers, 19, 49, 142, 144
B-52 bombers, 142, 159
Backfire bombers, Soviet, 159, 164–65, 179, 186
Bader, William, 11, 13
Baker, William O., 101, 102, 104
Barnett, Frank, 29
Baroody, William, 98
Bartley, Robert, 9, 10–11
Basic Principles of Relations Between the United States of America and the Union of Soviet Socialist Republics, 51, 54
Beecher, William, 156, 176–77
Berkowitz, Bruce, 90
Bialer, Seweryn, 68–69
Biemiller, Andrew, 37, 43
Binder, David, 161, 178–79, 183, 186
BNE (Board of National Estimates), 98, 106, 107

Board of Consultants on Foreign Intelligence Activities, 100–101
Board of National Estimates (BNE), 98, 106
Boston Globe, 176
Bowie, Robert, 14, 187
Bradsher, Henry S., 136
Brands, H. W., 36
Brett, John, 144
Brezhnev, Leonid, 1, 7, 21, 22, 40, 42, 46, 190, 193
    and Ford, 57–58, 60
    reaction to on Jackson-Vanik amendment, 44
    reasons for support of detente, 18
    talks with Kissinger, 8–9, 56
    wheat trade and, 37
Brzezinski, Zbigniew, 187
Buckley, William F., 80
building-block method, 132–34
Bulletin of Atomic Scientists, 42, 62
Bureau of Intelligence and Research, 15, 89, 98, 172
Bush, George H. W., 53, 178–79, 189
    on adversarial positions, 171–72
    Binder interview with, 179, 186
    briefing on track record study, 130
    Carter and, 84
    as CIA DCI, 122, 123, 124, 130, 137, 153, 160, 162, 185–86
    CIA information support for Team B and, 157
    communication with Cherne, 139, 151, 152, 155, 161, 177–78
    communication with Keegan, 155
    Graham and, 177
    Hyland and, 139
    PFIAB and, 102, 138
    response to Team A/B final reports and, 160–62, 171, 173–74
    support for competitive threat assessment, 127
    support for parallel NIE experiment, 139
    support for Team A, 160
    Team A/B final reports and, 159–60
    Team B and, 151, 155, 157, 160–62
Byers, Wheaton, 103, 117, 118

Cabell, Charles Pease, 90
California Arms Control Seminar, 11
Cambodia, 2, 34, 52, 57, 152, 156
Canavan, Gregory, 167

Carter, James E. (Jimmy), 88, 144, 154, 155, 162, 178, 180, 182, 188
    abolishment of PFIAB, 102, 179
    Bush and, 84
    CIA and, 92
    defense policy of, 49
    in 1976 elections, 28, 158
    Presidential Review Memorandum-10, 187
    reaction to Team B report, 187
    SALT II and, 186
Carver, George, 139
    CIA ground rules for Team A/B and, 152
    on function of intelligence estimates, 124–25
    on parallel NIE, 131
    at PFIAB, NSC, CIA meeting, 117–18
    support for parallel NIE, 138
    track record study and, 128, 130
Casey, William J., 30, 45, 84
Castro, Fidel, 75, 79
CENTO, 33
Central Intelligence Agency. *See* CIA
CEP (circular error probability), 93–94, 145, 146–47, 159
Chaiken, Sol, 27
Chain, John T., 163–64
Cheney, Richard, 123, 190
Cherne, Leo, 101, 111, 125
    Bush communication with, 151, 152, 155, 161, 177–78
    on conservatives' view of arms race, 53
    as member of PFIAB, 110
    PFIAB time logs of, 103, 104
    on proposed parallel NIE process, 139
    on Team B experiment, 160
Chicago Council on Foreign Relations, 15
Chile, 54, 75
China, 3, 49, 55
CIA Authorization Bill, Team B-inspired amendments to, 189–90
CIA (Central Intelligence Agency), 1–2, 15–16, 22. *See also* Schlesinger, James: as CIA DCI; Team A
    assassination schemes of, 75, 79–80, 102
    attacks on analysts of, 82–85
    building-block methodology of, 132–34
    congressional concerns with, 81–82, 181
    covert activities report, 78–81
    creation of, 70
    critics of, 71–72 (*see also* NIEs [National Intelligence Estimates])

decline of consensus support for, 71–73
Directorate for Plans, 76, 78
directors of, 76, 84, 185–86, 197 (*see also*
    names of individual directors)
estimations of Soviet military expenditures,
    132–37, 167–68
"family jewels" secrets of, 79–80, 102
Foster and, 114–15
ground rules for parallel NIE, 152–55, 182
Hughes-Ryan amendment and, 56
Inspector General's Report of 1967 and, 79
Kissinger and, 74, 75–78, 97
military and, 91
National Intelligence Estimates of (*see* NIEs
    [National Intelligence Estimates])
navy and, 126–27
Nixon animosity toward, 73–75, 76
Operation Chaos of, 78–79
outside review of CIA estimates and, 136–39,
    171–72, 183–84
PFIAB and, 102, 107, 110, 117, 124, 129–31
Phoenix and, 71
press on, 79–80
response to Wohlstetter articles, 107–9
Rockefeller Commission and, 80–81, 102
Senate Select Committee and, 180–82
SR 76-10053, 135
SS-9 and, 93–99
supporters of, 73
Team B and (*see* Team B)
Teller and, 125
track record study of, 121, 127, 128–32
use of defectors by, 134–35, 194
Watergate and, 73
CINCSAC, 116
circular error probability (CEP), 93–94, 145,
    146–47, 159
Clifford, Clark, 94, 101
Cline, Ray, 22, 89
Clinton, William J. (Bill), 44, 61, 102, 191
"Clocking the Strategic Arms Race" (Wohlstet-
    ter), 64
Coalition for a Democratic Majority, 26, 27
Codevilla, Angelo, 181
Colby, William
    abolishment of BNE by, 106
    Binder interview with, 178
    on Defense Intelligence Agency, 107
    establishment of NIOs by, 106–7
    firing of, 81, 121

first NIE of, 109–11
Ford and, 122–24
Kissinger and, 75, 117, 118–20
length of DCI service of, 84
opposition to parallel NIE, 119, 186
PFIAB and, 105, 110–11, 116
report on CIA covert activities, 78–82
response to Kissinger memo, 118–20
on Soviet Union military expenditures,
    134–35
on Team B exercise, 172
on Wohlstetter articles, 15, 107
Collins, John, 67
Colson, Charles, 77
Commission on CIA Activities Within the U.S.
    (Rockefeller Commission), 80–82, 102
Committee for a Sane Nuclear Policy (SANE),
    35
Committee on NIE Evaluation, 112
Committee on the Present Danger. *See* CPD
"Common Sense and Common Danger" (CPD),
    188
"Common Understandings" (SALT and ABM
    treaties), 64
The "Community." *See* intelligence community
Conant, James, 28–29
Conference on Security and Cooperation in Eu-
    rope (CSCE), 57–58
Congress, and CIA, 49, 56, 81–82, 180–84. *See
    also entries beginning with* "House"; *entries
    beginning with* "Senate"; Jackson, Henry M.
    (Scoop)
Connally, John, 104
Connor, John T., 80
Conolly, Richard L., 101
conservatives, on detente, 9, 15, 26–30, 53–54,
    59, 185, 186, 196
conventional forces, numerical balance of, 13
Copper-Church amendment, 56
CPD (Committee on the Present Danger), 28–
    30, 184, 188–89, 191
cruise missiles, 142–43, 187
CSCE (Conference on Security and Coopera-
    tion in Europe), 57–58
Cuba, 55, 82

Davies, Spencer, 178
Davis, Lynn, 13
DeBruler, Henson R., 114, 117, 147

decade-of-neglect argument, 67–68
Decter, Midge, 26
defectors, CIA use of, 134–35, 194
Defense Department (DOD), 1, 11, 24, 47, 83, 95, 96, 105, 112, 171. *See also* Pentagon
Defense Intelligence Agency (DIA), 15
 on Backfire bombers, 165
 Colby and, 107
 estimations of Soviet military expenditures, 133, 134
 PFIAB and, 115
 projections of Soviet SS-9s by, 98
 on Soviet nuclear capabilities, 173
 on Soviet procurement slowdown, 168
Defense Posture Panel, 12
Defense Research and Engineering (DR&E), 95, 96
Defense Science Board, 12, 112
defense spending, 1974 public opinion on, 7. *See also* Soviet Union: military expenditures of
detente. *See also* detente, international causes of demise of
 critics of, 4, 9, 15–16, 20, 22, 23, 26, 29–30, 32, 186
 definition of, 1, 8, 56–57
 myth of, 27, 29
 reasons for, 2–3, 8, 17–18
 reasons for demise of, 2, 68–69, 185
 selling of, 21–22, 49, 51–52
 support for, 8, 45–46
detente, domestic opposition to, 17–49
 administrative foes of, 17–49
 background of, 17–18
 conservatives and, 26–30, 185
 early, 18–20
 effect of domestic politics on, 45–49
 impact of Solzhenitsyn, 32–33
 influential foes, 25–26
 Jackson and (*see* Jackson, Henry M. [Scoop])
 labor and, 36–39
 liberals and, 34–36
 neocons and, 30–31
 unification of diverse forces in, 45
detente, international causes of demise of, 50–69
 background of, 50–51
 CSCE and Helsinki accords, 57–60
 effect of U.S. foreign policy on, 52–54, 56, 58
 Soviet compliance with arms control and, 62–64

Third World revolutions and interventions and, 50–69
 Vladivostok and, 60–62
DIA (Defense Intelligence Agency). *See* Defense Intelligence Agency
Digby, James, 9–10, 14
Digby, Mary Jane, 9
Dillon, C. Douglas, 80
directed energy weapons, 166, 167
Directorate for Intelligence (CIA), 82, 83
Directorate for Operations (CIA), 78, 82, 83
Directorate for Plans (CIA), 76, 78
dissidents, 31, 35, 41, 45, 158, 193, 194–95. *See also* human rights; Sakharov, Andrei; Solzhenitsyn, Alexandr
Dobrynin, Anatoly F., 8, 33, 35
 on Angola, 55
 on delay of signing of PNET, 48
 meetings with Ford, 43, 46
 on Nixon-Kissinger treatment of Rogers, 21
 on reasons for demise of detente, 69
Doolittle, James H. "Jimmy," 101
Drake, James, 141, 151, 160
Draper, Theodore, 36, 80
DR&E (Defense Research and Engineering), 95, 96
Drell, Sidney, 13
Duckett, Carl, 98
Duffy, Bob, 144
Dulles, Allen, 101

Eberstadt, Nick, 132
education tax, Soviet Union and, 39–41
Eisenhower, Dwight D., 3, 4, 36, 90, 100, 101
elections
 1968, 94–95
 1976, 5, 47–48, 123, 158
"equals-aggregate" approach, 68
equivalent megatonnage, 64–65
Ermarth, Fritz, 156–57
Estimates Evaluation Committee, 177
Ethiopia, 54
Eurocommunism, 52–53
Evans, Rowland, 59
"evil empire," and U.S. remilitarization, 16, 138
Export-Import Bank, 40, 44–45

Fairless, Benjamin F., 101
"family jewels" secrets, of CIA, 78–81, 102, 185
FB-111 bombers, 142, 164
FBI (Federal Bureau of Investigation), 15

Federation of American Scientists, 35
Feshbach, Murray, 192
Fink, Dan, 141, 142
Finney, John, 95–96
Firth, Noel, 91
Flax, Alexander, 149, 150
Flieger, Howard, 61–62
FNLA (Frente Nacional de Liberação de Angola), 55
footnotes, in NIEs. *See* NIEs (National Intelligence Estimates): footnotes in
footprint theory, 96–97
Ford, Gerald R., 79, 160, 185
    approval ratings of, 122, 124
    Bush and, 84
    Colby and, 81, 118, 122–24
    creation of Commission on CIA Activities Within the U.S., 80
    critics of, 38
    Halloween Massacre and, 123–24
    Helsinki Final Act and, 57–59
    on Jackson, 40
    on Jackson-Vanik amendment, 43, 44
    Kissinger and, 46, 123
    meetings with Dobrynin, 43, 46
    meetings with Gromyko, 46
    1976 elections, 47–48, 123, 158
    Nixon's pardon, 6
    on Portugal, 52
    Reagan challenge to, 5, 46, 47–48, 62
    SALT and, 46–47, 60–61, 185
    Schlesinger and, 23–24, 25, 47, 122
    Solzhenitsyn and, 32, 33, 48
    on Soviet arms objectives, 186–87
    on Soviet compliance with arms control, 62–63
    support for detente, 45–46
    at Vladivostok, 60–61
Ford, Harold, 180–82
forecasts, reservations about, 144, 168
Foreign Affairs, 66
Foreign Policy, 14–15, 107
Foreign Policy Task Force (Coalition for a Democratic Majority), 27
Foreign Technologies Division, 94, 95
Fossum, Robert, 150
Foster, John, 139, 151, 152
    creation of parallel NIE by, 111–15
    criticisms of NIEs, 117–18, 125–26
    Kissinger support for MIRV theory of, 96–97

    as member of PFIAB, 104
    MIRV theory of, 98–99
    on need for worst-case scenario, 124–25
    role in Team B review panel selection, 154
    role in Team B selection, 99, 141, 144, 147, 149, 154
    on Safeguard system, 95
Foster, Richard, 157
Fowler, Henry, 27
fratricide, 145
Frente Nacional de Liberação de Angola (FNLA), 55
Fromm, Joseph, 9, 10
Frye, Alton, 13–14
Fulbright, J. William, 42

Gaffney, Frank, 190
Gaither Committee, 3–4
Gaither Report, 4, 86, 136, 152
Gallup polls, on American opinion of Soviet Union, 7. *See also* public opinion
Galvin, Robert, 104, 113, 125, 139
    on ASW vulnerability, 127
    creation of parallel NIE by, 112
    ground rules for Team A/B and, 152, 153
    as member of PFIAB, 104
    on Team B ground rules, 182
    track record study and, 128, 130
Garthoff, Raymond, 20, 68, 164
Gates, Robert, 92, 167–68
Germany, 6, 8, 14, 29, 33, 137
Gleason, Thomas W., 37
Goldwater, Barry, 185
Goure, Leon, 29
Graham, Daniel, 151
    on building block methodology, 134
    as candidate for Team B, 150
    criticisms of NIEs, 83–84
    as possible Team B report leaker, 176, 177, 178
    as Reagan adviser, 189
    on Senate report on Team B, 181–82
    Team B recommendations and, 169
    on Wohlstetter article, 107–8
Gray, Gordon, 104
Great Britain, 29, 70, 137
Great Caspian Sea Monster, 65
Greece, 52
Griswold, Erwin N., 80
Gromyko, Andrei A., 9, 46, 56

Gulf of Tonkin Resolution, 2
Gullion, Edmund, 27

Haig, Alexander, 24
Haile Selassie, 54
Haldeman, H. R., 40, 74
"Halloween Massacre," 123–24
Harlow, Bryce, 122
Hart, Gary, 84, 183
Hartzell, Craig, 141
Helms, Jesse, 32, 99, 189
Helms, Richard
    firing of, 77
    length of service as DCI of, 84
    management of CIA by, 76
    NIEs and, 97–98
    Nixon and, 74, 75, 77
Helsinki conference, 47, 57
Helsinki Final Act, 48, 53, 57–60
Herbst, Roland, 151
    on Bush response to Team B report, 160
    presentation of Team B Missile Accuracy
        Panel report, 159
    as Team B candidate, 144
    on Team B methodology, 145, 146
Heritage Foundation, 191
Hersh, Seymour, 79–80
Herzfeld, Charles, 147, 149, 150
Hewitt, Robert L., 128, 130
Hoffman, Hank, 141
Hoffman, Stanley, 20
Holbrooke, Richard, 14
Holloway, Bruce, 141
Holloway, James L., III, 47
Holst, Johan, 9, 10
Hoover Commission on the Reorganization of
    Government, 100
Horelick, Arnold, 149
House Armed Services Subcommittee on Arms
    Control, 25
House Permanent Select Committee on Intelli-
    gence, 136, 190
Hughes, Thomas, 98
Hughes-Ryan amendment, 56
Huizenga, John, 71, 72, 106
Hull, John E., 101
human rights, 31, 33–35, 39–45, 58, 59, 185.
    See also dissidents
Humphrey, Hubert H., 53–54, 94
Hunt, E. Howard, 73, 78

Hyland, William
    on Bush response to final Team A/B report,
        160
    as deputy national security adviser, 123, 139,
        151, 178
    on Kissinger selling of detente, 21
    on Kissinger's strategic superiority comments,
        66

ICBMs (intercontinental ballistic missiles), 13,
    18, 50, 72, 93, 94, 108, 109, 116, 117, 124,
    128, 129, 144, 145, 146, 173, 175, 186
the Igloo, 159
Ikle, Fred, 19–20, 47, 62
Inman, Bobby, 126–27
Inouye, Daniel K., 33, 182
intelligence community, 4, 5, 15, 22, 76, 77, 84,
    89–90, 111, 120, 121, 128, 129, 130, 132,
    134, 145, 146, 175, 186
intercontinental ballistic missiles. See ICBMs
    (intercontinental ballistic missiles)
International Longshoremen's Association, 37
International Security Council, 190
Internet, as example of netting, 142
"Intraagency Intelligence Memoranda" (CIA),
    105
Iran, 54, 77, 92
Iraq, 54
isolationism, 31–32
Israel, 30–31, 39

Jackson, Henry M. (Scoop), 39–45, 148. See also
    Jackson-Vanik amendment
    on effect of Soviet military build up, 192–93
    on Helsinki Final Act, 58
    Kissinger and, 19, 40
    labor and, 36–37
    Laird and, 19
    linkage of trade bill with Jewish emigration,
        40–43
    Nixon and, 19
    on parity, 64
    presidential ambitions of, 39
    on SALT and ABM treaties, 18–19, 20, 49,
        68
    Schlesinger and, 22
    Solzhenitsyn and, 33
    supporters of, 26
    Vietnam and, 19
    on Vladivostok, 61
Jackson-Vanik amendment, 5, 19, 41, 43–44, 49

Javits, Jacob, 33, 44
Jewish emigration, from Soviet Union, 16, 39–45
  education tax and, 39, 41
  Jackson linkage of trade bill with, 40–43
  quotas for, 43
  scientists' support for, 42–43
Johnson, Lyndon B., 27, 36, 94
Joint Chiefs of Staff, 66
Joint Congressional Committee on Intelligence, 101
Joint Economic Committee, 191, 192

Kampelman, Max, 26, 27, 30
Karalekas, Anne, 82–83
Keegan, George, 177, 178
  Air Force Intelligence and, 91
  briefings on directed-energy weapons, 111, 156
  communication with Bush, 155
  impact on NIEs, 125–26, 174
  intelligence post-mortem, 128
  opposition to parallel NIEs, 120
  overestimation errors of, 167
  as possible Team B report leaker, 176
  on Soviet objectives included in NIEs, 127
  on Team B Missile Accuracy Panel report, 159
Kennedy, John F., 39, 101
Kennedy, Joseph P., 101
Kent, Sherman, 157, 175
Khrushchev, Nikita, 36, 61
Killian, James, 101
Kirk, John, 144
Kirkland, Lane, 26, 27, 80
Kirkpatrick, Jeane, 30
Kissinger, Henry A.
  CIA and, 74, 75–78, 97
  Colby and, 75, 117, 118–20
  conservatives and, 26, 186
  critics of, 20, 25, 27, 31
  Ford and, 46, 123
  human rights and, 34–35
  introduction to Nixon, 104 (see also Nixon, Richard M.)
  Jackson and, 19, 40
  Jackson-Vanik amendment and, 43–44
  memo to Colby on NIE process, 117, 118–20
  on MIRV theory, 96–97
  at 1972 Moscow summit, 40

  Nitze and, 25, 26
  PFIAB and, 22, 117, 138
  press and, 26
  Reagan and, 47
  rivalry with Schlesinger, 24, 122
  Rogers and, 21–22
  SALT and, 20, 46–47, 56
  on selling detente, 21, 52
  on Soviet compliance with arms control, 62–63
  on Soviet economic and social decline, 195
  on Soviet military superiority, 66
  Soviet Union role in Vietnam and, 2–3, 17
  SS-9 controversy and, 96, 97, 98
  suppression of intelligence by, 22
  talks with Brezhnev, 8–9, 56
  Team B and, 187
  trip to Iran, 54
  U.S. Department of State and, 21–22, 24
  vision of detente of, 56–57
  Weiss and, 148
  on wheat trade issue, 38
Kistiakowsky, George, 90–91
Knoche, E. Henry, 138, 177, 178
Kohler, Foy, 148–49, 150, 154, 169, 176, 188, 189
Kosygin, Aleksei, 193
Kraft, Joseph, 9, 10
Kristol, Irving, 31

labor, and detente, 36–39
LaFeber, Walter, 17, 37
Laird, Melvin
  Jackson amendments and, 19
  on Soviet economy, 193
  on Soviet violations on SALT and ABM treaties, 63
  on SS-9 controversy, 95, 96–97, 98
  support of CIA by, 73
  Team B review panel and, 154
Land, Edwin, 104
Latter, Richard, 112, 127, 144–45, 147, 154
Leahy, Patrick, 84
Lee, William, 134
Lehman, John, 30, 151
Lehman, Richard, 177, 178
Leites, Nathan, 13
LeMay, Curtis, 64
Lemnitzer, Lyman L., 29, 80
Lerch, Charles, 141–42, 151, 180

Levine, Paul, 144
liberals, on detente, 34–36, 42
Library of Congress, study on Soviet military su-
    periority, 67
Limited Test Ban Treaty, 112
Lisagor, Peter, 66
Livermore Laboratory, 112, 114, 151
Lodal, Jan, 8
Long, Frank, 62
Los Alamos National Laboratory, 114, 167
Lourie, Richard, 35
Lovett, Robert, 101
Luce, Clare Boothe, 53, 104, 105, 130
Lynn, Laurence, 96

Main Political Directorate of the Armed Forces,
    166
Mansfield, Mike, 81, 101
Marder, Murrey, 179
Marsh, Jack, 32
Marshall, Andrew, 156
Marshall, Charles Burton, 27
Martinez, Eugenio, 73
McCarthy, Eugene, 82
McClellan, John, 135
McCord, James, 73
McCormick, Thomas J., 31
McGovern, George, 19
McIntryre, Thomas, 84
McManus, Deborah, 9
McManus, Jason, 9, 10
McNamara, Robert, 94, 151
Meany, George, 36, 37, 38, 41, 43, 45, 66
Mengistu, Haile-Mariam, 54
Merrick, Jim, 144
MFN (most favored-nation) status, 38–39, 40,
    41, 45. See also trade, and detente
military, distrust of CIA estimates, 91
Miller, William, 102, 178, 182
Milligan, John H., 128
Minuteman missiles, 67, 91, 93, 95, 96, 97, 98,
    116, 124, 126, 129, 145, 173, 175
"mirror-imaging," 164, 169–70
MIRV Panel, 96
MIRVs (multiple independently targetable reen-
    try vehicles), 50, 61, 93–94, 96–97, 98–99,
    129
Missile Accuracy Panel, 142, 144–47, 159
Molander, Roger, 117, 118, 147
Moscow summit (1972), 18, 40, 49–51, 54

most favored-nation (MFN) status. See MFN
Movimiento Popular de Liberação de Angola
    (MPLA), 55
Moynihan, Daniel Patrick, 183–84
MRVs (multiple targetable reentry vehicles),
    93–94, 96–98
multiple independently targetable reentry vehi-
    cles. See MIRVs (multiple independently
    targetable reentry vehicles)
multiple targetable reentry vehicles. See MRVs
    (multiple targetable reentry vehicles)
Murphy, Daniel, 127, 159

National Center for Jewish Policy Studies, 39
National Foreign Intelligence Board (NFIB),
    87–89, 97, 153, 159, 166, 172, 179
National Intelligence Estimates. See NIEs (Na-
    tional Intelligence Estimates)
National Intelligence Officers (NIOs), 106–8,
    171
National Review, 80
National Security Agency, 15, 87, 102, 115, 142
National Security Council (NSC), 47, 74, 117–
    18, 161
National Security Information Center, 29
National Security Intelligence Committee, 76
NATO (North Atlantic Treaty Organization),
    33, 52, 67, 137, 168, 187–88, 196
Naval Intelligence, 15, 115, 173
Negus, Gordon, 156
neocons, on detente, 30–31
net assessments, 114, 115, 117, 119, 171, 181
Net Technical Assessment Group, 115
netting, Internet as example of, 142
Neuberger, Egon, 191–92
New Alternatives Workshops, 151
New Republic, 32, 34
New York Times, 51, 58, 59, 61, 80, 95, 179
Newsweek, 80
NFIB (National Foreign Intelligence Board),
    87–89, 159, 172
Ngo Dinh Diem, 79
NIEs (National Intelligence Estimates), 15, 83–
    84, 86–99. See also Strategic Objectives
    Panel Report
    about, 87–89
    on adversarial positions, 114, 117, 171
    arrangement of, 170
    audiences for, 91, 163

bureaucratic politics in, 89–91
CIA track record study of, 127, 128–32
congress on, 183
creation of parallel, 111–15, 117–18, 125–26,
    131, 138, 139
criticisms of, 83–84, 88, 109–11, 112, 114,
    115–16, 118, 153–54, 166, 169
Eisenhower on, 90
first Colby, 109–11
focus of, 117
footnotes in, 88, 98, 125–26, 172–73, 186
Foster on, 111–13
functions of, 86, 87–89, 124–25
influences on, 90, 173–74, 186–88
Kissinger rejection of, 88, 117, 118–20
military distrust of, 91
multiagency input into, 107
NIE 11-3/8, 86, 87, 88, 120
NIE 11-3/8-68, 93–94, 97
NIE 11-3/8-69, 98
NIE 11-3/8-73, 170
NIE 11-3/8-74, 114, 115, 118, 119
NIE 11-3/8-75, 114, 115, 118, 119, 124, 125
NIE 11-3/8-76, 145, 152, 153, 170, 172–76,
    186; differences from previous NIEs,
    174–75 (see also Strategic Objectives Panel
    Report)
opposition to parallel, 119, 120, 186
outside review panels for, 136–37, 154, 171–
    72, 183–84
PFIAB under, 101–2
policymakers and, 91–93
power of, 92
preparation of, 87
revisions of, 97
SS-9 controversy and, 93–99
Team B study of (see Strategic Objectives
    Panel Report; Team B)
terminology in, 175
track record study conclusions about, 128–29
Truman on, 90
uncertainty in, 88–89
NIOs (National Intelligence Officers), 106–7
Nitze, Paul, 24, 27, 142, 149, 151, 176, 186
as author of NSC 68 and Gaither Report, 4,
    152
background of, 10
first Strategic Objectives Panel meeting and,
    158
Kissinger and, 25, 26

Pipes and, 150
press interviews with, 188
on previous NIEs, 154
resignation from SALT negotiations, 25
on Senate report on Team B, 181–82
on Soviet military superiority, 66
Team B recommendations and, 169
on U.S. underestimation of Soviet forces, 14
Wohlstetter and, 9, 25
Nixon, Richard M., 1, 7, 20, 51, 78, 101, 102
after 1972 elections, 77
animosity toward CIA, 73–75, 76
introduction to Kissinger, 104 (see also Kis-
    singer, Henry A.)
Jackson and, 19
1968 elections, 94–95
R. Helms and, 74, 75, 77
reasons for rapprochement with China, 3, 49
resignation of, 6, 79, 115
Rogers and, 21–22
on SALT leaks, 156
Soviet Union role in Vietnam and, 2–3, 17
on SS-9 controversy, 96–97
trip to Iran, 54
U.S. Department of State and, 21
vision of detente of, 8, 56–57
wheat trade and, 37
Nolan, Chris, 141
North Atlantic Treaty Organization. See NATO
North Vietnam, 55, 63
Novak, Robert, 59
NSC (National Security Council), 21, 117–19
NSC 68, 3, 4, 10, 136, 152
nuclear issues
    Agreement on the Prevention of Nuclear
        War, 49, 51
    Partial Nuclear Test Ban Treaty, 64
    Peaceful Nuclear Explosives Treaty (PNET),
        48
    Soviet debate about nature of nuclear war,
        166
    Soviet desire for nuclear war, 165
    Soviet nuclear capabilities, 173

Ober, Richard, 117
Odom, William, 92
Office of National Estimates, 72, 106
Office of Net Assessment, 171
Office of Strategic Services (OSS), 70
Olmer, Lionel, 103, 117, 129–30, 147, 154–55

Operation Chaos, 78–79
"Optimal Ways to Confuse Ourselves" (Wohlstetter), 14–15
Osborne, John, 34

Packard, David, 27, 97
Paisley, John
  as liaison between Team A and B, 139–40, 147
  Graham and, 177
  on Pipes security clearance, 155
  selection of Team B and, 149, 150
  Team B document requests by, 157
  Van Cleave and, 156
Pakistan, 34
parity, in arms race, 61, 62, 64, 67, 111, 165
Parker, Patrick J., 150
Partial Nuclear Test Ban Treaty, 64
Peaceful Nuclear Explosives Treaty (PNET), 48
Pentagon, 19, 23, 24, 66–67, 105, 108, 136, 156.
  See also Defense Department
Peretz, Martin, 31
Perle, Richard, 30, 40, 44, 148, 150
Pershing missile, 187
PFIAB (President's Foreign Intelligence Advisory Board), 5, 53, 100–120. See also Strategic Objectives Panel Report; Team B
  under Bush, 102, 138
  under Carter, 102, 179
  CIA ground rules for Team A/B and, 152–55, 182
  CIA track record study and, 129–31
  under Clinton, 102
  Colby and, 105, 110–11, 116
  composition of, 104–5
  criticisms of, 105
  DCIs and, 105–7
  Defense Intelligence Agency and, 115
  dissolution and reactivation of, 101, 102
  under Eisenhower, 101
  formation of NIE alternative, 111–15, 117–18, 125–26, 131, 138, 139
  history of, 100–103
  under Kennedy, 101
  Kissinger and, 22, 117, 138
  meetings of, 103, 114, 117
  1976 budget of, 103
  under Nixon, 101–2
  NSC and, 118–19
  objections to NIEs, 110, 115–16
  purpose of, 100–101
  under Reagan, 102
  review panel for Team B report, 154
  right-wing composition of, 104–5
  Schlesinger and, 105–6
  threat assessments of, 103
  three major NIE concerns of, 117
  U.S. State Department on, 105
Phillips, Samuel C., 66–67, 154
Pike, John, 167
Pipes, Richard, 151, 156, 159, 188
  as author of Team B report, 4, 163
  Binder interview with, 179
  on Bush reaction to Team B report, 161
  as candidate for Team B, 147
  as chairman for Team B Strategic Objectives Panel, 148–49
  on confrontation between Teams A and B, 158
  CPD and, 28
  on declassification of Team B report, 176
  on influence of Team B on NIE 11-3/8-76, 173–74
  Nitze and, 150
  as Reagan adviser, 189
  security clearance for, 155
  Senate report on Team B and, 180–82
  on Soviet desire for nuclear war, 165
  Strategic Objectives Panel and, 157
  on Team B ground rules, 153–54
  Team B recommendations and, 169
  "What Is the Soviet Union Up To?," 29, 188
Ploymate, Ben, 154
Podgorny, Nikolai, 193
Podhoretz, Norman, 26, 31
Polaris/Poseidon submarine, 65, 98
Portugal, 47, 52, 53, 54, 59, 60, 63, 101
Powers, Thomas, 74, 83, 90
Pravda, 51
Presidential Review Memorandum-10 (Carter), 187
President's Foreign Intelligence Advisory Board. See PFIAB (President's Foreign Intelligence Advisory Board)
press. See also names of specific publications
  on CIA, 79–80
  on CPD policy statement, 188
  on "Halloween Massacre," 124
  Kissinger and, 26
  leaks from Team B report and, 162, 176–79

on Soviet defense spending, 136
on SS-9 controversy, 95–96
use of by opponents of detente, 29–30, 32
on Vladivostok, 61
The Price of Peace and Freedom (film), 29
Proctor, Edward, 22
The Progressive, 80
Proxmire, William, 180
Psychological Strategy Board, 104–5
public opinion, American
    about arms race, 68
    about Soviet Union, 1, 7–8, 58–59, 191
    on defense spending, 7, 135–36
    on Helsinki Final Act, 58–59

Quadripartite Agreement, 63

Ralston, Theodore, 180
Ranelagh, John, 84
RDA, 141, 144
Reagan, Ronald W., 27, 80, 81, 186
    administration members of CPD of, 30
    attacks on Ford-Kissinger foreign policy, 47
    challenge to Ford, 5, 46, 47–48, 62, 124
    defense policy of, 49
    on Ford firing of Schlesinger, 25, 47
    on Helsinki Final Act, 58
    PFIAB and, 102
    on Sonnenfeldt Doctrine, 59
    on Soviet military expenditures, 132
    Team B advisers of, 189
Reagan Doctrine, 55
Republican National Committee, 185
Reston, James, 59–60
Ribicoff, Abraham, 44
Richardson, Elliott, 78
Richelson, Jeffrey, 87
Rockefeller, Nelson A., 80, 104, 123
Rockefeller Commission (Commission on CIA
    Activities Within the U.S.), 80–81, 102
Rodham, Peter W., 8–9
Rogers, William P., 21–22
Rosefielde, Steven, 134
Rosenblum, Louis, 39
Rostow, Eugene, 26–27
    on CIA estimates of Soviet military expendi-
    tures, 134
    on detente, 26
    formation of Committee on the Present Dan-
    ger, 27–28

as member of National Security Information
    Center, 29
    press interviews with, 188
    Team B and, 149
Rumsfeld, Donald, 46–47, 54, 123
Rusk, Dean, 28
Russell, Richard, 81
Ryerson, Edward, 101

Safeguard, 95, 96, 98
Safire, William, 40, 190–91
Sakharov, Andrei, 35, 41–42, 193–94
SALT (Strategic Arms Limitation Talks), 7, 46–
    47, 50, 60–61, 185
SALT I Treaty
    Ford and, 46–47, 60–61
    Jackson amendments to, 18–19, 20, 37, 49, 68
    leaks on, 156
    negotiations on, 57, 64
    provisions of, 50–51
SALT II, 20, 24, 27
    Carter and, 186
    Ford and, 185
    Kissinger and, 56, 187
    Nitze resignation from negotiations for, 25
    Team B members on, 189
Saltonstall, Leverett, 81–82
SAMs (surface-to-air missiles), 166, 186
SANE (Committee for a Sane Nuclear Policy),
    35
Savimbi, Jonas, 55
Scheer, Robert, 157
Schlesinger, Arthur, 42
Schlesinger, James, 26, 27, 33
    on CIA analyses, 72
    as CIA DCI, 77–78, 83, 84, 185
    critics of, 23
    Ford on, 23–24, 25, 47
    Jackson and, 22
    on NIE 11-3/8-74, 118
    PFIAB and, 105–6
    review of intelligence community by, 76
    rivalry with Kissinger, 24, 122
    as secretary of defense, 22–23, 156
    on Soviet military expenditures, 134, 135–36
    on Soviet violations of arms control agree-
    ments, 62
    Team B review panel and, 154
    Time cover story on, 65
Schorr, Daniel, 81

Schroeder, Gertrude, 192
scientists, and detente, 42–43, 61–62
Scop, Peter, 143–44
Scoville, Herbert (Pete), 90
Scowcroft, Brent, 48, 123, 155
Scowcroft Commission Report, 86
SDIO (Strategic Defense Initiative Office), 167
sea-launched ballistic missiles (SLBMs), 128, 175
SEATO, 33
security clearances, and Team B, 150, 155–56
Semipalatinsk, 167
Senate Armed Services Committee, 84
    CIA subcommittee of the, 82
Senate Defense Appropriations Subcommittee, 180
Senate Foreign Relations Committee, 180
    Subcommittee of the, 95
Senate Intelligence Committee on Collection, Production, and Quality of Intelligence, 180
Senate Select Committee on Intelligence, 82, 102, 178, 181
Senate Select Committee to Study Governmental Operations with Respect to Intelligence Activities, 82
Shannon, Edgar F., Jr., 81
short-range attack missles (SRAMs), 142, 143
Shulsky, Abe, 182
Shultz, George, 27, 54, 104
Sidey, Hugh, 186
Slocombe, Walter, 87–88
Slocum, Marianna, 192
Smith, Abbot, 97
Smith, Gerard, 19
Solzhenitsyn, Alexandr, 5, 6, 29, 35, 47
    Ford and, 32, 33, 48
    on Helsinki Final Act, 58
    impact on opposition to detente, 32–33, 49
    intellectuals' support for, 42
    Jackson and, 32
Somalia, 54
Sonnenfeldt, Helmut, 56, 59, 113
Sonnenfeldt Doctrine, 47, 59
Soviet Union
    alleged American underestimation of forces of, 11–15
    alleged military superiority of, 14, 66, 67, 144, 165, 193
    alleged violations of SALT and ABM treaties, 62–64

American public opinion about, 7–8, 58–59
Angola and, 55–56
armed forces in, 169
China and, 3
CIA analysis of threat of, 72
Committee on the Present Danger on, 29
compliance with arms control, 62–64
debate about nature of nuclear war, 166
dissidents in, 35, 193, 194–95 (see also Sakharov, Andrei; Solzhenitsyn, Alexandr)
early signs of decline of, 191–95
economy of, 18
education tax of, 39–41
Helsinki Final Act and, 59–60
interpretation of peaceful coexistence by, 51
Jewish emigration from, 39–45
liberals and, 34–35
military doctrine of, 166, 170
military expenditures of, 132–37, 167–68
1974 weapons inventory of, 13
role in Vietnam, 2–3, 17
Schlesinger and, 23, 62
"science of winning" of, 164
SS-9 controversy and, 93–99
support for wars of national liberation, 57
testing of detente limits by, 23
Third World involvement of, 52, 55–56, 57
trade issues of, 37–38, 39–45
vision of detente of, 57
Spain, 52, 53
Sputnik, 4
SS-18, 67, 145
SS-19, 67, 145, 146–47
SS-9 controversy, 93–99, 111, 112
    ABM and, 95
    circular error probability in, 93–94, 145
    Kissinger and, 96, 97, 98
    Laird and, 95, 96–97, 98
    MRV versus MIRV, 93–94, 96–97
    Nixon and, 97
    press on, 95–96
    Soviet numbers of, 95
    Soviet tests on, 96
State Department. See U.S. Department of State
Stein, Herbert, 28
Stern, Paula, 39, 40
Stevens, Sayre, 138, 142
Stevenson, Adali, III, 33, 44–45, 180, 181
Stevenson amendment, 45, 49
Stimson, Henry, 70

Stoertz, Howard, 114
  on consultants, 172
  on forecasts about Soviet defense system, 144
  on influence of Team B on NIE 11-3/8-76,
    174
  on making material available to Team B, 157
  opposition to parallel NIE, 119, 138
  on previous NIEs, 153–54
  on Soviet military doctrine, 170
  on Team A and B confrontation, 158
  on Team A and B presentation, 159, 166
Stone, I. F., 42
Stowe, Chuck, 144
Strategic Arms Limitation Talks. See SALT
    (Strategic Arms Limitation Talks)
Strategic Defense Initiative Office (SDIO), 167
Strategic Objectives Panel, 146, 147–52, 156–
    58. See also Strategic Objectives Panel Re-
    port
Strategic Objectives Panel Report, 163–84. See
    also Team A; Team B
  "A Critique of NIE Interpretations Of Cer-
    tain Soviet Strategic Developments," 166
  annex to, 169
  Bush response to, 160–62, 173–74
  capability-versus-intention argument in,
    163–64
  congressional response to, 180–84
  influence on NIE 11-3/8-76, 173–74, 186–88
  leaks of, 176–79
  mirror-imaging in, 164–65, 166, 169–70
  on net assessments, 171
  on outside review panels for NIEs, 171–72,
    183–84
  on previous NIEs, 169
  recommendations of, 169–72
  on Soviet desire for nuclear war, 165
  on Soviet military doctrine, 170
  on Soviet military expenditures, 167–68
  Soviet "science of conquest," 164
  "Soviet Strategic Objectives" in, 168–69
  on Soviet strategic thinking, 166
  worst-case scenario focus of, 166–67
Studies in Intelligence, 108–9
Sulzberger, C. L., 59
Suvorov, A. V., 164

Taylor, Maxwell, 101
Team A, 4
  Bush support for, 160–62

  composition of, 139, 142
  controversy with Team B, 142
  meetings with Team B, 143–44, 146, 158
  Missile Accuracy Panel of, 145–46
  presentation of final report of, 159–60
  Soviet Air Defense Panel of, 142–43
  Stoertz on, 174
  Strategic Objectives Panel of, 158
  Strategic Objectives Panel Report of (see NIE
    11-3/8-76; Strategic Objectives Panel Re-
    port)
Team B, 4, 16. See also Foster, John; Graham,
    Daniel; Herbst, Roland; Pipes, Richard;
    Van Cleave, William; Weiss, Seymour;
    Wohlstetter, Albert
  assessment of, 195–96
  Bush and, 151, 155, 157, 160–62
  Carter and, 187
  CIA information support for, 157
  Colby and, 172
  composition of, 139, 141, 144, 147–50, 154
  conclusions about, 172, 182–83
  congressional response to, 180–84
  controversy with Team A, 142
  estimated costs of, 140
  failure to look at Soviet social and economic
    conditions, 194
  ground rules controversy and, 153–54
  ground rules for, 152–53, 182
  inaccuracies in analysis by, 146–47
  influence on NIE 11-3/8-76, 173–74, 186–88
  Kissinger and, 187
  leaks about, 162, 176–79
  legacy of, 189–91
  meetings with Team A, 143–44, 146, 158
  Missile Accuracy Panel of, 142, 144–47, 159
  negative impact of, 191–96
  origins of, 111–13
  personal relationships among, 151–52
  planning for, 113–15
  presentation of final report of, 159–60
  press leaks from, 162
  purpose of, 153
  Reagan and, 189
  review panel for, 154
  SALT and, 189
  security clearances for, 150, 155–56
  selection of, 141, 144, 147, 149, 150
  Senate report on, 181–83
  Soviet Air Defense Panel of, 141, 143

on Soviet military doctrine, 170
Strategic Objectives Panel of, 146, 147–50, 156–58
Strategic Objectives Panel Report of (*see* Strategic Objectives Panel Report)
supporters of, 184, 189
Teller, Edward, 104, 105, 151, 152
creation of parallel NIE and, 112, 118, 127
criticism of NIEs by, 125, 130
meeting with CIA on NIE 11-3/8-74, 114
on need for worst-case scenarios in NIEs, 113, 125
support for Vladivostok agreement, 61–62
Third World politics, effect on detente, 50–69
threat assessments, 1, 5. *See also* NIEs (National Intelligence Estimates)
Gaither Report as, 4
NSC 68 as, 3, 4
"throw weight," 24, 129
Time, 10, 65, 186
track record study, of CIA, 121, 127, 128–32
trade, and detente, 37–38, 39–45
Trident submarine, 19, 49, 65
Trujillo, Rafael, 79
Truman, Harry S., 70, 90, 104
TRW, 96
Tucker, Gardiner, 147–48, 149, 154
Turkey, 52
Turner, Stansfield, 92, 162, 181, 187
Tyroler, Charles, 27, 28

Uniâo Nacional para a Independência Total de Angola (UNITA), 55
"Unilateral Statements," 64
Union of Councils for Soviet Jewry, 39
U.S. Air Force, 10, 90, 94, 98, 145
U.S. Army, 94
U.S. Department of State, 90
Kissinger and, 21–22, 24
Nixon and, 21
on PFIAB, 105
Weiss and, 148
U.S. House of Representatives, 41, 56, 82
U.S. Intelligence Board (USIB), 97, 98
U.S. Navy, 94, 126–27
U.S. Senate, 19, 41, 44, 56, 82, 97, 98, 124
USA Institute, 166

Van Cleave, William, 176
Binder interview with, 178
as candidate for Team B, 147, 148, 149–50

CPD and, 188
Paisley and, 156
personality of, 152
on purpose of Team B, 153
as Reagan adviser, 189
security clearance of, 155–56
Senate report on Team B and, 181
on senior review panel, 154
Team B recommendations and, 169
Van Slyck, Forrest, 90
Vanik, Charles, 41, 44
Vaughan, David, 144
Verification Panel, 96
Vietnam, 2, 3, 57, 67, 71, 79, 152, 185
Vietnam War, 52, 73
and detente, 8
CIA interpretation of, 71
Jackson support of, 19
opposition to, 34, 36, 39, 71
Soviet Union role in, 2–3, 17, 40
Vladivostok Accord, 40, 46, 49, 60–62, 187
Vogt, John, 150, 151, 176, 177
personality of, 152
on purpose of Team B, 153
as Reagan adviser, 189
Team B recommendations and, 169

Walesa, Lech, 69
Walker, Charls E., 27
Wall Street Journal, 58, 64
Wallop, Malcolm, 181, 183, 184
Walsh, John, 154
Walters, Vernon, 22
Warnke, Paul, 186
Warsaw Pact, 13, 67, 137
Washington Post, 179
Washington Star, 130
Watergate, 6, 20–21, 25, 73, 77, 78, 79, 115, 123
Wattenberg, Ben, 31
Webster, William, 190
Weinberger, Casper, 1–2
Weiss, Seymour, 151, 152, 176
Binder interview with, 178
as candidate for Team B, 147–48, 149, 150
Kissinger and, 148
as Reagan adviser, 189
Team B recommendations and, 169
Welch, D., 144
Welch, Jasper, 150, 151, 153, 169, 176

Whalen, Richard J., 26
"What Is the Soviet Union Up To?" (Pipes), 29,
     188
wheat trade issues, 37–38, 193
Wheelon, Albert, 12
Wohlstetter, Albert, 9, 151, 152
  on arms race, 11–13, 16, 64–65, 85, 89, 109
  background of, 10
  as candidate for Team B, 147, 150, 154
  CIA response to, 107–9
  criticisms of, 108
  Foreign Policy articles of, 14–15, 107, 115
  on NIEs, 88

Nitze and, 9, 25
  reactions to, 13–14
Wohlstetter, Roberta, 9
Wolfe, Thomas, 150, 151, 156, 169, 176, 178
Wolfowitz, Paul, 150, 151, 165, 169, 176
Working Group on National Aims, Interna-
     tional Agreement, and Strategic Forces, 11
worst-case scenarios, 113, 124–25, 131, 166–67,
     183

Yahya Khan, Agha M., 34
Yom Kippur War, 30–31, 36, 54, 68

Zumwalt, Elmo, 27, 91